W9-CZT-404

THE
GLOBAL
GOURMET

©1992 Concordia Language Villages
All rights reserved
Published in the United States
by Concordia Language Villages

No part of this book may be reproduced in any form or by any means
without permission in writing from the publisher.

Library of Congress Catalog Number: 92-74044

ISBN 0-9615951-7-5

Director, Concordia Language Villages: Christine Schulze
Assistant Director for Public Relations, Concordia Language Villages:
  Beth Johnson Holod

Project Coordinator: Patricia Meyers
Editor/Copywriter: Heather Randall King
Recipe Editor: Betsy Norum, Certified Home Economist
Editorial Assistants: Stephanie Hillman, Kathie Fargione
Production Advisor: Mary Meuwissen
Creative Director: Jane Eschweiler
Cover Design: Heather Randall King and April Grande
Photography: John Borge and Hetland Ltd.

Printed by Bolger Publications/Creative Printing, Minneapolis, MN

4   3   2   1
95 94 93 92

Table of Contents

An Affirmation of Diversity. . .

The curriculum of the Concordia Language Villages is deeply rooted in affirmation of diversity. Its programs, reflecting the positive cultural and ethnic contrasts of our world, create a global environment for participatory experience-based learning.

A highlight and hallmark of this immersion in language and living is a thirty-year tradition of sharing and exploring authentic foods and dining customs of other countries. Village chefs have introduced favorite ethnic dishes to more than 60,000 young people representing all fifty states and many foreign countries.

Each of the ten villages — Chinese, Danish, Finnish, French, German, Japanese, Norwegian, Russian, Spanish and Swedish, has a select culinary staff dedicated to promoting the important link between language and culture. At mealtimes, villagers feast on sumptuous "souvenirs" of other lands, along with generous "helpings" of traditions, history, geography, economics and of course, language. Differences are regarded as prized opportunities to promote global understanding and responsible world citizenship.

With this recipe collection, we proudly invite you to join us at our international tables. And, we urge you to recreate these cherished recipes from our kitchens, from villagers, parents, restaurateurs, celebrities and other program supporters. Savor with us exotic ingredients of Asia and the Mideast, robust classics with Russian roots, subtle French interpretations, stouthearted German fare, bold and spicy Spanish creations, the bounties of Scandinavia and more. All in all, we've included hundreds of mouth-watering reasons for you to travel tastefully around the world, relishing the offerings of haute and humble, rural and urban cuisine. Adventure lies ahead — we promise you!

Bon voyage and bon appetit!

Christine Schulze

Christine Schulze, Director
Concordia Language Villages

Looking Back, Looking Ahead . . .

In 1960, two Concordia College faculty members, Dr. Gerhard Haukebo of the Education Department and Raymond Miesnicks of the German Department, suggested that the college initiate an experimental program in language instruction based on immersion teaching techniques. One year later, the idea became reality when the college sponsored the first German session, "Camp Waldsee," using rented facilities on Lake Carlos north of Alexandria, MN. Erhard Friedrichsmeyer, a former Concordia faculty member, was the first "dean" of this unique concept.

The program was a resounding success and received wide recognition for the language-centered, cultural-immersion opportunity offered to young people. As interest increased, more language "camps" were organized. Modeled after the original "Camp Waldsee," there are now ten villages: Waldsee (German), Lac du Bois (French), El Lago del Bosque (Spanish), Skogfjorden (Norwegian), Lesnoe Ozero (Russian), Sjölunden (Swedish), Salolampi (Finnish), Skovsøen (Danish), Sen Lin Hu (Chinese) and Mori-No-Ike (Japanese). All the village names loosely translate as "Lake in the Woods."

In 1966, Concordia College purchased an 800-acre tract of woodland with three miles of shoreline on Turtle River Lake, near Bemidji, MN. Plans call for construction of all the villages around the lake shore, reflecting architectural styles of village cultures. Several permanent facilities have been completed; other programs currently operate at leased lakeside sites in northern and central Minnesota.

Almost 70 percent of the villagers are enrolled in two-week sessions. In addition, one and four-week programs are also available plus village-sponsored trips abroad. The four-week sessions are available for a full year of high school language credit. Previous language training and experience are not required. Since levels of instruction are appropriately tailored to all language backgrounds from novice to fluent speaker, villagers feel comfortable with whatever their levels of expertise. Fifty percent of villagers return year after year for the unique encounter with nature and a world language. Annually, more than 5,300 young people from age 7 to 18 travel to the villages from all 50 states and many foreign countries.

The program is ever optimistic about the human enterprise. Building on the richness of the past, it embodies a vision of a world of peace. The ultimate goal is to send young people into society charged with global concern, energized to have positive impact and filled with hope for the future.

The Global Gourmet

is dedicated to the Concordia Language
Villages culinary staff, past and present, who
have enhanced the program and its mission
with their expertise, ingenuity and enthusiasm.
Through their untiring efforts, foods of the
world have provided nourishment and cultural
enrichment to villagers for over three decades.

Inquiries and orders should be addressed to:
Concordia Language Villages
Attn: The Global Gourmet
901 South Eighth Street
Moorhead, Minnesota 56562

For information on the Concordia Language Villages program,
write or call:
Concordia Language Villages
901 South Eighth Street
Moorhead, Minnesota 56562
800/247-1044 (in Minnesota)
800/222-4750 (out of state)

Mardi Gras masks Arts and crafts
are used in all the Language Villages to
teach vocabulary and cultural charac-
teristics. These "villagers" wear masks
made in preparation for the French
Village's Mardi Gras celebration.

Flag-raising Morning flag-raising is
a daily event at many villages. Here
a staff member and "villager" unfurl
the Norwegian flag over the first
permanent site, built in 1970.

*When Beth Johnson Holod, St. Paul, MN., returned from a year in France, she delighted her family by preparing this traditional terrine. It should be made at least a day ahead of serving for optimum flavor. When a pâté mixture is cooked in a bacon-lined dish rather than in a crust, it is called a **terrine** after the earthenware cooking vessel in which it bakes.*

Country Pâté

½	pound bacon
2	tablespoons margarine
1	bunch scallions, chopped
1	pound lean ground pork
1	pound ground veal
2	eggs
½	pound chicken livers, chopped
½	cup Calvados or apple brandy
¾	cup fresh white bread crumbs (2 slices)
⅓	cup milk
1½	teaspoons salt
½	teaspoon nutmeg
¼	teaspoon pepper

Heat oven to 350°. Line 9x5x3-inch pan with bacon strips, reserving 3 strips for top. Melt margarine in small skillet. Add scallions and sauté until golden. Place scallions in large bowl. Add pork and remaining ingredients; mix well. Pack mixture firmly into lined pan. Place 3 reserved bacon strips on top. Cover pan tightly with foil. Bake 1 hour. Remove foil and bake 45 minutes longer or until a meat thermometer inserted in center of loaf registers 170°. Remove from oven and drain off fat. Allow to cool in pan. When cool, remove from pan; wrap tightly in foil and refrigerate overnight.

18 (½-INCH) SLICES.

In an inviting northwoods atmosphere, restaurateur Shelly Jacobs presides over the original woodroast cooking of specialties such as this. Shelly's Woodroast is located in St. Louis Park, MN., a suburb of Minneapolis. At the request of appreciative patrons, he has adapted this recipe for easy home kitchen preparation.

Walleye Fingers

6   (6 to 8-ounce) skinless walleye fillets

12 eggs, well beaten

¼   cup honey

1   (8-ounce) package buttery round crackers

    Vegetable oil

    Tartar sauce

Lay fillets flat on cutting board and cut at angle to make strips about 1½ inches wide. Combine eggs and honey; mix well with fork. (Do not use electric mixer.) Roll, blend or crumble crackers in food processor; set aside. Stir egg and honey mixture again with fork. Dip each piece of fish in egg mixture; dredge in crumbs to coat completely. Let stand 10 to 30 minutes in refrigerator. Heat oil to high temperature in skillet. Pan-fry fish until crisp and golden brown. Drain on paper towels. Serve with tartar sauce.

6 SERVINGS.

The aroma of this popular appetizer being grilled draws hungry crowds at Japanese train stations where it is sold at stands. Mirin is a sweet rice cooking wine available at most Asian markets. Watch chicken carefully while grilling to avoid overcooking; baste and turn as needed to keep ingredients moist.

Yakitori

SAUCE

1   tablespoon sugar

¼   cup mirin

½   cup soy sauce

½   cup sake

KABOBS

10   ounces skinned, boned chicken

4   green bell peppers

2   leeks

25 to 30 skewers*

Heat barbecue or grill. Combine sauce ingredients in saucepan; simmer 10 to 15 minutes or until volume decreases by about ⅓ of the original. Cut chicken, green peppers and leeks into 1-inch pieces. Thread on skewers. Grill until chicken is light brown. Brush with sauce and continue grilling until chicken is done. Brush with sauce 2 or 3 more times while grilling.

25 TO 30 APPETIZERS.

*Tip: *If using bamboo skewers, soak in water about 20 minutes before grilling to prevent bamboo from burning.*

This is one marvelous example of Spanish appetizers called "tapas". Jennifer Teichmann, Spanish Village head cook, shares the recipe from El Lago del Bosque and explains that tapas are a tasty tradition throughout Spain, where people gather to visit, sip wines of the country and savor a sampling of appetizers.

Garlic Shrimp

6   tablespoons butter

4   cloves garlic, sliced

1   dried red chile pepper, cut into 2 pieces, seeds removed

1   pound small or medium shrimp, shelled

     Salt to taste

     Garlic powder to taste, if desired

Melt butter in large skillet. Add garlic and chile pepper. When garlic begins to turn golden, add shrimp and cook over high heat about 3 minutes, stirring constantly. Adjust seasoning. Serve immediately.

6 SERVINGS.

Diane Syme, Edina, MN., shares a spicy spread from Costa Rica. Colorful confetti-like bits of vegetable add color, texture and great flavor.

Tuna Ceviche

1   (6½-ounce) can white tuna, drained

1   medium tomato, finely chopped

1   medium onion, finely chopped

½   red or green bell pepper, seeded, finely chopped

1   or 2 jalapeño peppers, seeded, finely chopped

1   stalk celery, finely chopped

1   clove garlic, finely chopped

¼   cup fresh lime juice

2   tablespoons mayonnaise

1   teaspoon prepared mustard

    Salt and pepper to taste

    Crackers

Break tuna into small pieces in bowl; lightly toss vegetables with tuna. Combine lime juice, mayonnaise, mustard, salt and pepper; stir into tuna mixture. Cover and refrigerate at least 2 hours. Serve with crackers.

4 TO 6 SERVINGS.

"Double the recipe," advises contributor, Eric Peterson, Amherst, WI. "It's great for parties," he adds. Testers, Kay and Robert Kallos, Atlanta, GA., anchored roll-ups with toothpicks and added an olive to each for color.

Tempting Tortilla Roll-Ups

1   (8-ounce) package cream cheese, softened

½   cup chunky mild or medium salsa

½   cup chopped green onions

1   clove garlic, minced

12   (6-inch) flour tortillas

Beat cream cheese until smooth. Add remaining ingredients except tortillas; mix well. Spread 1 heaping tablespoon of cream cheese mixture on each tortilla, covering entire surface. Roll up tightly. Place seam side down in shallow dish or pan. Cover and refrigerate at least 2 hours. Cut each tortilla into 1-inch pieces (or serve whole).

4 TO 5 DOZEN APPETIZERS.

Mary Dickson, Northfield, MN., first sampled this melted cheese creation while working in Mexico City with American Study Travel Abroad. Now, she and her husband, Jim, share it with family and friends along with students in her conversational Spanish class. Tester Carrie Rocke, Davis, CA., reported raves "even from the picky eater" in her family.

Queso Fundido

4	ounces hot Mexican sausage (chorizo)
5	ounces (1¼ cups) shredded Monterey jack or Mexican white cheese
4	ounces (1 cup) shredded longhorn cheese
2	jalapeño peppers, thinly sliced
	Dried epazote (Mexican herb), to taste

Cook and stir sausage over low heat until brown and crumbly. Heat broiler. Combine cheeses and jalapeño peppers in broiler-proof dish. Sprinkle with epazote. Garnish with cooked sausage. Place under broiler until bubbly and golden brown. Serve with tortilla chips or on small plate with a fork.

2 TO 4 SERVINGS.

Tip: Place tortillas in shallow baking pan. Top with remaining ingredients. Broil until bubbly and golden brown.

Gail Tsuboi, Moraga, CA., includes this festive appetizer on Mexican menus or serves it as a snack. Although cilantro resembles parsley, it has a more robust flavor and should be used soon after purchasing for peak freshness. Julie Bernstein, Grand Blanc, MI., who tested the dip proclaimed it "the best we've ever had!"

Zesty Guacamole and Chips

2	large ripe avocados, peeled and seeded
1	ripe medium tomato, peeled, seeded and chopped
½	small onion, minced
1	to 2 fresh or canned serrano or jalapeño peppers, finely chopped
	Dash of sugar
	Salt and pepper to taste
1	to 2 tablespoons finely chopped fresh cilantro, if desired
	Tortilla chips*

Mash avocados. Combine with remaining ingredients except tortilla chips; mix well. If made ahead of serving time, press plastic wrap tightly onto surface to cover; refrigerate. Serve with tortilla chips.

4 TO 8 SERVINGS.

*Tip: *To make lowfat tortilla chips, brush corn or flour tortillas with a light coating of vegetable oil; cut each tortilla into 8 wedges. Place on a cookie sheet and broil until crisp, turning once.*

For this dip from Nicolle Pata, Danville, CA., try using avocados grown in her home state. They are smaller, darker green in color and a bit more flavorful than the East Coast variety. Once called butter pears, avocados were enjoyed by ancient Aztec and Inca civilizations.

California Guacamole

1	medium ripe avocado, peeled and seeded
2	medium ripe tomatoes, finely chopped
2	teaspoons minced onion or 1 teaspoon dry minced onion
1½	tablespoons dairy sour cream
1	teaspoon lemon juice
¾	teaspoon salt
½	teaspoon lemon pepper
½	teaspoon dry minced garlic
6	drops hot pepper sauce

Mash avocado. Combine with remaining ingredients; mix well. Serve with chimichangas or as a dip with tortilla chips.

4 TO 6 SERVINGS.

*Joanna Christensen, Council Bluffs, IA., prepares this **hot** dip in seconds. "It's quick and easy and we had none left over," reports tester Janelle Lamb, Altoona, IA. "Don't overblend," she cautions.*

Picante Sauce

1	(24-ounce) can stewed tomatoes
6	jalapeño peppers (less if you do not want it so hot)
4	(4-inch) green onions
1	teaspoon garlic salt
½	teaspoon garlic powder
1	teaspoon seasoned salt
1	teaspoon wine vinegar or apple cider vinegar

Combine all ingredients in blender or food processor; process until desired texture.

2 CUPS.

Jean Hughes, Superior, WI., dubs this rich specialty of Lorraine, France, "delicious and decadent." Allow quiche to set after baking for easy serving. "Best served warm," advises tester Gerda Weninger, Boise, ID.

Appetizer Quiche

CRUST

1	cup all-purpose flour
½	teaspoon baking powder
½	teaspoon salt
2	heaping tablespoons lard, at room temperature
	Ice water

FILLING

10	slices bacon, crisply cooked and crumbled
4	ounces (1 cup) shredded Swiss cheese
3	small eggs
1	cup whipping cream
1	tablespoon butter

Heat oven to 350°. Combine flour, baking powder and salt; cut in lard until mixture is crumbly. Sprinkle with just enough ice water to make a dough that can be rolled. Roll out dough to fit 8-inch pie plate; fit into pie plate. Prick bottom and side thoroughly with fork. Flute edge. Bake 6 minutes. Cool.

Sprinkle crumbled bacon over crust; sprinkle with cheese. Lightly beat eggs with wire whisk; whisk in cream. Pour over bacon and cheese. Dot with butter. Bake 40 to 45 minutes or until set. Serve cold, cut into small wedges as an appetizer or serve large wedges hot as a main dish. Refrigerate any leftovers.

12 APPETIZER SERVINGS; 6 MAIN DISH SERVINGS.

Tip: Freezes well. Thaw and warm to serve.

Dip into this versatile favorite of Madison, WI., residents, Eileen and Heather Cumming. "Adapt ingredients to suit your taste," they suggest, "and try as an entrée or side dish with tortillas." Tester Susan Hall, Osakis, MN., "loved it" as did her guests.

Ensalada Dip

1½ to 2 (8-ounce) packages cream cheese, softened

1½ to 2 (9-ounce) cans bean dip

1 (12-ounce) jar thick chunky salsa

4 ounces (1 cup) shredded mild Cheddar cheese

4 to 5 lettuce leaves, chopped or shredded

2 to 3 medium tomatoes, chopped

1 (6-ounce) can pitted ripe olives, sliced

1 small bunch fresh cilantro

1 (16-ounce) package tortilla chips

Spread cream cheese evenly on bottom of 12½-inch round platter or pan with rim. Spread bean dip over cream cheese. Spread salsa over bean layer. Sprinkle with cheese, reserving about 2 table-spoons. Sprinkle with lettuce, reserved cheese, tomatoes, olive slices and cilantro. Serve with tortilla chips, or as an entrée or side dish with tortillas.

10 TO 12 APPETIZER SERVINGS;
6 TO 8 MAIN DISH SERVINGS.

Curry the favor of your guests by offering this with crisp raw vegetables. Wonderful as a dipping sauce for beef and chicken fondue, too. Tester Ruthann Lewis, Madison, WI., rated it "excellent" and spent only 10 minutes preparation time.

Curry Dip

1 cup mayonnaise (not salad dressing)

1 teaspoon tarragon or apple cider vinegar

½ teaspoon garlic powder or salt*

½ teaspoon onion powder or salt*

1 teaspoon ground horseradish

2 teaspoons to 2 tablespoons curry powder

Combine all ingredients; mix well. Cover and refrigerate 30 minutes or overnight.

1 CUP.

Tip: Use just one powder and one salt or it will be too salty.

*Hats off to Alan Wax, Evergreen Park, IL., for a colorful, hearty fiesta snack. Vary
amounts according to number of servings needed.*

Sombrero Snacks

1   loaf white or whole wheat
      sandwich bread, frozen
      Butter
      Hard salami rounds
      Softened butter or margarine
      Frilly toothpicks

Cut two 1¾-inch rounds from each slice of
frozen bread with a cookie cutter. Spread
rounds with butter. Cut a slit in each
salami round, from center to edge. Form
into cone or tent shape. Pinch ends and roll
edges up to create a brim. Place one on
each bread round. Add a toothpick frill on
diagonal on bottom seam of salami.

ABOUT 30 APPETIZERS.

*Tip: Softened colored cream cheese can be
piped in a zigzag border on bread
rounds with a #16 pastry tube. With a
#352 tube, a feather can be added in
place of the toothpick.*

*While on one of their annual scuba diving trips to Cozumel, Mexico, Peggy and Jim
Baumgaertner, LaCrosse, WI., watched a Mayan woman prepare this piquant sauce in a
backyard kitchen. Since then, the Baumgaertners "consume a quart in less than a week,
using it in scrambled eggs, on grilled fish, with cottage cheese and in many other dishes."*

Cozumel Salsa

5   large tomatoes, diced
1   large onion, diced
4   to 6 jalapeño peppers, finely
     chopped
¼   cup finely-chopped fresh cilantro
1   (8-ounce) bottle lime juice

Combine all ingredients; mix well. Cover
and refrigerate 8 hours or overnight.

1 QUART.

*Tip: To use as a base for Ceviche —
combine 2 pounds fresh, firm fish such
as sole, pompano, snapper or flaked
crab with salsa in glass dish. Cover
and refrigerate 4 hours. Serve with
tortilla chips.*

This picture-pretty hors d'oeuvre for special occasions should be called "disappearing spread" because it is devoured so eagerly. Contributor Betsy Norum, Minneapolis, MN., is past president of the Minnesota Home Economics Association and for years has lent her expertise to the publication of cookbooks for numerous non-profit organizations and food companies.

Curried Shrimp Spread

1	(8-ounce) package cream cheese, softened
¼	cup mayonnaise
½	teaspoon curry powder
	Salt and pepper, if desired
1	(4½-ounce) can shrimp, drained, rinsed, chopped
¼	cup sliced green onions
1	egg, hard-cooked, separated, chopped
	Norwegian flat bread

Blend cream cheese, mayonnaise, curry powder, salt and pepper until smooth. Spread cheese mixture ½ inch thick in shallow dish or plate. Arrange shrimp on cheese mixture, leaving ½ inch margin at outer edge; press lightly into cheese. Top shrimp with green onions and egg white, leaving margins at outer edges of each. Arrange chopped or sieved egg yolk in center. Chill several hours or overnight. Serve at room temperature with flat bread.

8 TO 10 SERVINGS.

A marvelous spring and summertime first course, particularly festive during the Easter season. Spoon sauce over each egg half to completely cover. Serve with small slices of buttered pumpernickel cocktail bread.

Eggs à la Russe

12	eggs, hard-cooked
1	cup mayonnaise
½	cup chili sauce
1	teaspoon dry mustard
1	teaspoon onion juice
¼	teaspoon salt
⅛	teaspoon white pepper
	Bibb lettuce leaves
2	tablespoons snipped fresh parsley
	Fresh parsley sprigs or anchovy fillets for garnish

Peel eggs carefully; refrigerate. Combine remaining ingredients except lettuce and parsley until well mixed. Cover and refrigerate several hours. To serve, line small salad plates with lettuce leaves. Halve eggs lengthwise. Place 2 halves, rounded side up, on each plate. Cover each egg with a spoonful of the sauce. Garnish with parsley or anchovy.

12 SERVINGS.

Tester Roma Hoff, Eau Claire, WI., served this delicate French treat to guests from Holland, Costa Rica, Panama and Honduras and was pleased to report "they all liked it!" Kathy Watts, Freehold, NJ., the recipe contributor, suggests serving it on lettuce leaves for a luncheon as well as for an appetizer.

Salmon Mousse

1	(10¾-ounce) can condensed tomato soup
1	(8-ounce) package cream cheese, cut up
2	envelopes unflavored gelatin
½	cup cold water
1	cup mayonnaise
1	tablespoon lemon juice
1	teaspoon horseradish
	Salt and pepper to taste
2	(6-ounce) cans pink salmon
1	cup finely-chopped celery
1	tablespoon finely-chopped onion
	Round buttery crackers

Heat soup in a saucepan until smooth. Stir in cream cheese until melted; set aside. Soften gelatin in water; stir into soup mixture. Cool. In blender combine mayonnaise, lemon juice, horseradish, salt and pepper; add soup mixture and blend. Mash salmon; stir in celery and onion. Stir in soup mixture by hand, mixing well to avoid lumps. Pour into 4½-cup greased mold. Refrigerate 1 hour; cover and refrigerate 8 hours or overnight. Serve with crackers.

10 SERVINGS.

A versatile, inviting dip or sauce from Gary Mark, Newberry, MI. Tester Charla Beukema, Marquette, MI., advises, "This won't last long — there are so many ways to enjoy it." She suggests serving it warm as a dip for shrimp, meatballs and meat fondue. Gary favors it with ham dinners and as a sandwich spread.

Saucy Mustard Dip

2	eggs, beaten
½	cup sugar
¼	cup dry mustard
½	cup vinegar
½	cup evaporated milk
2	tablespoons butter

Combine all ingredients except butter in top of double boiler. Stir over hot water until thickened. Stir in butter; cover and cool in refrigerator several hours or overnight. Sauce will thicken as it cools.

ABOUT 2 CUPS.

Ruby Bauer, Hudson, WI., keeps ingredients on hand for this quick-to-fix, big-batch **starter** *for Scandinavian menus. "Try with soups and salads, too," she suggests. Onion soup amount can be adjusted to suit tastes.*

Onion-Topped Crispbread

1   pint mayonnaise

1   envelope dry onion soup mix

1   (8½-ounce) package thin-style Norwegian crispbread

Dry Parmesan cheese

Combine mayonnaise and onion soup mix; refrigerate until spreading consistency. Heat oven to 350°. Spread mixture evenly on each piece; place on cookie sheet. Sprinkle with Parmesan cheese. Bake about 5 minutes. Watch carefully. While still warm cut each piece into halves, thirds or quarters for bite-size canapés.

102 TO 216 APPETIZERS.

Tip: Cool, cover tightly and refrigerate or freeze. Warm to serve.

Ann Zavoral, Fargo, ND., suggests using a high-quality mustard for these unique canapés she and her daughter, Sara, enjoyed at a gathering of friends in Sweden. Party rye bread works well for appetizers; larger bread slices can be used for luncheon sandwiches. Tester Pam Fredericksen, Davenport, IA., tried a variety of cheeses and spices and found "all equally delicious."

Smörgås

Small dark rye, limpa or other deli-style bread

Prepared mustard

Banana slices

Slices of Gruyère or other cheese

Curry powder, paprika and/or garlic powder

Heat broiler or oven to 400°. Spread mustard on bread slices. Place banana slices on bread. Place cheese slices over banana slices; sprinkle with spice. Broil or bake several minutes or until lightly browned and hot.

5 TO 6 SERVINGS

These colorful, creative roll-ups must be thoroughly chilled before slicing to set the filling. So, assemble the night before serving, if you wish. Arrange on chilled plate and keep extras in the refrigerator until ready to use.

Jalapeño Ham Rolls

1	(10-ounce) jar green jalapeño jelly
1	(8-ounce) package cream cheese, softened
24	slices boiled ham
	Toothpicks

Spoon about ¾ of jelly into bowl. Add cream cheese and mix well. Place boiled ham slices on paper towels to absorb moisture. Spread 1 spoonful cheese mixture on each ham slice. Roll up, starting with the short edge. Spread and roll all ham slices; arrange on flat cookie sheet or shallow pan; cover with plastic wrap and refrigerate 8 hours or overnight. Chill serving plate. Cut each roll into 4 pieces. Pierce each piece with a toothpick. Serve on chilled plate.

8 SERVINGS.

"Easy to make and well liked by all my family," reports Barbara Francis, Blytheville, AR. Tester Bonita English, Red Cloud, NE., echoed Barbara's pleasure. Be sure to select tomato and avocado which are fully ripe but firm for this colorful dip.

Pica de Gallo

1	large tomato, finely chopped
1	medium avocado, peeled, seeded, finely chopped
½	onion, finely chopped
4	chili peppers, finely chopped
2	tablespoons vinegar
1	tablespoon vegetable oil
1	teaspoon lime juice
½	teaspoon salt
¼	teaspoon garlic powder
¼	teaspoon sugar
	Tortilla chips

Combine all ingredients except tortilla chips;. Cover and refrigerate. Serve with tortilla chips.

ABOUT 2½ CUPS.

Katherine Bradbury, Edina, MN., enjoys cooking so much she has shared some of her kitchen secrets with friends through cooking classes and in several cookbooks for non-profit organizations. This Greek recipe takes time and a little patience to prepare, but the results are worth the extra effort. "Very impressive," remarked our testers.

Spanakopitta

1   large onion, minced

1   bunch scallions, including tops, chopped

1   pound butter, melted

3   (10-ounce) packages, frozen chopped spinach, thawed, drained, squeezed dry

6   eggs, slightly beaten

8   ounces feta cheese, crumbled or grated

10 ounces (2½ cups) mozzarella cheese, shredded

½   cup fine dry bread crumbs

½   cup chopped fresh parsley

½   cup minced fresh dill or 2 teaspoons dried dill
    Salt
    Freshly ground pepper
    Nutmeg

1   cup fine dry bread crumbs (homemade or herb flavored)

1   (16-ounce) package filo, thawed
    Fresh parsley

Tip: If mold is made the day before serving, refrigerate until ready to bake. Mold can also be made several days ahead. Wrap well; freeze. Mold can be baked right from the freezer, but baking time will have to be lengthened.

Sauté onion and scallions in 2 tablespoons of the butter. Add spinach; cook over low heat, stirring occasionally until onion is soft and spinach moisture has evaporated. Cool slightly. Pour mixture into large bowl; add eggs, cheeses; ½ cup crumbs, chopped parsley, dill, salt, pepper and nutmeg. Stir well. Grease 2 to 3-quart ring mold or Bundt pan.

Heat oven to 350°. Unfold filo; cut in half lengthwise. Place on waxed paper; cover with another sheet of waxed paper and a damp towel. Place 1 sheet of filo diagonally across mold, allowing it to extend about 1½ inches over sides of pan and over center opening. Press against side of mold. Brush filo with butter. Cover other side of mold in same fashion. Sprinkle with a very thin layer of bread crumbs. Continue layering filo, butter and crumbs until you have used 16 pieces of dough.

Fill mold with spinach mixture; cut out filo that is still covering hole in center of mold. Fold overhanging pastry over filling; brushing with butter. If desired, add a couple more layers of filo on top to make a thicker bottom crust. Place pan on cookie sheet to catch any butter drips. Bake 1¼ hours. Let rest at least 15 minutes before turning out of pan.

10 SERVINGS.

Scouting a new idea for make-ahead holiday menus? Vasthi Christensen, Council Bluffs, IA., describes her contribution as "festive and fancy." Tester Karen Michael, Eden Prairie, MN., trimmed calories by using "fat-free deli ham and lowfat cream cheese."

Holiday Ham Dip Wreath

1	(2-ounce) jar pimento pieces (not chopped), drained
1	(8-ounce) package cream cheese, softened
12	ounces luncheon ham, ground
2	tablespoons ground onion
2	teaspoons Worcestershire sauce
1	tablespoon lemon juice
	Snipped fresh parsley
	Rye or other crackers

Using largest piece of pimento, cut enough ¼-inch strips to make loop bow for decoration. Chop remaining pimento. Whip cream cheese until smooth and creamy. Combine with ham, onion, Worcestershire sauce, lemon juice and chopped pimento; mix well. Fill and lightly pack mixture into lightly greased 20-ounce ring mold. Cover and refrigerate 2 to 3 hours or overnight. Unmold onto serving plate; sprinkle with parsley and decorate with pimento bow. Serve with crackers.

ABOUT 2½ CUPS.

This Japanese version of American fried chicken is a popular appetizer at the Japanese Language Village. It is served at the first meal of every session and wins over any who are shy about sampling Asian cuisine.

Tori no Karage

2	tablespoons soy sauce
1	tablespoon sake
1	teaspoon ginger juice*
14	ounces skinless, boneless chicken breasts, cut into 1-inch pieces
	Vegetable oil for deep frying
	Cornstarch

Combine soy sauce, sake and ginger juice; marinate chicken in sauce 20 minutes. Heat oil to 320°. Toss chicken lightly in cornstarch; deep fry 3 to 4 minutes or until golden brown.

4 SERVINGS.

*Tip: *Peel and grate fresh gingerroot, then squeeze.*

This prize-winning recipe shared by Juneko Grilley, Madison, WI., is a perfect warm-up for a meatless main dish. Japanese in origin, the recipe has been adapted for western palates.

Pickled Beef

2	pounds beef tenderloin or sirloin steak
1½	cups soy sauce
1½	cups rice vinegar
2	cloves garlic, crushed
3	walnut-size pieces of fresh gingerroot, grated
2	medium onions, sliced, separated into rings
1	lemon, sliced

Heat oven to 325°. Trim fat from meat. Roll meat into a log; tie with string. Roast meat to rare (internal temperature 140°), about 35 minutes. Meanwhile, combine soy sauce, vinegar, garlic and gingerroot; add onion rings and lemon slices. Rinse meat under cool running water; pat dry with paper towel. Marinate meat in sauce in refrigerator 2 to 3 days*. Slice pickled meat just before serving and garnish with pickled lemon and onion rings.

16 SERVINGS.

*Tip: *Use a plastic bag for marinating; place meat and sauce in bag, seal securely and turn occasionally.*

Perfect for a cocktail buffet when placed in chafing dish or other warming server. Easily doubled to serve an open house crowd.

Oriental Cocktail Franks

1	cup packed brown sugar
3	tablespoons flour
2	teaspoons dry mustard
1	cup unsweetened pineapple juice
½	cup vinegar
2	tablespoons soy sauce
	Cocktail franks, sliced frankfurters or sausage pieces

Blend brown sugar, flour and mustard in saucepan. Stir in pineapple juice, vinegar and soy sauce. Cook and stir until thickened and bubbly. Heat franks separately to serve as *dippers* or add franks to sauce and place in chafing dish to keep hot.

2 CUPS SAUCE.

Count on a guaranteed crowd-pleaser with this layered southwest sensation. Contributed by Bonnie Damkroger, Bloomington, MN., it was enthusiastically taste-tested and eagerly consumed at several parties.

Tex-Mex Torte

1   (8-ounce) package cream cheese, softened
1   (8-ounce) carton dairy sour cream
2   medium to large ripe avocados, peeled, seeded
1   tablespoon seasoned salt
2   (16-ounce) cans refried beans
1   (2¼-ounce) chopped ripe olives, drained
    Chopped lettuce
1   medium onion or 2 bunches green onions, finely chopped
2   medium to large tomatoes, chopped
6   ounces (1½ cups) shredded Cheddar cheese
    Dorito chips or tostados

Blend cream cheese, sour cream, avocados and seasoned salt. (Add a little mayonnaise if mixture is too thick.) Spread beans on large platter; spread with cream cheese mixture. Layer with olives, lettuce, onions, tomatoes and cheese. Serve with Dorito chips or tostados.

12 SERVINGS.

Home economist, Diana Gulden, Minneapolis, MN., and her Spanish-born husband, José, first sampled this appetizer or "tapa" at a Madrid restaurant. It tastefully showcases the abundant, economical sweet red peppers grown in Spain. Diana prefers using fresh peppers, but says good quality pimentos found in jars can be substituted. For variety, try as a unique side dish for grilled meats, fish or poultry.

Roasted Red Peppers and Garlic

2 to 3 large red bell peppers or 1 (11.5-ounce) jar whole roasted pimentos

2 tablespoons olive oil

2 cloves garlic, finely chopped (not pressed)

Salt

Thinly-sliced, toasted French bread

If using fresh peppers, broil whole peppers, turning frequently until completely charred and blistered; cool. Peel, remove seeds and cut into ¼-inch wide strips. If using jarred roasted pimentos, drain liquid from peppers, remove seeds and pat peppers dry with paper towels. Cut into ¼-inch wide strips.

Heat oil in skillet; sauté garlic about 30 seconds. Reduce heat; add peppers and salt. Gently stir pepper strips in oil mixture until thoroughly heated, about 5 minutes. Serve with French bread.

4 TO 6 SERVINGS.

"Serve this Bavarian specialty with German dark bread and a stouthearted beer or wine," suggests Gary Tucker, Ogden, UT. "And, be prepared for the bold flavor," he advises. Tester Dianne Curtiss, Battle Creek, MI., liked it with Brie as well as Camembert.

Obatzten

2 (4-ounce) Camembert cheeses, softened

1 large onion, finely chopped

2 egg yolks, if desired

¼ cup butter or margarine

3 to 4 tablespoons dry mustard

1 tablespoon garlic powder or fresh garlic, minced

Dash of cayenne pepper

About 2 tablespoons paprika

Mash all ingredients together until stiff cheese spread consistency. Let stand 1 hour to blend flavors. Spread on crackers or dark bread or serve with pretzels.

8 SERVINGS.

Take a tasty tip from the French who savor snails in a multitude of ways. Here is an impressive curtain-raiser for your most elegant dinner party from Linda Norderhaug, Brookfield, WI. In Burgundy, snails feed on grape leaves before making menu appearances.

Mushrooms Escargots

2   dozen good-sized mushroom caps
4   dozen snails
1   cup butter, softened
2 to 3 tablespoons chopped shallots
2 to 3 cloves garlic, finely chopped
¼   cup chopped fresh parsley
     Salt and freshly-ground pepper
¼   cup chopped black walnuts
24   toast rounds, sautéed in butter

Heat broiler. Wipe mushroom caps with a damp cloth. Drain snails. Cream butter with shallots, garlic, parsley, salt and pepper. Rub mushroom caps lightly with seasoned butter and place hollow-side-down on broiler pan. Broil 2 minutes. Remove, turn mushroom caps over and put 2 snails in each cap. Reduce oven temperature to 450°. Sprinkle mushroom caps with chopped walnuts; divide remaining seasoned butter among mushrooms. Bake about 8 minutes. Remove from oven and place each mushroom on a round of sautéed toast.

6 SERVINGS.

A favored harvest-time appetizer when eating apples are in their prime. At least a day before serving, prepare cheese mixture to mellow flavors. Spread can be placed in a crock surrounded by apple slices and crackers so guests can help themselves.

Roquefort-Cognac Crisps

6   ounces Roquefort cheese, softened
¼   cup butter, softened
¼   cup brandy
6   red apples
     Lemon juice
     Assorted crackers

Combine cheese, butter and brandy; cover and refrigerate at least 8 hours. Core apples; do not peel. Cut into ½-inch slices and dip quickly into lemon juice to prevent darkening. (If you want apple slices that lie flat, cut each cored apple in half lengthwise; place each half on its cut side and slice crosswise.) Spread slices with cheese mixture and serve with crackers.

8 SERVINGS.

Ribbons of colorful peppers highlight this sherry-laced Spanish appetizer. Spanish villagers celebrate "Banquet Night" by sampling a variety of "tapas" along with imported apple and grape juices. For a main dish marry this recipe with rice and a salad of lightly-dressed romaine.

Garlic Shrimp with Peppers

2   tablespoons olive oil

1   tablespoon minced garlic

1   medium yellow onion, cut into half circles

1   red bell pepper, cut into strips

1   yellow bell pepper, cut into strips

1   green bell pepper, cut into strips

15 to 20 medium shrimp, peeled, deveined

1   tablespoon sherry

     Salt

     Romaine lettuce leaves

     Paprika

Heat oil in skillet until hot. Sauté garlic and onion about 30 seconds. Add peppers and cook about 1 minute. Add shrimp and sherry; cook 3 to 5 minutes. Salt to taste. Serve on Romaine lettuce leaves and sprinkle with paprika.

4 TO 6 SERVINGS.

Why buy this ready-made when you can prepare it so easily at home? Be sure the herbs are fresh and flavorful for this do-ahead spread for crackers or French bread rounds.

Mock Boursin au Poivre

1   (8-ounce) package cream cheese, softened

1   clove garlic, crushed

1   teaspoon caraway seed

1   teaspoon snipped fresh basil leaves

1   teaspoon snipped fresh dill weed

1   teaspoon snipped fresh chives

     Lemon pepper

     Assorted crackers

Blend all ingredients except lemon pepper and crackers. Pat into flat round on a piece of waxed paper. Sprinkle another piece of waxed paper with lemon pepper. Roll all sides of cheese in lemon pepper. Wrap and refrigerate at least 1 day before serving to blend flavors. Serve with crackers.

6 TO 8 SERVINGS.

Judith Larson, Bayport, MN., enjoys ethnic cooking as well as entrepreneurial duties as owner of Everything Kitchen & Coffee in Edina, MN. This favorite Greek appetizer is quite easy to make and freezes beautifully. Keep pastry sheets covered until you are ready to work with them so the delicate texture remains pliable.

Tiropetes

1 (8-ounce) package cream cheese or 1 (3-ounce) package cream cheese and ⅓ pound feta cheese

3 ounces Gruyère cheese, finely shredded

1 egg

2 tablespoons snipped fresh parsley

5 to 6 sheets filo dough (about 14x20 inches)

½ cup butter, melted

Heat oven to 375°. Cream the cream cheese (and feta cheese, if used) until light; mix in Gruyère. Add egg and beat until blended. Mix in parsley. Lay out 1 sheet of filo and brush lightly with melted butter. Cut into 14x3-inch strips. Place 1 heaping teaspoon of cheese mixture in one corner of a strip; fold over, making a triangle. Continue folding, making sure the bottom edge is always perpendicular to the alternate side edge until you come to the end of the strip. Place on ungreased cookie sheets. Bake 10 minutes or until puffed and golden brown. After baking, tiropetes can be cooled and frozen. To reheat, place frozen pastries on cookie sheet; heat at 375° for 10 to 15 minutes.

ABOUT 3 DOZEN APPETIZERS.

With your sharpest French chef knife, go to work on the mushroom chopping. The blender does the rest and you can refrigerate the savory results for several days before serving.

French Mushroom Pâté

16 ounces fresh mushrooms, finely chopped

2 tablespoons unsalted butter

1 tablespoon dry sherry

4 ounces semi-soft boursin cheese spread with garlic and spices

4 ounces cream cheese

Sauté mushrooms in butter and sherry 5 to 10 minutes or until tender and almost all liquid has evaporated. Place in blender or food processor with cheeses. Process until well blended. Cover and refrigerate at least 3 hours before serving.

ABOUT 1½ CUPS.

Sidney A. Rand, former President of St. Olaf College and one-time Ambassador to Norway, and his wife, Lois, were served this elegant appetizer at a dinner party. It was hosted by General Sir Anthony Farrar-Hockley, a British general who was Commander of NATO forces in Norway, and this is his own recipe. Since that memorable dinner, Lois has served it often "with great success." Tester, Ingrid Lenz Harrison, Wayzata, MN., reported delicious results in "less than 30 minutes" of preparation time.

Sardine Pâté in Lemon Cases

4	large lemons
1	(7-ounce) can sardines, tuna or salmon
6	ounces cream cheese, softened
6	tablespoons dairy sour cream or plain yogurt
½	teaspoon Dijon mustard
1	teaspoon finely-chopped onion
½	teaspoon paprika
¼	teaspoon salt
	Freshly ground black pepper
	Dash of cayenne pepper
1	egg white
4	sprigs fresh thyme, parsley, basil or celery leaves

Cut tops from lemons; reserve. Remove lemon pulp with grapefruit knife or spoon. Discard seeds and membrane; reserve pulp and juice of 1 lemon. (Use remaining juice and pulp for other purposes.) Trim bottoms of lemons so they will stand upright. (If skins are very thick, remove excess from insides.) Mash fish, cream cheese, sour cream and mustard together until smooth. Add onion, paprika, salt, black and cayenne peppers. Adjust seasoning if necessary. Strain juice and pulp of 1 lemon into mixture; blend. Beat egg white until stiff; fold into fish mixture. Spoon pâté into lemons, heaping slightly. Top with lemon caps. Cover and refrigerate. Just before serving tuck a sprig of green into top of each lemon.

4 SERVINGS.

This taste of spring is served by German Villager Bryan Rubbelke, Arden Hills, MN., at some of the many ethnic dinners his family enjoys hosting. Serve with small plates and forks for easy eating. Tester Barbara Des Camps, Casper, WY., suggests using fresh asparagus, blanched, when it is in season.

Ham and Asparagus Rolls

6	thin slices boiled ham
1	(15-ounce) can (12 spears) asparagus, well drained, reserve liquid
	Pimento strips
1	cup asparagus liquid
¼	teaspoon dried thyme leaves
	Dash of salt
1½	teaspoons (½ envelope) unflavored gelatin
2	tablespoons cold water
	Few drops lemon juice

Place ham slices flat; place 2 asparagus spears on each slice. Roll ham around asparagus; place pimento on top. Heat asparagus liquid, thyme and salt to boiling. Soften gelatin in cold water; pour hot liquid through a strainer over gelatin; stir to dissolve. Add lemon juice; cool. Spoon a little of cooled, but still liquid, gelatin over top of each roll. Refrigerate to chill; add another layer of gelatin; chill again. Repeat for a third layer. Keep refrigerated until serving. Serve on small plates with forks.

6 SERVINGS.

Another choice chafing dish appetizer is this elegant Greek repast. **Sagnaki** *is Greek for* **hot pan**. *This could also be served as a main dish with rice.*

Shrimp Sagnaki

2	pounds medium sized raw shrimp
2	(8-ounce) packages frozen artichoke hearts
⅓ to ½	cup olive oil
8	ounces small whole mushrooms
4	cloves garlic, finely minced
1	teaspoon salt
	Freshly-ground pepper
1	teaspoon dried oregano leaves, crumbled
¼	cup fresh lemon juice
¼	cup finely-chopped parsley

Peel and devein shrimp. Blanch artichoke hearts 2 minutes in boiling, salted water; drain. Heat olive oil in skillet; add shrimp and mushrooms; cook, stirring constantly until shrimp turn pink. Add artichoke hearts, garlic, salt, pepper and oregano. Cook until thoroughly heated. Sprinkle with lemon juice and stir lightly to blend flavors. Serve in chafing dish; garnish with parsley.

10 SERVINGS.

Definitely deluxe for special occasion open houses and dinner parties. Make a day ahead of serving and unmold onto a pretty pedestal plate; border with parsley sprigs alternating with lemon wedges.

Red Caviar Mousse

1	(8-ounce) package cream cheese, softened
2	tablespoons mayonnaise
2	tablespoons dairy sour cream
½	teaspoon lemon juice
¼	teaspoon onion powder
¼	teaspoon dill weed
¼	teaspoon salt
1½	teaspoons unflavored gelatin
½	cup milk
¼	teaspoon Maggi seasoning or Worcestershire sauce
1	(4-ounce) jar red caviar
	Fresh parsley sprigs
	Lemon wedges
	Assorted crackers and/or small rye bread rounds

Blend cream cheese, mayonnaise, sour cream, lemon juice, onion powder, dill weed and salt; mix until very smooth. Combine gelatin with milk in small saucepan; let stand 5 minutes. Place over low heat and stir until gelatin is dissolved. Blend in Maggi and cheese mixture. Fold in caviar gently to avoid breaking. Pour into greased 2-cup mold; Refrigerate until set. Unmold onto serving plate; garnish with parsley and lemon. Serve with crackers and rye rounds.

10 SERVINGS.

From the Chinese Village comes a delectable dim sum staple. Wonton wrappers should be kept covered before and after filling so they do not dry out before cooking. If you are making Pot Stickers an hour or so ahead of cooking, cover completely with plastic wrap and refrigerate.

Pot Stickers

½	pound Chinese cabbage, bok choy or celery cabbage
1	pound ground pork
1	teaspoon mashed fresh gingerroot
1	tablespoon dry sherry
1	tablespoon soy sauce
1	tablespoon sesame oil
4	dozen wonton wrappers cut into circles
	Peanut oil
1	cup chicken broth
¼	cup soy sauce
2	tablespoons rice vinegar

Finely chop cabbage; squeeze to extract water. Combine with pork, gingerroot, sherry, 1 tablespoon soy sauce and sesame oil. Dampen edge of 1 wonton with water; put 1 teaspoon of filling in center. Press edges together to seal completely. Repeat with remaining wrappers and filling. Heat large skillet over high heat; coat bottom with peanut oil. Fry one side of dumplings. Pour in chicken broth almost to cover. Cover and cook until liquid is evaporated and bottom of dumplings are crisp. Combine ¼ cup soy sauce and rice vinegar. Serve with dumplings.

4 DOZEN APPETIZERS.

Tip: Dumplings can be frozen; cook frozen or thawed.

Corinne Matney, Northfield, MN., describes these hearty meat-filled pastry foldovers as "spicy, tasty and enjoyed by all." For serving with soup or salad for lunch or supper, just increase size of puffs. Corinne suggests adding chopped leftover cooked vegetables to filling, if desired. For a vegetarian version, substitute lentils and rice for the meat.

Indian Pastry Puffs

FILLING

½	onion, chopped
1	clove garlic, minced
2	tablespoons margarine or vegetable oil
2	teaspoons ground coriander
¼	teaspoon cayenne pepper
¼	teaspoon ginger
¼	teaspoon cinnamon
¼	cup chopped tomatoes
1½	cups ground lamb or beef
1¼	teaspoon salt
¼	cup water
2	teaspoons fresh lemon juice

PASTRY

2	cups all-purpose flour
1	teaspoon salt
¼	cup margarine, melted
7	tablespoons plain yogurt
1	egg white, slightly beaten

Sauté onion and garlic in margarine until onion is translucent. Add coriander, cayenne, ginger and cinnamon; stir and cook 1 minute. Add tomatoes, lamb and 1¼ teaspoons salt; cook and stir until meat is browned. Add water and lemon juice; cook and stir until water has disappeared. Drain and cool.

Heat oven to 400°.* Combine flour and salt; stir in margarine; mix well. Gradually stir in yogurt, working it in with hands, about 5 minutes. Knead until dough is satiny and smooth. Roll out pastry very thin on lightly-floured surface. Cut into 2½-inch circles with cookie cutter. Brush edges lightly with egg white. Place 1 rounded tablespoon of filling for large size or 1 rounded teaspoon of filling for small size on each circle. Fold dough over and crimp edges with fork, being sure to seal well. Bake 12 to 15 minutes. Serve with yogurt or chutney, if desired.

**3 TO 4 DOZEN APPETIZERS;
4 TO 6 MAIN DISH SERVINGS.**

*Tip: *Puffs can also be deep fried in oil heated to 375°. Fry until golden brown; drain on paper towels.*

Goes together in minutes and is delicious atop thinly-sliced French bread, toasted pita triangles or sturdy crackers. Let stand a bit at room temperature before serving for easy spreading consistency and best flavor.

Sherried Beef-Olive Spread

1	teaspoon dried minced onion
1	tablespoon dry sherry
1	(8-ounce) package cream cheese, softened
2	tablespoons mayonnaise
1	(3-ounce) package finely snipped smoked sliced beef
¼	cup chopped stuffed olives

Soften onion in sherry; blend in remaining ingredients. Cover and refrigerate.

6 SERVINGS.

Marjorie Delin, Minneapolis, MN., says these are a huge success every time she serves them. She suggests preparing them when bread is fresh for easy rolling. Make ahead and freeze, if you wish.

Toasted Mushroom Canapés

20	slices thinly-sliced white sandwich bread
8	ounces fresh mushrooms, finely chopped
	Seasoned salt
1	tablespoon butter or margarine
1	(8-ounce) package cream cheese, softened
½	teaspoon salt, if desired
5	tablespoons butter or margarine, melted

Cut crusts off bread slices; flatten slices with rolling pin. In skillet, sauté mushrooms and seasoned salt in 1 tablespoon butter. Remove from heat. Blend in cream cheese and salt. Spread mixture evenly on each slice of bread; roll up. Spread or brush melted butter on outside of each roll. Cover cookie sheet with foil. Place rolls on cookie sheet; freeze. Package in batches; do not layer. To serve, thaw slightly and cut each roll into thirds. Place cut side down on boiler pan. Broil each side about 3 minutes, watching carefully, until light brown.

60 APPETIZERS.

Favorite Greek ingredients — feta, shrimp, garlic and mint — combine for a terrific-tasting topping. Watch very carefully during broiling step to avoid overcooking.

Feta-Shrimp Triangles

4   (5 to 6-inch) pita breads
    Unsalted butter, softened
8   ounces feta cheese
8   ounces baby or medium shrimp, chopped
2   large cloves garlic, crushed
½   cup mayonnaise
½   teaspoon chili powder
½   teaspoon ground cumin
2   tablespoons snipped fresh mint
    Sesame seed
    Paprika

Heat oven to 300°. Slip knife into edge of pita breads, dividing them in half horizontally. Spread each half with butter; cut into 5 to 6 triangles. (If bread is large, cut into 8 to 10 triangles.) Place triangles on cookie sheet. Bake 15 to 20 minutes or until light brown; remove from oven. Heat broiler.

Meanwhile crumble feta cheese into medium bowl; add remaining ingredients except sesame seed and paprika, mixing with a fork until blended. Spread topping generously on toasted triangles. Sprinkle tops with sesame seed and sprinkle with paprika. Place on broiler pan and broil until tops are brown and bubbly.

ABOUT 40 APPETIZERS.

Tip: Triangles can be frozen. Reheat on cookie sheet at 450° for 5 to 10 minutes or until thoroughly heated.

Whether you're of English descent or not, you can toast the health of holiday guests with this traditional hot punch. **Wassail** *comes from the Saxon words* **wass hael** *meaning* **be whole** *or* **be well.** *Heather Randall King, Edina, MN., keeps this on hand in December to heat up in quantity or by cupfuls in the microwave, depending on the number of visitors.*

Olde English Wassail

½ cup water

1 cup sugar

4 (3-inch) cinnamon sticks

1 lemon, sliced

2 cups pineapple juice

2 cups fresh orange juice

½ cup fresh lemon juice

6 cups claret wine

1 cup dry sherry

Heat water, sugar, cinnamon sticks and lemon slices to boiling in large pan. Reduce heat and simmer 5 minutes. Add juices, claret and sherry. Heat and stir until drinking temperature; do not boil. Remove lemon slices and cinnamon sticks before serving.

20 SERVINGS.

A refreshing change from the heartier red wine version, this cooler is the perfect complement for Spanish appetizers or tapas. If desired, combine all ingredients ahead except for soda water. Add that just before serving to preserve effervescence.

Sangria Blanca

½ cup sugar

½ cup fresh lemon juice

1 lemon

1 (750 mL.) bottle Chablis

1 (10-ounce) bottle club soda

½ cup fresh orange juice

¼ cup Curaçao (or other orange liqueur)

   Ice cubes

   Fresh mint leaves

In large nonmetal pitcher dissolve sugar in lemon juice. Cut lemon into cartwheel slices. Add Chablis, club soda, orange juice, Curaçao, lemons and ice cubes to lemon juice mixture; stir well. Garnish with mint.

12 SERVINGS.

Marlis Runnberg, Silver Bay, MN., shares this special sipper served for celebrations of the Finland-Minnesota Historical Society. Tester, Doris Ann Girerd, Palo Alto, CA., deemed it festive enough to serve "in a very elegant crystal punch bowl" to faculty members. Together they toasted Stanford University's 100 years.

Fruit Juice Glögg

4	oranges
1	gallon apple cider
2	quarts (64 ounces) white grape juice
1	cup sugar
4	(3-inch) cinnamon sticks
32	whole cloves
2⅔	cups raisins
2⅔	cups slivered blanched almonds

Cut peel from each orange in a single spiral, if possible. (Save orange pulp for another use.) In Dutch oven or large kettle, combine all ingredients. Cover and let stand 4 hours. Heat to boiling over medium heat. Reduce heat to low and simmer 30 minutes. Serve warm including some raisins and almonds in each serving.

48 (½-CUP) SERVINGS.

Incorporate French flag colors in this sparkling celebration punch. If desired, freeze mounds of sherbet on a cookie sheet ahead of time and add to punch bowl with fresh blueberries just before serving.

Bastille Day Punch

2	(10-ounce) packages frozen red raspberries in syrup, thawed
½	cup lemon juice
½	cup sugar
1	(750 mL.) bottle red rosé wine, chilled
1	quart raspberry sherbet
1	(750 mL.) bottle champagne, chilled
1	pint fresh blueberries

In blender, purée raspberries. In punch bowl, combine puréed raspberries, lemon juice, sugar and wine; stir until sugar is dissolved. Just before serving, scoop sherbet into punch bowl; add champagne. Stir gently. Float blueberries on top.

ABOUT 3 QUARTS.

Ralph Larson, Bayport, MN., has created his own special version of the mulled Swedish drink, so popular during the holidays. Not surprisingly, the Larsons find that their guests appreciate this warm welcome all winter long.

Glögg

12	blanched almonds, halved
12	ounces raisins
	Peel of 1 orange, cut into quarters
15	whole cloves
2	(3-inch) cinnamon sticks
1	small piece fresh gingerroot
12	cardamom pods
4	cups water
1	gallon port wine
1	4/5-quart bourbon
¾	cup sugar

Put almonds, raisins, orange peel, cloves, cinnamon, gingerroot, cardamom and water in saucepan; cover and simmer about 45 minutes.

Pour into large kettle; add wine. Cover tightly and heat to just below boiling point. Turn off heat and carefully add bourbon. Cover and heat again to just below boiling point. Keep covered and let cool about 5 minutes. Remove cover. Light a match and carefully hold over wine mixture to light surface. Let burn 1 to 2 seconds. Quickly cover tightly to smother flame. Again, light for 1 to 2 seconds. Cover to smother flame. Stir in sugar. Strain out fruit. Serve warm in punch cups.

1½ GALLONS.

Despite all the singing and dancing, there's a nip in the autumn air and a warming brew hits the spot. Be sure to allow for the 1 hour of standing time for the syrup. This can be heated on the stove and served from a slow-cooker to maintain proper serving temperature.

Oktoberfest Warmer

½	cup sugar
2	cups water
1	(3-inch) cinnamon stick
5	whole cloves
1	teaspoon ground allspice
2	cups orange juice
1	cup lemon juice
1	quart apple juice or cider

In large saucepan, combine sugar and water. Heat to boiling over medium-high heat; boil 5 minutes. Remove from heat; add cinnamon, cloves and allspice. Cover and let syrup stand 1 hour. Strain into a bowl. When ready to serve combine syrup and fruit juices in large saucepan. Simmer until piping hot. Serve immediately.

ABOUT 16 (½-CUP) SERVINGS.

Two warm weather refreshers from Kafté in the Edina, MN., Galleria sooth and invigorate visitors at the elegant shopping complex. Fine French roast coffee — double strength — gives these sippers robust personality.

Iced Kafté Frothy

2 cups double strength French roast coffee

2 cups 2% milk

3 tablespoons sugar

1 tablespoon vanilla

Crushed ice or ice cubes

Combine all ingredients except ice in blender; whip 15 seconds. Serve over ice.

3 TO 4 SERVINGS.

Iced Granita Latte

¼ cup half & half

¼ cup whole milk

¾ cup double strength French roast coffee

1 teaspoon vanilla

1 tablespoon sugar

Ice cubes

Whipped cream

Unsweetened cocoa or nutmeg

Combine half & half, milk, coffee, vanilla and sugar in blender. Add enough ice cubes to cover the mixture (almost to top of blender). Blend until ice is finely chopped (do not purée). Pour over cubes. Top with whipped cream and sprinkle with cocoa or nutmeg.

1 SERVING

Russian store Dollars and cents are exchanged at the village bank for authentic currency from the target country. "Villagers" can then shop at their village's store for souvenirs and gifts like this *Matryoshka* doll from the Russian republic.

Stavkirke The Language Villages uses architecture to enhance the feeling of living in another country. The Stavkirke, a three-quarter-size replica of a 950-year-old stave church, adds to the Norwegian Village's architectural authenticity.

Select tender young spinach leaves for this India-inspired salad. Because the greens wilt quickly after dressing is added, wait until just before serving to toss. And, since apples darken soon after slicing, leave this step until end of preparation.

Spinach Salad with Chutney Dressing

SALAD

1	cup pecan halves
1½	pounds fresh spinach
2	red-skinned eating apples
½	cup raisins
½	cup chopped green onions

DRESSING

½	cup vegetable oil
¼	cup mango-ginger chutney
1	teaspoon curry powder
1	teaspoon dry mustard
½	teaspoon salt
2	tablespoons lemon juice

Heat oven to 300°. Spread pecans on cookie sheet; toast about 12 minutes. Wash, stem and dry spinach. Core unpeeled apples; halve and cut crosswise into thin slices. Combine all salad ingredients in large bowl; toss to mix. Combine all dressing ingredients in small bowl. Stir until well mixed. Add to salad mixture and toss gently to coat. Serve immediately.

4 SERVINGS.

Diana Gulden, Minneapolis, MN., treasures this "beautiful recipe" served to her in a Spanish home. "On a recent trip to my husband's native country we were served pomegranates in a salad, for dessert and as a garnish," she recalls. "They are a popular, versatile Spanish staple."

Pomegranate and Escarole Salad

1	medium head escarole (curly endive), torn into bite-sized pieces
¼	cup pomegranate seeds
¼	cup olive oil
2	tablespoons white wine vinegar
	Salt and pepper to taste

Place escarole and pomegranate seeds in salad bowl. Shake remaining ingredients together in tightly covered container. Just before serving, pour dressing over salad and toss.

4 TO 6 SERVINGS.

Dotted with ripe olives and little white onions, this mixed green salad is tossed with a flavorful, Roquefort-sparked dressing. Combine dressing ingredients at least several hours ahead to maximize flavor.

Black and White Salad

DRESSING

½   cup French dressing

¼   cup crumbled Roquefort cheese

1   clove garlic, crushed

SALAD

½   head lettuce, torn into bite-sized pieces

4   endive leaves, torn into bite-sized pieces

6   spinach leaves, torn into bite-sized pieces

½   cup sliced ripe olives

1   (3-ounce) jar pickled onions, drained

Combine all dressing ingredients in tightly-covered container. Toss all salad ingredients together. Just before serving, combine dressing with salad.

4 SERVINGS.

This North African combo contributed by Linda Church, Oxford, OH., received A + in every testing category by Kitty Winn, Edina, MN. "Although the salad sounds unusual, I'm so glad we tried it," she says. "It's amazingly easy, incredibly tasty and very attractive!"

Orange and Radish Delight

6   tablespoons lemon juice

2   tablespoons sugar
    Dash of salt

4   medium navel oranges

10   large radishes, coarsely shredded

Combine lemon juice, sugar and salt in a small bowl; stir until sugar and salt dissolve. With a sharp knife, peel oranges, removing white membrane. Cut oranges into segments by cutting on both sides of each section. Combine oranges, radishes and dressing. Serve at once or refrigerate.

4 TO 6 SERVINGS.

"This is one of the most requested recipes at Maplelag and is served almost every Saturday night during the ski season," reports Mary Richards, Callaway, MN. She and her husband, Jim, own and operate this ski resort and conference center, which hosts Swedish and Russian Language Villages during the summer and elderhostels focusing on foreign languages in the spring.

Greek Spinach Salad

DRESSING

1½   cups vegetable and/or olive oil or combination

½   cup lemon juice

5   large garlic cloves, minced

1   teaspoon salt

SALAD

10 to 12 cups torn iceberg lettuce, fresh spinach or romaine lettuce, torn into bite-sized pieces

2   tomatoes, cut into 1/16-inch slices

1   cucumber, halved, cut into chunks

¼ to ½ cup crumbled feta cheese

¼   cup Greek olives

Sliced radishes and/or green onions, if desired

Combine all dressing ingredients in blender; blend until creamy. Combine all salad ingredients; toss with dressing until lightly coated.

10 SERVINGS.

Cinnamon dusts this "quick and easy" honey-sweetened salad, also from the recipe file of Mary Richards. She plans half an apple per person when figuring number of servings.

Scandinavian Apple Salad

¾   cup half & half

3   tablespoons lemon juice

3   teaspoons honey or sugar

½   teaspoon cinnamon

4   tart apples, sliced

Combine all ingredients except apples. Pour sauce over apples; toss slightly. Refrigerate to chill. Sprinkle with additional cinnamon before serving, if desired.

6 TO 8 SERVINGS.

For a patio lunch on a warm day, Gail Tsuboi, Moraga, CA., offers this refreshing, choose-your-own-topping creation. Main ingredients in Chinese cuisine include: freshness, complementary colors and textures, a sweet agreeable flavor, purity and artful presentation. Certainly all can be satisfyingly incorporated here.

Chinese Cold Noodle Salad

16   ounces Chinese chow mein noodles (fresh or dry)

1   tablespoon sesame oil
Toppings: cooked tiny shrimp, julienned ham, shredded cooked chicken, chopped hard-cooked egg; blanched broccoli flowerets, julienne red and/or green bell pepper strips, 2-inch pieces of blanched green beans, blanched Chinese pea pods, sliced green onions, fresh or frozen peas, thinly-sliced cucumber, roasted sesame seed

DRESSING

¼   cup vegetable oil

1   tablespoon sesame oil

6   tablespoons soy sauce

6   tablespoons rice wine vinegar

3   tablespoons sugar

Place noodles in boiling water; when water returns to a boil, add 1 cup cold water. At second boil, remove from heat and rinse twice in cold water; let soak 5 minutes in cold water to which 1 table-spoon sesame oil has been added. Drain, cover and refrigerate until chilled. (Can be done ahead.)

Combine all dressing ingredients in bowl; stir until sugar is dissolved. To serve, set out a large bowl of chilled noodles, small bowl or pitcher of dressing and your choice of toppings in separate bowls. Guests assemble their own salads, placing ¾ to 1 cup noodles in bowl or on plate; top with desired toppings and dressing.

4 TO 6 SERVINGS.

The Good Earth Restaurant, located in the Galleria shopping complex, Edina, MN., is famous for this unusual main dish salad. Tamari, a pure naturally-fermented soy sauce that contains no artificial colorings or flavorings, is a popular substitute for salt in the Orient. We suggest adding dressing gradually so you end up with just the right amount to suit your tastes.

Spicy Oriental Noodle Salad

ORIENTAL PEANUT SAUCE

2	cups canola oil
1	cup peanut butter
2	tablespoons sesame oil
2	tablespoons fresh lemon juice
2	ounces grated fresh ginger
1	clove garlic, crushed
2½	tablespoons red wine vinegar
2½	tablespoons tamari
2	tablespoons crushed red pepper
1½	teaspoons hot chili oil

SALAD

1¼	pounds cooked turkey breast, julienned
¾	cup chopped green onions
¼	cup snipped fresh cilantro
16	ounces spaghetti, cooked and drained
¾	cup sesame seed
1¼	pounds carrots, julienned
	Lettuce
	Roasted peanuts
	Red bell peppers, cut into rings

Combine all Oriental Peanut Sauce ingredients; set aside. Combine turkey, green onions, cilantro, spaghetti, sesame seed and carrots with 2 to 3 cups sauce. Serve on a bed of chilled lettuce. Top with peanuts and sliced red pepper rings.

6 SERVINGS.

A no-fuss make-ahead featuring only four ingredients and very little effort. Richard and Enid Roehrner, Laguna Hills, CA., recall this being an integral part of a German salad sampling. "On a warm evening, the family would move a dining table outside under the apple trees to enjoy recipes such as this and have an opportunity to chat with neighbors strolling by."

Simple Sauerkraut Salad

1	(27-ounce) can sauerkraut, drained	Rinse and drain sauerkraut again. Combine with remaining ingredients. Cover and refrigerate overnight.
½ to 1 teaspoon ground pepper		
2	tablespoons capers	10 SERVINGS.
1	cup dairy sour cream	

The Roehrners also enjoy this more elaborate version which "is a big hit at potlucks." Combine ingredients and refrigerate overnight for flavor blending and convenience. Great to have on hand for house guests — just add a cold meat and cheese platter and bread or sandwich buns.

Overnight Sauerkraut Salad

1   (27-ounce) can sauerkraut, drained, rinsed

1   medium white onion, diced

1   small green bell pepper, diced

1   small red bell pepper, diced

1   cup diced celery

½   teaspoon ground pepper

½   cup vegetable oil

½   cup white vinegar

½   cup sugar

Combine sauerkraut with onion, bell peppers, celery and ground pepper in bowl. In small saucepan, heat oil, vinegar and sugar to boiling; cool 15 minutes. Pour over sauerkraut mixture; cover and refrigerate overnight.

10 SERVINGS.

The nutty flavor of sesame seed and a soy-sparked dressing are delightfully congenial with garden-fresh cucumbers. For variety, try the dressing with blanched, drained watercress or bean sprouts.

Korean Cucumber Salad

3	cucumbers
	Salt
3	green onions, chopped
1	large clove garlic, chopped
3	tablespoons soy sauce
3	tablespoons sesame seed
1 to 2	teaspoons salt
1 to 2	teaspoons pepper
	Dash of cayenne pepper
2	tablespoons sugar
2	tablespoons vinegar

Peel cucumbers, leaving alternating lengthwise strips of green. Cut in half; remove seeds with spoon. Cut into ¼-inch slices. Sprinkle with salt; let drain. Combine remaining ingredients with drained cucumbers.

6 TO 8 SERVINGS.

Beth Johnson Holod, Assistant Director for Public Relations for the Villages, recalls, "There was hardly a meal I ate in Denmark which didn't feature some form of cucumber. They were so fresh and versatile." Beth urges use of fresh lemon juice for authenticity.

Danish Cucumber Salad

1	large cucumber (about 1 pound)
1	cup water
½	cup fresh lemon juice or 1 cup vinegar
1	tablespoon sugar
1	teaspoon ground black pepper

Peel cucumber only if skin is thick and rubbery. (Fresh garden cucumbers rarely need peeling.) Cut cucumber into very thin slices. Combine water, lemon juice and sugar in bowl; add cucumber and sprinkle with pepper. Let stand at least 1 hour before serving.

6 SERVINGS.

From Alice Matsumoto, Woodbury, MN., comes a low-cal combo that is as refreshing as it is nutritious. Tester Nancy Bros, Edina, MN., suggests elevating it to main dish status for serving at warm weather luncheons and suppers.

Japanese Cucumber Salad

1	large cucumber
½	teaspoon salt
½ to 1 cup cooked shrimp

SAUCE

⅓	cup Japanese vinegar or ½ cup white vinegar and 2 tablespoons water
¼	cup sugar
¼	teaspoon salt

Peel cucumber, leaving alternating length-wise strips of green. Cut in half and remove seeds with spoon. Cut into very thin slices. Combine slices with ½ teaspoon salt in bowl; let stand 15 minutes. Meanwhile, combine sauce ingredients. Squeeze cucumber and drain off liquid. Combine half of sauce with cucumber. Just before serving, drain liquid from cucumber; combine cucumber with shrimp and remaining sauce. Serve in individual bowls. Garnish with parsley, if desired.

5 TO 6 SERVINGS.

When garden-grown tomatoes are ripe for the picking, Angela Klus, Mason City, IA., enhances them with a French accent. Freshly-snipped herbs make this simple garlic-laced mixture memorable.

Tomatoes Vinaigrette

6	ripe medium tomatoes, peeled, thinly sliced*
1	sweet onion, sliced
2½	tablespoons olive or corn oil
1	tablespoon lemon juice
1	clove garlic, finely chopped
2	tablespoons snipped fresh basil
2	tablespoons snipped fresh parsley
1	teaspoon salt
¼	teaspoon pepper

Combine tomatoes and onion in bowl. In separate bowl, combine remaining ingredients. Pour over tomatoes and let stand at room temperature at least 15 minutes.

4 TO 6 SERVINGS

*Tip: *To easily peel tomatoes, dip in boiling water for 1 to 2 minutes; drain and rinse in cold water.*

A year-around salad sensation reminiscent of the authentic Italian antipasto platters. Make ahead for best flavor.

Antipasto Salad

1	medium head cauliflower
1	medium bunch broccoli
1	(6-ounce) can pitted medium ripe olives, drained
2	(6-ounce) jars whole button mushrooms, drained
1	cup diagonally-sliced celery
4 to	6 green onions, chopped
1	pint cherry tomatoes
1	(12-ounce) bottle Italian or Romano cheese salad dressing
	Seasonings to taste (salt, pepper, instant minced garlic, Italian herbs, etc.)

Break cauliflower and broccoli into bite-sized flowerets. In large bowl, combine all ingredients; cover and refrigerate at least 4 hours to marinate vegetables. Serve in glass bowl to show off colors.

8 SERVINGS

Patricia Meyers, Edina, MN., offers a choice vegetable salad to add color and nutrients to almost any menu. No need to cook frozen corn, just thaw and drain thoroughly.

Calico Corn Salad

2	(10-ounce) packages frozen corn
½	cup mayonnaise
¼	cup dairy sour cream
2	tablespoons fresh lemon juice
½	teaspoon salt
¼	teaspoon Tabasco
1	cup finely-chopped celery
⅓	cup finely-chopped red or sweet onion

Let corn thaw to room temperature; drain in colander. In medium bowl, blend mayonnaise, sour cream, lemon juice, salt and Tabasco; stir in celery and onion. Pour into corn and mix well. Cover with plastic wrap and refrigerate up to 24 hours.

4 SERVINGS.

Ene Vogel, Fargo, ND., and her mother, Aino Koivastik, Beaverton, OR., brought this Estonian delight from their homeland years ago. "I remember it always being a part of every celebration," says Ene. "Use as a main dish or accompaniment to a salad buffet and a meat and cheese platter," she suggests. Begin preparation at least four hours before serving and show off the rosy hues in a pretty glass serving bowl.

Rosolje

4	medium red potatoes, cooked in skins
1	medium onion, chopped
1	(16-ounce) can diced beets, drained
⅔	pound cooked roast beef or Argentina beef, cut up
1	small herring or 1 (8-ounce) jar herring in wine sauce, drained
⅔	cup chopped dill pickles (2 to 3)
3	eggs, hard-cooked, cut up
	Salt
1	cup dairy sour cream
½	cup salad dressing
1	apple, cubed, if desired

Cool potatoes; cut into cubes about the size of the beets. Four or five hours before serving, combine potatoes with onion, beets, roast beef, herring, pickles and eggs. Salt to taste. Combine sour cream and salad dressing; stir into potato mixture. Cover and refrigerate until serving. Stir in cubed apple. Garnish as desired.

8 TO 10 SERVINGS.

*Phyllis Hanes, food editor of **The Christian Science Monitor**, brought this recipe back from a trip to Santiago after finding it served at almost every meal. "The tomatoes and onions are always sliced paper-thin," she observes. "What sets Chilean food apart is the surprise of flavors — the combination of unusual tastes that come from ingredients familiar to North Americans."*

Chilean Salad

4	cups thinly-sliced onions
4	tomatoes, peeled, thinly sliced
	Salt and pepper
3	tablespoons olive oil
¼	cup snipped fresh coriander

Rinse onions in cold water; drain. Mix with tomatoes and season to taste with salt and pepper. Add olive oil and mix well. Sprinkle with coriander just before serving.

6 TO 8 SERVINGS.

This is a special favorite of Sjölunden's (Swedish Village) vegetarians. Therese Hennemann, head cook, suggests pairing it with dark bread or crusty rolls for an inviting warm weather main dish.

Sallad Vegetaro

½	head iceberg lettuce
2	tablespoons prepared mustard
1½	tablespoons vegetable oil
2	tablespoons lemon juice
½	teaspoon herb salt
	Dash of powdered ginger
2	cups cold cooked rice, brown preferred
1	cucumber
6	ounces creamed cottage cheese
2	tablespoons snipped chives

Rinse and dry lettuce; thinly slice or shred. Arrange in bottom of large salad bowl. Combine mustard, oil, lemon juice, herb salt and ginger with a wire whisk, or in tightly-covered container. Toss rice with dressing to coat; arrange mixture on bed of lettuce. Peel cucumber if skin is tough; chop cucumber into bite-sized pieces and arrange over rice. Top salad with dollops of cottage cheese; garnish with chives.

4 SERVINGS.

Linda Norderhaug, Brookfield, WI., sautés the garlic in a tiny bit of olive oil before combining it with other ingredients. "This minimizes any bitter after-taste," she explains. This trendy make-ahead is a splendid accompaniment for barbecued meats and poultry.

Pasta Salad with Sun-Dried Tomatoes

1	pound penne pasta (small tube-like shapes)
2	medium cloves garlic, minced
15 to 20	large sun-dried tomatoes in olive oil, drained, minced
4	large green onions (green part only), finely-chopped
¾	cup finely-chopped fresh parsley
½	cup olive oil
	Salt and freshly-ground black pepper to taste
½	cup freshly-grated Parmesan cheese

Cook pasta to desired doneness as directed on package; drain. Toss with a little olive oil to prevent sticking. Combine all ingredients in large bowl. Toss gently. Refrigerate several hours to blend flavors.

10 SERVINGS.

St. Paul Pioneer Press food writer, Eleanor Ostman, "raided the refrigerator" to invent this prize winner in a recipe contest for food writers across the country. "Pardon my bragging," comments Eleanor, "but the hot pepper cheese and curry combine into salad dynamite!" She mixes the dressing with a hand-held blender to emulsify the oil and vinegar into a thick mixture, but a whisk and some energetic beating work just as well. With an eye to healthful eating, she uses low fat ham and salt-free soup mix. The wild rice, raw vegetables and nuts provide fiber.

Salad on the Wild Side

SALAD

1	cup uncooked wild rice
3	cups hot water
2	tablespoons salt-free chicken flavor instant soup mix
4	ounces 96% fat-free ham or turkey ham, cut into julienne strips
¾	cup hot pepper cheese, cut into julienne strips
¾	cup broccoli flowerets, broken into small pieces
1	(5 to 6-inch) carrot, sliced into thin rounds
¾	cup walnut halves
¾	cup red bell pepper strips
4	green onions, cut into thin rounds
	Freshly-ground pepper, if desired

DRESSING

½	cup vegetable oil
2	tablespoons lemon juice
2	tablespoons white wine vinegar
½	teaspoon dry mustard
½	teaspoon curry powder (or more)

Rinse rice with hot water; drain. Cook rice in 3 cups hot water with instant soup mix. Heat to boiling; reduce heat, cover and simmer 35 to 45 minutes or until water is absorbed and rice is tender. Cool.

In large bowl, toss rice with remaining salad ingredients. In small bowl, beat dressing ingredients until emulsified. Pour over salad and toss to mix well. Cover and refrigerate to chill.

4 TO 6 SERVINGS.

Patricia Lund, Edina, MN., has an educated palate, to be sure. She serves as Board of Directors Chair for Lund's Food Stores in the Twin Cities' area. This mid-eastern salad is just one tasty example of the many ethnic recipes gleaned from her world travels — recipes she incorporates in the store's monthly newsletter to share with shoppers. Pat suggests serving it with crisp lettuce leaves for scooping up the mint-refreshed mixture.

Tabbouleh

8	cups boiling water
1½	cups bulgur wheat
1	cup finely-chopped parsley
¼	cup snipped fresh mint
½	cup chopped green onions
2	large tomatoes, chopped
3	tablespoons chopped green bell pepper
½	cup lemon juice
½	cup olive oil
2	tablespoons salt and freshly-ground pepper to taste

Pour boiling water over bulgur in large bowl. Cover and let stand several hours or until bulgur is tender and fluffy. Drain off any excess water. Stir in remaining ingredients. Cover and refrigerate until serving time.

10 TO 12 SERVINGS.

Enjoy this al fresco as the Greeks do, sitting at little tables under an arbour or beside the sea. Success depends on use of fresh ingredients and preparing at least several hours ahead of serving.

Aegean Salad

8	large or 10 medium tomatoes
4	cucumbers
1	cup crumbled feta cheese
1	cup pitted ripe olives
6	tablespoons olive oil
1	teaspoon salt
	Freshly-ground pepper
1	teaspoon dried oregano leaves, crumbled

Peel and slice tomatoes and cucumbers. Arrange slices in shallow serving bowl. Sprinkle with cheese and olives. Combine remaining ingredients in tightly covered container. Pour over salad. Cover and refrigerate until serving time.

10 SERVINGS.

Helen Couper, Ponte Vedra Beach, FL., offers a salad for two that can easily be expanded to serve more for a main dish luncheon or supper salad. Busy hosts will appreciate the make-ahead possibility and preparation ease.

Italian Bean and Tuna Salad

1   (6½-ounce) can solid pack tuna, drained, rinsed
1   (15½-ounce) can cannellini beans, drained, rinsed
3   green onions, thinly sliced
2   tablespoons snipped fresh parsley
1   clove garlic, minced
3   tablespoons fresh lemon juice
3   tablespoons olive oil
    Freshly-ground black pepper
    Shredded lettuce or lettuce leaves
    Tomato wedges, if desired
    Green bell pepper rings, if desired

Place tuna in bowl and break up into coarse chunks. Combine gently with beans. Combine onions, parsley, garlic, lemon juice, olive oil and pepper; mix well. Pour over tuna mixture. Refrigerate at least 2 hours. Stir gently once or twice. Arrange tuna mixture over lettuce and garnish with tomato and green pepper.

2 VERY GENEROUS SERVINGS.

Daniel Palmquist, a professional chef, introduced this nutritional, make-ahead to Villagers with superior results. He brings authenticity to his cooking, having lived in Spain and studied cooking in Madrid. Varied textures and colors make this particularly inviting.

Spanish Cabbage Salad

1   head green cabbage, shredded
2   carrots, cut into julienne strips
1   green bell pepper, cut into julienne strips
3   tablespoons raisins
¼   cup olive oil
2   tablespoons white wine vinegar
2   teaspoons Dijon mustard
    Salt and pepper, to taste

Combine vegetables and raisins in bowl. In separate bowl, whisk remaining ingredients together; taste to adjust seasoning. Stir into vegetables; refrigerate several hours before serving.

8 SERVINGS.

Ann Bose, St. Louis Park, MN., relates that "Grandma didn't write this recipe down until it was requested by a grandson. She then made it three times before perfecting it. And since she never wasted a morsel, she insisted that Grandpa eat all three test batches." Tester, Dorothea Ofstedal, Williston, ND., and her family appreciated Grandma's triple testing.

Grandma Fleck's German Potato Salad

5	pounds red potatoes (5 cups, cooked)
¼	pound bacon, diced
1	small onion, chopped, if desired
¾	cup sugar
1	teaspoon salt
2	tablespoons cornstarch
½	cup water
½	cup vinegar

Cook potatoes with skins on until tender but firm. Peel potatoes; slice thinly and set aside. Fry bacon until crisp. Remove from skillet, drain on paper towels and crumble, leaving drippings in skillet. Add bacon and onion to potatoes. Combine remaining ingredients in bowl; whisk to mix well. Stir into bacon drippings in skillet; simmer until sauce is thickened. Pour over potatoes; toss gently to coat potatoes with dressing.

ABOUT 12 SERVINGS.

Quite different from the American version, this Parmesan-topped vegetable combo is marinated with Italian dressing. If you don't have a microwave, simply boil potatoes conventionally until tender but still firm.

Italian Potato Salad

1	pound new red potatoes
¼	cup water
½	teaspoon salt
1	small red onion, thinly sliced
⅓	cup sliced ripe olives
½	cup chopped green bell pepper
1	tomato, chopped
½	cup Italian dressing
2	tablespoons snipped fresh parsley
1	tablespoon grated Parmesan cheese

Scrub potatoes; cut crosswise into ¼-inch slices. Place in 1½-quart microwave-safe casserole. Add water and salt. Cover with casserole lid. Microwave on HIGH for 9 to 10 minutes or until potatoes are tender, stirring once. Drain; let stand uncovered to cool. Add remaining ingredients except cheese; mix lightly to coat evenly. Cover; refrigerate until chilled. Stir before serving; sprinkle with cheese.

6 SERVINGS.

This family recipe "treasured for at least three generations" comes from Mary Schlieckert, Bloomington, MN. "Save time," she suggests, "by leaving potatoes unpeeled."

German Potato Salad

8	medium potatoes
2	eggs, hard-cooked, sliced*
½ to ¾	cup diced celery
1	medium onion, diced or ½ cup sliced green onions
1½	teaspoons salt
¼	teaspoon pepper
6	slices bacon, diced, crisply cooked, drained (reserve drippings)
¼	cup vinegar
¼	cup sugar
¼	cup chopped fresh parsley

Peel potatoes, slice lengthwise, then crosswise into ¼-inch slices. Cook until tender but not crumbly, 15 to 20 minutes. Place potatoes, eggs, celery and onion in bowl. Sprinkle with salt and pepper. Sprinkle with bacon, pour bacon drippings over potato mixture. Heat vinegar and sugar until sugar is dissolved. Pour over potato mixture; mix gently to keep potatoes from crumbling. Sprinkle with parsley; serve warm.

8 SERVINGS.

*Tip: *To hard cook eggs: place in pan with cold water to cover by 1 inch. Heat to boiling; remove pan from heat. Let stand 15 minutes. Pour off hot water; cover with cold water. Peel under running water.*

From the Swedish Village comes a nutritious main or side dish salad starring lentils, a favorite European ingredient. Cook just until tender to avoid a mushy consistency.

Lentil Salad

1	small leek
½	head iceberg lettuce
1	green bell pepper
2	cups cooked lentils
¼	cup vegetable oil
½	cup fresh dill weed, snipped
	Herb or seasoned salt to taste

Cut leek lengthwise; rinse thoroughly under running water. Remove root end and dark green portion of top; cut into julienne strips, about 2 inches long. Rinse and dry lettuce; thinly slice or shred. Remove stem and seeds of green pepper; dice. Blend all ingredients.

4 SERVINGS.

Also called Gado-Gado, this Indonesian medley is a favorite of Arlene Lombard, Dallas, TX. In fact, she is so fond of the dressing, she prepares it in quantity for freezing. Vegetables can be readied ahead, but add dressing just before serving.

Vegetable Salad with Peanut Dressing

2	medium new potatoes
3	eggs, hard-cooked
4	ounces fresh green beans
1	large carrot
¼	head small cabbage
4	ounces bean sprouts, if desired
2	teaspoons salt
5	ounces cauliflower, broken into flowerets
1	small cucumber, peeled, cut into round slices

PEANUT DRESSING

1¼	cups roasted peanuts
2	tablespoons vegetable oil
3	medium shallots or ½ small onion, finely chopped
2	cloves garlic, finely chopped
2	cups water
½	teaspoon cayenne pepper
½	teaspoon salt
2	teaspoons dark brown sugar
	Freshly-ground black pepper
4 to 5	teaspoons lime or lemon juice

Cook potatoes until tender; cool but do not refrigerate. Peel and cut into ¼-inch slices. Cut eggs lengthwise into quarters. Keep all raw vegetables separate. Trim beans; cut into 2-inch lengths. Cut carrot crosswise into 2-inch sections; halve or quarter to match beans in size. Cut cabbage into fine long shreds. Break off thread-like tails of bean sprouts and rinse sprouts well in bowl of water; drain.

Place bowl near the stove with a sieve balanced on it and several plates to hold the different vegetables as they are cooked. Heat 2 quarts water (2 teaspoons salt) to boiling in medium saucepan. Cook green beans and carrot together until water comes to a boil again; boil rapidly 3 minutes. Drain vegetables in colander, reserving hot water. Rinse vegetables under cold running water and place on plate. Reheat water to rolling boil. Cook cauliflowerets (1½ minutes), cabbage (1 minute) and bean sprouts (30 seconds) in same way. Rinse in cold water and place on separate plates. Squeeze excess moisture from cabbage and bean sprouts; separate strands.

In food processor, chop peanuts as fine as possible. Heat oil in small pan over medium heat. Add shallots and garlic; stir and fry about 1 minute or until medium brown. Add water, cayenne, salt, brown sugar and ground peanuts. Stir and heat to boiling. Reduce heat to medium-low; simmer 15 to 20 minutes or until sauce has thickened to consistency of creamy dressing, stirring occasionally. Cool dressing; beat in black pepper and lime juice. Taste for seasoning. Arrange potatoes, eggs and vegetables side by side on 4 individual plates. Just before serving, pour ¼ of dressing evenly over each serving.

**4 MAIN COURSE OR
8 APPETIZER SERVINGS.**

Quite different from what Americans refer to as "Hot German Potato Salad" is this classic version where potatoes are thinly sliced and marinated at least several hours or overnight. You can use regular vinegar but our testers preferred the more subtle flavor of tarragon vinegar. Although salad must be refrigerated for food safety reasons, it should be brought to room temperature for serving.

German Village Potato Salad

2	pounds unpeeled red potatoes
1	tablespoon sugar
2	teaspoons salt
1	cup tarragon vinegar
1	teaspoon pepper
1	teaspoon bouquet garni
1	cup vegetable oil
1	medium onion, finely chopped

Cook potatoes until tender. Cool slightly; peel and cut into thin slices. Set aside. Dissolve sugar and salt in vinegar; add pepper and bouquet garni. Blend in oil; stir in onion. Pour enough dressing over potatoes to moisten well; toss gently. (Save remaining dressing for another use.) Cover and refrigerate at least 2 hours to blend flavors. About 30 minutes before serving, remove salad from refrigerator and let stand at room temperature. Retoss gently just before serving.

6 TO 8 SERVINGS.

This unique Syrian salad was served to brides to "fatten them up," according to Sue Reider, Cedar Rapids, IA. Allow ample time for marinating step and for peak flavor, use fresh mint and parsley and vine-ripened tomatoes.

Bride's Bread Salad

½   cup olive oil
½   cup lemon juice
¼   teaspoon garlic powder
1   large cucumber, chopped
4   medium tomatoes, chopped
1   small onion, chopped, if desired
2   tablespoons snipped fresh parsley
    or parsley flakes
2   tablespoons snipped fresh mint or
    1 tablespoon dried mint, crushed
6   slices bread, toasted*

Combine olive oil, lemon juice and garlic powder. In separate bowl, combine cucumber, tomatoes, onion, parsley and mint. Add oil mixture to vegetables; stir gently to coat. Cover and refrigerate 6 to 12 hours to blend flavors. Break toast into small pieces; combine with vegetable mixture. Let stand about 15 minutes before serving.

6 SERVINGS.

*Tip: *Dry bread can be substituted for toast; dampen slightly before adding to vegetables.*

David Erceg, Manager of Site and Support Services for the Villages, shares a recipe which originated with his Croation father. Combine dressing ingredients ahead and refrigerate. For an appealing crisp texture, wait until close to serving time to combine cabbage and dressing. Testers found the sage addition unique and flavorful.

Kraut Salat with Buttermilk Dressing

1   cup buttermilk
1   cup dairy sour cream
½   cup finely minced onion
1   teaspoon salt
½   teaspoon white pepper
½   teaspoon sage
1   medium head cabbage, shredded

In small bowl, gradually whisk buttermilk into sour cream. Stir in onion and seasonings. Pour dressing over cabbage; toss to coat evenly. Cover and refrigerate. Toss again just before serving.

6 TO 8 SERVINGS.

This is one of the many freshly-made take-out items available at the Rosebud Grocery in the Galleria of Edina, MN. Low in calories, high in flavor, the unique medley features beef, a leading product of Brazil.

Brazilian Beef Salad

DRESSING
1	clove garlic, minced
2	tablespoons lemon juice
2	tablespoons soy sauce
2	tablespoons olive oil
⅓	cup vegetable oil
	Salt and pepper to taste

SALAD
1	pound cooked roast beef, julienned
1	red onion, sliced
1	bunch green onions, sliced
1	red bell pepper, julienned
1	green bell pepper, julienned

Combine all dressing ingredients; set aside. Prepare salad ingredients; toss with dressing. Serve chilled.

6 SERVINGS.

Another variation of the popular basic oil and vinegar theme, this recipe features a subtle raspberry flavor. Add peak flavor and interest to tossed salads by combining greens which complement each other with different hues and textures. Tear gently to avoid bruising tender leaves.

Raspberry Vinaigrette

1	tablespoon raspberry vinegar
⅛	teaspoon salt
6	tablespoons olive or vegetable oil
	Dash of pepper
1 to	2 tablespoons minced green herbs

Beat vinegar with salt in small bowl until salt is dissolved. Beat oil in by droplets; season with pepper and herbs of choice.

ABOUT ½ CUP.

Fresh orange juice and peel add zest to a tasty fruit salad topping. Use low-fat mayo and yogurt if you are counting calories.

Orange Yogurt Dressing

¼	cup mayonnaise
¼	cup plain yogurt
3	tablespoons fresh orange juice
1	teaspoon grated fresh orange peel
1	teaspoon honey
¼	teaspoon salt

Combine all ingredients; cover and refrigerate 1 hour before serving.

ABOUT ¾ CUP.

A blended beauty using on-hand ingredients from Donna Nooleen, Edina, MN. Allow ingredients to meld by preparing at least a day ahead of serving.

Blender French Dressing

1	medium onion, cut up
¼ to ½	cup sugar
1	teaspoon salt
1	teaspoon paprika
½	cup vegetable oil
⅓	cup ketchup
¼	cup cider vinegar

Combine all ingredients in blender; blend about 2 minutes. Refrigerate at least 1 day before serving. Store in refrigerator.

ABOUT 2 CUPS.

Dress fresh greens for success with this easy, but elegant classic from Kim Lobert, Grosse Pointe Park, MI. Tester Julia Commons, Santa Barbara, CA., encourages use of the highest quality olive oil and suggests using champagne vinegar for variety. "It took only 10 minutes to make and tastes great," she adds.

Vinaigrette Simple

1	medium clove garlic or ¼ teaspoon garlic powder
2	tablespoons olive oil
2	tablespoons vegetable oil
2	tablespoons raspberry vinegar or red wine vinegar
	Salt and pepper

Mash garlic clove against bottom of bowl. (If using garlic powder, add with oil and vinegar.) Add remaining ingredients; mix well. Toss with salad greens just before serving.

MAKES 6 TABLESPOONS.

"Don't be put off by the amount of garlic," advise Doctors Paul and Roma Hoff, Eau Claire, WI. "The recipe was introduced to us by Yolanda from Madrid when she spent time here during high school. It always gets raves!" Tester Eileen Cumming, Madison, WI., agrees, calling it, in a word, "wonderful."

Gypsy Salad Dressing

4 to 5	cloves garlic, sliced
1½	teaspoons cumin seed
¾ to 1	teaspoon salt
¼	cup olive oil
2 to 3	tablespoons lime or lemon juice

Place garlic, cumin seed and salt in a mortar and mash firmly with pestle until mixture is the consistency of thick paste. Transfer to small glass or stainless bowl and add remaining ingredients; stir to mix. Prepare garden salad of your choice. Just before serving, pour dressing over salad; mix lightly.

ABOUT ½ CUP.

Tip: To make a larger quantity, double the oil and lime juice but not other ingredients.

SOUPS & STEWS

Map The mission of the Concordia Language Villages is to prepare young people for responsible citizenship in a global society. Part of being a responsible world citizen is being able to express empathy for one's neighbors in the global village. What better way to begin than by learning where these neighbors live?

At the Chinese Village, a geography lesson becomes a game. "Villagers" run to touch the country called out by a staff member—in Chinese!

Voyageur The Language Villages offers French and German-based wilderness programs that enable young people to develop their language skills while camping and canoeing. This "Voyageur" cooks over an open fire, experiencing the way French-Canadian fur traders lived during the 17th and 18th centuries.

When The Rev. Paul Ofstedal and family returned home to Williston, N.D., after touring East and West Germany in 1986, they improvised until they had created this savory memory of their trip. For variety, serve over rice or noodles.

Goulash Soup

3	strips bacon, cubed
1	medium onion, sliced
2	tablespoons paprika
1½	pounds boneless beef shank, cut into ½-inch cubes
½	teaspoon salt
	Pepper
1	clove garlic, finely chopped
1	large carrot, diced
1	stalk celery, chopped
1	small green bell pepper, diced
1	tablespoon dry sherry
1	(10½-ounce) can beef consommé
1	cup bouillon
1	teaspoon caraway seed
¼	cup flour
1	cup water

Cook bacon and onion in large kettle. Stir paprika into bacon drippings. Add beef and salt and pepper to taste; cook about 15 minutes over medium heat. Add remaining ingredients except flour and water. Heat to boiling; reduce heat and simmer about 1½ hours. Combine flour and water; mix well. Stir into soup. Heat to boiling; boil constantly 1 minute. Simmer about 5 minutes longer.

4 SERVINGS.

"This can be found on nearly every menu in Germany," reports Soraya Cornick, Albert Lea, MN. With the abundance of vegetables, hearty cubes of sirloin and bouquet of seasonings, it is made to order for chilly evenings and ravenous appetites. Soraya suggests rounding out the menu with crusty rolls.

Gulasch Suppe

3	tablespoons margarine
1½	cups chopped onions
1	tablespoon chopped garlic
1½	pounds cubed top sirloin (or more, if desired)
½	cup flour
2	tablespoons paprika
3	tablespoons tomato paste
1	(16-ounce) can tomatoes, undrained, chopped
8	cups water
8	teaspoons beef bouillon
2	tablespoons sugar
4	potatoes, diced
4	large carrots, diced
2	green bell peppers, diced
2	red bell peppers, diced
1	bay leaf
½	teaspoon dried marjoram leaves
½	teaspoon caraway seed
½	teaspoon salt
½	teaspoon pepper
¾	cup cream (or less, if desired)

Melt margarine in large soup kettle over medium-high heat. Add onions; cook until translucent. Stir in garlic and meat; cook and stir until meat is browned on all sides. Add flour, paprika and tomato paste; stir until smooth. Add tomatoes, water and bouillon; stir to separate meat. Add remaining ingredients except cream; stir to combine. Heat to boiling; reduce heat and simmer about 1 hour or until meat and vegetables are tender. Remove bay leaf; stir in cream. Remove from heat 30 minutes before serving.

8 SERVINGS.

East meets West in this sake and soy sauce-laced stew known as nikujaga. *Use a tender cut of beef for quick cooking and best flavor. This typical Japanese family meal can be table-ready in less than an hour.*

Japanese Beef Stew

10	ounces beef, thinly sliced*
3 to 4	potatoes
2	onions
4	tablespoons vegetable oil, divided
⅔	cup water
¼	cup sake
2	tablespoons sugar
3	tablespoons soy sauce

Cut beef into 1½-inch pieces. Peel potatoes, cut in quarters and soak in water 5 minutes. Cut onions in half lengthwise, then into thin moon shapes. Heat 2 tablespoons oil in heavy-bottomed pan; add beef and brown. Remove beef and set aside. Add remaining 2 tablespoons oil; sauté potatoes and onions about 2 minutes. Add water, sake and sugar. Boil until potatoes are half cooked; add soy sauce. Return beef to kettle and boil until potatoes are tender, about 15 minutes.

4 SERVINGS.

*Tip: *Partially freeze beef, or have butcher slice to get very thin slices.*

Chinese chefs delight in soups such as this and may serve more than one at a full-scale banquet. This is light enough to be appropriate for any season and it is delightful as a first course or an accompaniment for luncheon salads and sandwiches.

Chicken Consommé Oriental

4	cups homemade or canned chicken consommé
½	cup diced water chestnuts
½	cup sliced canned or fresh mushrooms
1	cup fresh spinach leaves, slivered
1	egg white
	Salt and white pepper

Heat consommé to boiling. Add water chestnuts and mushrooms; cook 1 minute. Add spinach; cook 1 minute only. Pour egg white in slowly, stirring with a fork. Taste and season with salt and white pepper as needed.

6 SERVINGS.

Called kalops *in Sweden, this stew is equally tasty with venison substituted for beef. Allspice, often thought to be a medley of spices, is a hard berry-like spice that emits fragrances and tastes of cloves, nutmeg and cinnamon. It is commonly used in Scandinavian meat mixtures, with herring and in baked goods.*

Swedish Beef Stew

3	tablespoons butter or margarine
1	pound boneless beef rib, rump or round, cut into large bite-size chunks
3	tablespoons flour
1½	teaspoons salt
2½	cups water
4 to 5	carrots, cut into chunks
3 to 4	yellow onions, cut into wedges
10	whole allspice
2	bay leaves

Melt butter in large saucepan over medium-high heat. Add meat; brown well on all sides. Sprinkle with flour and salt; add water. Heat to simmering, stirring to loosen flavorful brown bits from bottom of pan. Add carrots, onions, allspice and bay leaves. Cover and simmer over medium-low heat 1½ to 2 hours or until meat is tender. Remove bay leaf. Serve with boiled potatoes, pickled beets or lingonberry jam and tossed salad, if desired.

4 TO 6 SERVINGS.

A Greek treasure light enough for a first course or tasty for lunch or supper with accompaniments. Take care not to boil mixture after adding eggs — curdling will result. And do use fresh lemon juice rather than bottled.

Avgolemono Soup

12	cups rich chicken broth or 9 (10½-ounce) cans broth and 8 tablespoons chicken stock base
1	cup uncooked regular rice
6	eggs
⅔	cup fresh lemon juice, strained
8 to 10	lemon slices
	Fresh snipped parsley

In soup kettle or Dutch oven, heat 12 cups broth to boiling. Add rice; cook 20 minutes or until rice is tender. Reduce heat so soup barely simmers. In bowl, beat eggs until light and frothy; stir in lemon juice. Very slowly, stir 4 cups of the broth into egg mixture, beating constantly. Stir egg mixture gradually into remaining broth. Heat thoroughly, but do not boil. Serve with a lemon slice and a little parsley floating in each bowl.

8 TO 10 SERVINGS.

Robert Schmid, Hibbing, MN., shares this prize-winning recipe for "mojakka", which he served at Ironworld USA's Finnish Day. Robert speaks fluent Finnish and has made five trips to the land of his ancestors. The word "mojakka" is mysterious because although it is used on the Iron Range to denote a "hearty hot soup or stew," it is not included in the formal Finnish language.

Finnish Beef Stew

1	gallon spring water
1	teaspoon salt
4½	pounds beef chuck roast
3	beef bones, trimmed of excess fat
30	whole allspice
10	whole peppercorns
2	bay leaves
4 to 5	fresh parsley sprigs
3	small onions, coarsely-chopped
3	celery stalks, coarsely-chopped
8	carrots, sliced
10	potatoes, cut into bite-size pieces
2	rutabagas, diced
3	leeks, sliced
1	bunch fresh parsley, minced

Heat water to lukewarm in soup kettle. Add salt, beef and bones. Heat to boiling; reduce heat and simmer, skimming off fat from time to time. Add allspice, peppercorns, bay leaves and several sprigs of parsley. Add onions, celery and carrots and continue simmering. When meat is tender, remove meat and bones. Cut meat into pieces. Stir potatoes, rutabagas, cut-up meat and leeks into stew. Continue cooking until meat and vegetables are tender. Remove bay leaves. Garnish with remaining parsley.

12 SERVINGS.

Tip: One way to remove fat from soup is to chill the stock in the refrigerator 6 to 8 hours. Then use a spoon to lift off the fat that solidifies on the surface of the stock.

When the next chilly day arrives, you will want a pot of this Scottish brew simmering on the stove. "An old family favorite," writes Helen Spencer, Great Falls, MT. Barley, one of the first cultivated grains, has been used in a variety of ways over the years — as a gift to Egyptian gods, for barter as a measuring system and for medication. Here it supplies good hearty eating.

Highland Mushroom Barley Soup

¼ cup vegetable oil

2 pounds beef short ribs

1 cup chopped onions

1 cup sliced carrots

7 cups water

2 (14½ or 16-ounce) cans whole tomatoes, undrained, crushed

3½ teaspoons salt

Marjoram and thyme to taste

¼ teaspoon ground black pepper

½ to 1 cup barley

16 ounces fresh mushrooms, sliced

½ cup chopped fresh parsley

Heat oil in large soup kettle. Add meat and brown. Add onions and carrots; cook and stir 5 minutes. Stir in water, tomatoes, seasonings and barley. Heat to boiling; reduce heat and simmer, covered, 1 hour. Add mushrooms; cover and simmer 30 minutes longer. Remove meat and bones from soup and cut meat into 1-inch cubes. Add meat and parsley to soup and heat thoroughly before serving.

12 SERVINGS (3 QUARTS).

A refreshing prelude to any summertime menu. Tester Patricia Meyers, Edina, MN., describes the light soup as, "Just delicious in addition to being low in fat and calories." She suggests making it a day ahead of serving for best flavor. Recipe is easily increased for additional servings.

Curried Zucchini-Buttermilk Soup

¼ cup dry sherry or white wine

½ cup sliced green onions, including tops

2 cups sliced unpeeled zucchini

1 tablespoon curry powder

½ teaspoon cumin (or to taste)

2 cups lowfat buttermilk

Salt and pepper to taste

Shredded zucchini

In skillet over medium heat, heat sherry to bubbling; add onions and sauté 2 minutes, stirring to prevent browning. Add sliced zucchini, curry and cumin. Continue cooking 5 minutes or until zucchini softens. Remove from heat; cool slightly. Purée in blender with buttermilk. Add salt and pepper. Cover and refrigerate several hours or overnight to blend flavors. Garnish with shredded zucchini.

4 SERVINGS.

A made-from-scratch specialty often served with Russian black bread. Select fresh beets that are small to medium in size and are firm with fresh-looking tops. They are rich in potassium and the tops, which can be steamed, are a great source of vitamin A.

Russian Village Borscht

2	pounds shin of beef with bone*
	About 8½ cups water
1	onion, quartered
1	carrot, quartered
1	stalk celery
1	bay leaf
	Few sprigs fresh parsley
	Dash of dried thyme leaves
1½	pounds beets**
½	pound cabbage, shredded
2	potatoes, peeled, sliced
1	tablespoon butter or margarine
1	tablespoon sugar
1	tablespoon vinegar
	Salt and pepper
1	large potato, shredded, if desired
1 to	1½ cups dairy sour cream

Make a stock with beef, water, onion, carrot, celery, bay leaf, parsley and thyme. Strain the stock, remove meat from bones. Cut up meat and return it and the marrow to the stock. Peel beets and cut all but 2 into small pieces. Lightly sauté cabbage and potatoes in butter. Add cabbage, potatoes and cut beets to the stock. Gently boil until tender. Add sugar and vinegar. Season to taste with salt and pepper. If slightly thicker soup is preferred, shred a large raw potato into the soup and boil rapidly for a few minutes. Shred the 2 remaining beets and make a red juice by pressing them through a sieve. Add this to the soup, but do not boil again or the color will be lost. Top each serving with a dollop of sour cream.

10 TO 12 SERVINGS.

Tips: *Use bouillon instead of making beef broth from scratch; add 1 to 2 ounces cubed beef per person.*
**Two (16-ounce) cans beets, drained, can be substituted for fresh beets. Add 5 minutes before serving; heat through.*

Lorraine Brown, St. Paul, MN., translates popular sandwich ingredients into a unique and hearty soup. Round out a luncheon or supper menu with crisp rye crackers and sherbet or fresh fruit for dessert.

Cream of Reuben Soup

½	cup beef broth
½	cup chicken broth
¼	cup coarsely-chopped celery
¼	cup coarsely-chopped onion
¼	cup coarsely-chopped green bell pepper
1	tablespoon cornstarch
2	tablespoons water
1	cup coarsely-chopped corned beef (about ¼ pound)
1	cup diced Swiss cheese
¾	cup sauerkraut, drained and rinsed
¼	cup butter
2	cups half & half

Combine broths, celery, onion and green pepper in large saucepan. Heat to boiling over high heat; reduce heat and simmer until vegetables are crisp-tender, about 5 minutes. Dissolve cornstarch in water; stir into soup mixture and continue cooking until soup thickens. Remove from heat and stir in corned beef, Swiss cheese and sauerkraut, blending well. Melt butter in large double boiler over medium heat. Stir in half & half. Stir in soup, blending until smooth. Heat thoroughly; do not boil.

8 SERVINGS.

Beverly LeBeau, Fayetteville, NY., offers a 20 minute solution for a hurry-up lunch or supper soup. Keep ingredients on your "emergency shelf" and then just heat, eat and enjoy!

Impromptu Crab Bisque

1	(7-ounce) can crab meat
1	(10¾-ounce) can tomato bisque soup
1	(10¾-ounce) can condensed chicken soup with rice
1	(13-ounce) can evaporated milk
2	tablespoons sherry
8	tablespoons unsweetened whipped cream

Combine crab, soups and milk in large saucepan. Heat to serving temperature (do not boil). Just before serving stir in sherry. Top each bowl of soup with dollop of whipped cream.

8 SERVINGS.

"This has long been a traditional stew among Indian and Spanish cultures," explains Jane Ahlin, Fargo, ND., "It is especially popular at Christmas and New Year's celebrations." Marilyn Whippl, who is affiliated with the American Embassy in Mexico City and tested the recipe, enjoyed "the semi-hot taste — just enough to give it a zing." Flavors are enhanced by making a day ahead of serving and leftovers adapt well to freezing.

New Mexican Posole

1	(3-pound) pork loin
2	pounds frozen posole*
2	quarts water
1	large onion, diced
2	teaspoons dried oregano leaves
1½	teaspoons garlic powder
½	teaspoon dried thyme leaves
2	tablespoons salt
1	teaspoon black pepper
4	(4-ounce) cans chopped green chiles

Boil pork loin until tender, 1½ to 2 hours. Cool and cut into 1-inch cubes. Rinse posole well. Place posole and water in large soup kettle; heat to boiling, reduce heat and simmer at least 1 hour or until posole kernels burst. Add pork cubes, onion and seasonings. Cover and simmer 6 hours, adding water if necessary. Add chiles during last hour of cooking.

8 to 10 SERVINGS.

Tip: *Two (32-ounce) cans white hominy can be substituted for frozen posole; drain well before adding. Simmer 3 hours instead of 6.

Use preparation time for this traditional made-from-scratch soup to look forward to rewarding results. Since the chicken is used only for flavoring the broth, you have the bonus of having it available for sandwich or casserole fixings. Broth can be made ahead and refrigerated or frozen and matzo balls can be prepared a day ahead of boiling.

Chicken Soup with Matzo Balls

SOUP

1	stewing chicken, about 5 pounds, cut up
6	quarts cold water
1	tablespoon salt
3	stalks celery with leaves, cut into 1-inch pieces
1	carrot, cut into 1-inch pieces
1	medium onion, stuck with 2 whole cloves
6	peppercorns
3	egg whites
	Cheesecloth
	Yellow food color, if desired

MATZO BALLS

6	eggs, separated
1½	teaspoons salt
⅛	teaspoon pepper
1	tablespoon snipped fresh parsley
2	tablespoons melted chicken fat (from soup)
1	cup matzo meal
4	quarts water
2	tablespoons salt
	Fresh parsley, if desired

Tips: *Cooked chicken is not used in the soup. Cover, refrigerate or freeze for another use.*

**Matzo balls can be covered and refrigerated up to 24 hours.*

Place chicken (including heart and neck) in large kettle; add water and salt. Heat to boiling over medium heat; reduce heat. Carefully skim; stir and skim again. Add vegetables and peppercorns. Cover and simmer until chicken is tender, 2½ to 3 hours. Strain broth; cover and refrigerate.* Remove all fat from top of chilled soup; reserve. Beat egg whites until frothy; stir into cold soup. Cook and stir over medium heat just until simmering. Remove from heat and let stand until egg whites coagulate. Skim egg whites from soup; pour soup through cheesecloth-lined strainer. (Soup should be very clear. If it is not a rich "chickeny yellow" color, add a few drops of yellow food color.) Refrigerate or freeze; reheat at serving time.

In large mixer bowl, beat 6 egg whites until stiff. Beat 6 egg yolks in small bowl until fluffy and lemon-colored. Stir in 1½ teaspoons salt, pepper, parsley and chicken fat; fold into egg whites. Fold in matzo meal, 1 tablespoon at a time. Refrigerate at least 1 hour. Form chilled mixture into 12 balls**. About 30 minutes before serving, heat water and 2 tablespoons salt to boiling. With slotted spoon, gently lower 1 ball at a time into water. Cover and reduce heat so water boils very slowly. Cook 30 minutes. Place 1 matzo ball in each soup bowl; ladle hot chicken soup over. Garnish with parsley.

12 SERVINGS.

70

A menu staple from Hotel Sofitel — rich, creamy and loaded with fresh mushrooms. Make your own bouquet garni in the true French fashion or purchase ready made. It is an essential ingredient.

Creme de Champignons

2	tablespoons butter
2	fresh shallots, finely chopped
	White of 1 leek, finely chopped
2	pounds fresh mushrooms, finely chopped
	Juice of 1 lemon
4	cups heavy cream
4	cups beef or chicken stock or canned beef consommé
	Bouquet garni*
	Salt and pepper

Melt butter in saucepan; sauté shallots and leek (but not until they change color). Add mushrooms and mix well; add lemon juice to keep mushrooms white. Cook 10 minutes. Stir in cream; heat to boiling and boil 5 minutes. Add stock, bouquet garni, salt and pepper to taste. Cook 25 minutes; remove bouquet garni before serving.

8 TO 10 SERVINGS.

*Tip: *Bouquet garni is thyme, celery, parsley and bay leaves, tied together or in cheesecloth bag.*

A mild, velvety soup to serve as a first course for elegant dinner parties. Preparation is uncomplicated with help from the blender and mixture can be combined a day ahead of serving. Take care not to boil in final heating step.

Cream of Scallop Soup

8	shallots, chopped
2	stalks celery, chopped
3½	cups chicken broth
1	cup (about 6 ounces) frozen scallops
½	cup dry white wine
1	pint light cream
	Salt and white pepper, to taste

Add shallots and celery to chicken broth; heat to boiling over high heat. Reduce heat and simmer 30 minutes. Add scallops; simmer 5 minutes. Purée until smooth. Strain into heavy saucepan or top of double boiler. Add wine and cream. Reheat to blend flavors but do not boil. Stir in salt and pepper. Serve immediately or refrigerate and reheat gently just before serving.

6 SERVINGS.

The Minneapolis restaurant, Yvette's, bowed to customer wishes and parted with this favorite recipe. Plum tomatoes are smaller than the usual garden-grown varieties, so adjust amount accordingly. This is perfect for late summer and fall preparation when tomatoes are plentiful.

Tomato-Basil Soup

1   large yellow onion, coarsely chopped

2   stalks celery, coarsely chopped

1   carrot, coarsely chopped

1   tablespoon dried thyme leaves

1   bay leaf

2   tablespoons unsalted butter

1½ teaspoons finely chopped fresh garlic

20 fresh plum tomatoes, cored and coarsely chopped

1   teaspoon cracked black pepper

½   cup unsalted butter, cubed

10 large fresh basil leaves, snipped Salt

In soup kettle, sauté onion, celery, carrot, thyme and bay leaf in 2 tablespoons butter over medium heat until thoroughly cooked, about 10 minutes. Turn heat to high; quickly stir garlic into vegetables. Add tomatoes and pepper; heat to simmer. Cook 15 minutes. Purée soup in blender or food processor. Strain through moderately fine sieve into kettle. Whisk in cubed butter and basil. Remove bay leaf. Salt to taste.

4 SERVINGS.

Carol Rueber and her family have grown to enjoy this recipe brought back by her husband from Peace Corps duty in Liberia, West Africa. Also called "ground nuts", peanuts are used generously in African dishes of all types from breads to main dishes. Served over rice, this becomes a hearty main dish.

Peanut Soup

½   onion, cut up
     Vegetable oil
½ to 1 chicken, cut into medium-sized
     pieces
     Hot water
¼   cup ground natural peanut
     butter*
½   (6-ounce) can tomato paste
2   chicken or beef bouillon cubes
     Dash of soy sauce
     Cut-up jalapeño or other hot
     peppers, to taste
     Salt
½ to 1 cup cut-up green beans, broccoli
     or cauliflower
     Cooked brown rice**

Brown onion in oil in 3-quart saucepan. Remove onion; add chicken pieces and cook until browned. Add onion and enough water to cover chicken. Heat to boiling; reduce heat to simmer. Add hot water gradually to peanut butter until it is the consistency of pea soup. Add peanut butter mixture to simmering chicken mixture. Add tomato paste, bouillon cubes, soy sauce and hot pepper. Boil vigorously until peanut oil rises to top of mixture, 20 to 30 minutes. (Soup can be thickened further, if desired, by continued boiling.) During last 15 minutes of cooking time, add vegetables. Serve over browned rice.

4 to 6 SERVINGS.

*Tips: *Cooked squash can be substituted for peanut butter and soy sauce.
**Allow about ½ cup uncooked rice per person.*

Readily-available vegetables combine with a creamy base and tiny shrimp for an inviting appetizer or first course offering with year-round appeal. Fresh or frozen shrimp, cooked and cut-up can be substituted for canned and add a little more texture.

Shrimp-Vegetable Bisque

16	ounces zucchini, sliced (3½ cups)
1	cup sliced carrots
½	cup chopped celery
½	cup sliced green onions
½	cup butter or margarine
1	tablespoon flour
1¾	cups milk
2	cups water
1	(10¾-ounce) can condensed cream of mushroom soup
½	cup dry white wine
½	cup dairy sour cream
2	teaspoons instant chicken bouillon granules
2	(4½-ounce) cans tiny shrimp, rinsed, drained
	Cucumber slices, if desired

Place vegetables and butter in Dutch oven; cover and cook until tender, about 20 minutes. Blend in flour; stir in milk. Cook and stir until bubbly; cook 1 minute, stirring constantly. Pour into blender container or food processor bowl; cover and blend until smooth. In same pan, combine water, canned soup, wine, sour cream and bouillon. Stir in puréed mixture and shrimp. Heat thoroughly; do not boil. Garnish with cucumber slices.

8 SERVINGS.

"A great way to 'Finnish' the day," comments tester Heni Lindberg, Warroad, MN. This is a "very aromatic soup, particularly flavorful with fresh dill and chives," she adds. Robert Schmid, recipe contributor, leaves ingredient amounts up to the chef's discretion.

Kekkonen's Chowder

Diced peeled potatoes
Onions, quartered
Bay leaf
Whole allspice
Salt
Salmon, whitefish or burbot
Butter
Rye flour, if desired
Chopped fresh dill and chives
Finely chopped onions
Melted butter

Put potatoes in large kettle of hot water. Add onions, bay leaf, allspice and salt. Cook potatoes until almost done. Add large pieces of fish and dabs of butter. Cook until fish is done. If desired, thicken soup Kainuu-style with flour or leave it clear. Remove bay leaf. Sprinkle with dill and chives. Serve in soup bowls and let each person add onions and melted butter.

"Very easy and very tasty," says Beverly Thorson about this conveniently combined concoction named after the Thorson's hometown. Tester Sonja Pavlik, Glendale, WI., says, "This light, lovely soup was the result of only 15 minutes of effort."

Bemidji Bisque

4	(10¾-ounce) cans condensed potato soup
2	(4-ounce) cans shrimp, drained
¼	cup chopped fresh parsley
2	soup cans half & half
1	soup can milk
1	(8-ounce) package frozen crab meat, thawed and drained
¼	cup butter or margarine
2	tablespoons minced onion
	Salt and pepper to taste

Combine all ingredients in large saucepan. Heat and serve.

8 SERVINGS.

"Nice light tuna flavor," responded tester Sharon Detert, Litchfield, MN., when she sampled this recipe from Linnea Eliason of Hibbing, MN. Most fish chowders, like this one, feature a seasoned milk base. Vegetables should be cooked just until tender to preserve texture and nutrition.

Tuna Chowder

¼   cup butter or margarine

1   cup chopped celery

1   cup chopped onion

1   cup chopped potato

1¼   teaspoons salt

¼   teaspoon pepper

¼   teaspoon dried thyme leaves, crushed

¼   teaspoon dill weed, if desired

2   tablespoons flour

1   (8-ounce) can tomatoes

3   cups milk

1   (6½-ounce) can tuna, drained, flaked

2   tablespoons snipped fresh parsley

1   cup (4 ounces) shredded Monterey jack or American cheese

In large saucepan, melt butter. Add celery, onion and potato. Cook and stir until vegetables are tender, about 15 minutes. Stir in seasonings and flour. Add tomatoes, milk, tuna and parsley. Heat to boiling, stirring constantly. Boil and stir 1 minute. Stir in cheese until melted.

4 SERVINGS.

Egg yolks and sherry are the final additions to this continental creation from Cindy Kryda, Marshfield, WI. Mild mushrooms are enhanced by seasonings found in every cook's pantry.

Sherried Mushroom Soup

16	ounces fresh mushrooms
4	green onions
⅓	cup butter or margarine
½	cup all-purpose flour
1½	teaspoons salt
¼	teaspoon white pepper
¼	teaspoon dry mustard
¼	teaspoon nutmeg
	Dash of cayenne pepper
4	cups milk or half & half, scalded, cooled
2	cups canned chicken broth
2	egg yolks, slightly beaten
½	cup dry sherry

Slice mushrooms; chop stems. Thinly slice onions; reserve tops for garnish. In large heavy saucepan, sauté white part of onions and mushrooms in butter; remove mushrooms. Blend flour and seasonings into butter in pan (add more butter, if necessary). Gradually stir in milk and broth. Cook, stirring constantly until slightly thickened.* Mix egg yolks and sherry; gradually add to soup, stirring constantly. Garnish with onion tops; serve immediately.

8 SERVINGS.

*Tip: *Recipe can be prepared to this point and refrigerated. To serve, reheat and proceed as above.*

"My family loves this hot or cold," says Amy White, Rapid City, SD. The leek, floral emblem of Wales, was a favorite flavoring of ancient Egyptians and Romans. It is said that Emperor Nero dined on leek soup daily, believing the vegetable would deepen his voice.

Potato-Carrot Potage

2	tablespoons butter or margarine
2	leeks, white part only, sliced
4	cups cubed potatoes
3	cups sliced carrots
6	cups chicken broth
1	teaspoon salt
⅛	teaspoon white pepper
2	cups half & half or milk
	Shredded carrot

Melt butter in large saucepan; add leeks and cook several minutes. Add potatoes, carrots, broth, salt and pepper. Heat to boiling. Reduce heat; simmer about 30 minutes or until vegetables are done. Carefully purée hot soup in blender or food processor. Return purée to saucepan. Add half & half; heat to serving temperature. Serve hot or chill soup several hours to blend flavors. Garnish with shredded carrot.

6 TO 8 SERVINGS.

From Douglas Holod, St. Paul, MN., and "a Polish auntie who served it at Easter," comes a rosy repast that can be served hot or cold. The dollop of sour cream is traditional and when lightly swirled into the soup, offers an attractive highlight.

Fresh Beet Borscht

1	bunch fresh red beets (about 2 pounds)
1	medium onion, grated
1 to 2	medium carrots, shredded
1	tablespoon chopped fresh dill
3	beef bouillon cubes
1	teaspoon salt
¼	teaspoon pepper
6	cups water
2½	tablespoons flour
½	cup cold water
3	tablespoons vinegar
2	tablespoons sugar
1¼	cups dairy sour cream

Cut beet greens from beets; wash about ¼ of the greens and cut into pieces about 1 inch wide. Wash, peel and shred beets. Place greens, beets, onion, carrots, dill, bouillon cubes, salt, pepper and 6 cups water in soup kettle or Dutch oven. Heat to boiling; simmer 35 to 45 minutes. Combine flour, ½ cup cold water, vinegar and sugar; stir into beet mixture. Heat to boiling; boil and stir 1 minute. Reduce heat; simmer about 10 minutes. Serve with 2 tablespoons sour cream blended into each bowl of soup.

10 SERVINGS.

Tip: Serve cold in the summer.

Treat yourself to this quick-to-fix refresher on a hot summer evening. Colorful, crunchy and wonderful with open-faced smoked salmon sandwiches. Judy Clifton, Urbana, IL., recreates a recipe she enjoyed while an exchange student in Russia.

Busy Day Borscht

3 to 4	cups pickled beet liquid
1	cup cubed pickled beets
½	cup cubed cucumber
¼	cup fresh dill, chopped
¼ to ½	cup dairy sour cream

Pour ¾ to 1 cup beet liquid into each soup bowl. Add ¼ cup beets and 2 tablespoons cucumber to each bowl. To serve, sprinkle each bowl with dill and top with 1 to 2 tablespoons sour cream.

4 SERVINGS.

"Hot summer days become instantly cool when you serve this elegant soup known as 'Soup-e-mast-o-Khiar'," comments Dr. John Giordano, associate director of the master's degree program in International Management at the University of St. Thomas, St. Paul., MN. Dr. Giordano was a Peace Corps trainer in Iran in the 70s and he remembers with pleasure the *"refined hospitality and sophisticated foods"* of that country. *"This is truly a carefree summertime recipe,"* he adds. *"Modify ingredient amounts according to preference."*

Iranian Yogurt Soup

4	cups plain yogurt
1	cup finely-shredded small unwaxed cucumbers
1	bunch green onions, finely chopped
¼	cup fresh dill, snipped
1	sprig fresh mint, snipped
1	small clove garlic, minced
½	cup walnut or pecan pieces
½	cup golden raisins
	Dash of salt
	Dash of pepper
2	cups ice-cold sparkling mineral water
	Ice cubes

Combine all ingredients except mineral water and ice cubes in large bowl; refrigerate. Just before serving add mineral water and stir. Float a few ice cubes in bowl to keep chilled.

4 TO 6 SERVINGS.

Another warm weather winner made easy with microwave and blender preparation. This makes a cooling substitute for salad or an appealing first course for summertime menus.

Cool-as-a-Cucumber Soup

3	cucumbers
1	small onion, chopped
1	tablespoon flour
1	(14½-ounce) can chicken broth
½	teaspoon salt
¼	teaspoon dill weed
¾	cup dairy sour cream

Peel 2½ cucumbers; set aside remaining unpeeled half. Quarter cucumbers and remove seeds. Chop cucumber; put into 2-quart microwave-safe bowl. Stir in onion and flour. Stir in chicken broth, salt and dill weed. Cover with plastic wrap. Microwave on HIGH for 13 to 14 minutes or until mixture boils and cucumbers are translucent, stirring twice. Let stand 10 minutes. Pour cucumber mixture into food processor bowl or blender container. Cover and process at medium speed until smooth. Return to bowl; cool. Blend in sour cream until smooth. With tines of fork, score peel of reserved cucumber half. Quarter and slice cucumber; stir into soup. Cover and refrigerate until chilled.

ABOUT 5 SERVINGS.

This is so popular at the Edina (MN.) Country Club, members and guests request the recipe so they can prepare it at home. Colorful, satisfying and much lower in calories than the milk-based variety, this soup works very well using canned clams. Executive Chef Jerry Cegla, C.F.B.E., has adapted it for family-size serving. Leftovers can be frozen.

Manhattan Clam Chowder

2	cups (½-inch) diced potatoes
4	cups chicken stock
2	tablespoons butter
2	tablespoons olive oil
1	cup (½-inch) diced carrots
1	cup (½-inch) diced celery
1	cup (½-inch) diced onions
¼	teaspoon dried thyme leaves
¼	teaspoon dried oregano leaves
½	teaspoon chopped garlic
½	teaspoon snipped fresh parsley
2	cups diced tomatoes, with juice
2	cups tomato sauce
6	cups chopped canned or fresh clams, with juice
	Salt and pepper to taste

Cook potatoes in chicken stock; remove potatoes from stock when about ¾ cooked (about 15 minutes). Add butter and oil to stock; thoroughly heat. Stir in carrots, celery, onions, thyme, oregano, garlic and parsley; cook until tender. Stir in tomatoes, tomato sauce, clams, potatoes, salt and pepper; thoroughly heat.

10 TO 12 SERVINGS.

When Tim Haugen, Fargo, ND., returned from a Concordia College French class trip to St. Boniface, Manitoba, he brought a recipe his family has enjoyed ever since. Tester Evelyn Bress, Spencer, IA., notes that "in spite of simple ingredients, this soup is quite elegant."

French Canadian Vegetable Soup

½	cup butter or margarine
1	cup thinly-sliced carrots
1	cup thinly-sliced turnips
1	cup thinly-sliced leeks
1	cup thinly-sliced celery
1	cup thinly-sliced potatoes
1	teaspoon salt
4	cups water
2	tablespoons butter or margarine
1	carrot, finely chopped
1	small turnip, finely chopped
1	stalk celery, finely chopped
1	cup whipping cream

Melt ½ cup butter in large soup kettle or Dutch oven. Add finely sliced vegetables and salt. Cover tightly and simmer gently over very low heat until vegetables are soft, about 20 minutes. Add water and heat to boiling. Reduce heat, cover and simmer 20 minutes. Place soup in blender; process at highest speed until all vegetables are puréed. Return soup to kettle. Melt 2 tablespoons butter in a skillet; add chopped vegetables. Brown lightly. Add to puréed soup. Stir in whipping cream. Heat to serving temperature or refrigerate to serve later. Do not boil.

6 TO 8 SERVINGS.

"Serve warm or cold," urges Beverly Deeds, Edina, MN., "Great for lunch with cinnamon rolls," she adds. Tester Nancy Witt, New York Mills, MN., says she enjoys preparing it as much as her family enjoys the results. "Even my 12-year-old 'fussy eater' liked it!"

Norwegian Fruit Soup

2	quarts water
½	cup tapioca
1	cup raisins
1	cup pitted prunes
1	cup dried apricots
1	lemon, thinly sliced
2	(3-inch) cinnamon sticks
1	tablespoon vinegar
1	cup sugar
1½	to 2 cups grape juice

Combine water, tapioca, raisins, prunes and apricots; soak overnight. Cook slowly 1 hour. Add remaining ingredients, except grape juice; simmer 30 minutes. Add juice; simmer 15 minutes. Remove cinnamon sticks. Serve warm or cold.

8 TO 10 SERVINGS.

"This traditional Russian soup can be served as a main dish or first course," comments Donna Kastner, Russian Village head cook. Cabbage, readily available in Russia, is credited for its high fiber content along with Vitamin C and potassium.

Schie

1	(2-pound) head cabbage
2	carrots, sliced
2	stalks celery, sliced
1	turnip, quartered
6	cups beef bouillon
1	(15-ounce) can Italian tomato sauce
	Salt and pepper to taste
2	onions
1	clove garlic
3	tablespoons bacon drippings
3	medium potatoes
	Dairy sour cream
	Chopped fresh dill
	Chopped fresh parsley

Simmer cabbage, carrots, celery and turnip in bouillon in large soup kettle. Add tomato sauce, salt and pepper. Heat to boiling; reduce heat, cover and simmer 2 to 3 hours. Cook and stir onions and garlic in bacon drippings; add to soup with potatoes. Simmer about 30 minutes longer. Serve in a large tureen with accompanying bowls of sour cream, dill and parsley for toppings.

8 SERVINGS.

Even folks who usually don't like spinach enjoy this flavorful cream soup. Make a day ahead of serving, if desired, up to point of cream and nutmeg addition. Just before serving, reheat and add those final ingredients. For fewer servings, just halve ingredient amounts.

Potage Creme d'Epinards

4	(10-ounce) packages frozen chopped spinach
1	large onion, sliced
1	cup water
6	tablespoons butter
¼	cup flour
2	teaspoons salt
½	teaspoon pepper
6	cups chicken broth
2	cups light cream
½	teaspoon nutmeg
8 to	10 lemon slices
4	hard-cooked egg yolks, sieved

Cook spinach, onion and 1 cup water 10 minutes. Purée mixture, several cups at a time, in blender or food processor. Melt butter in large saucepan; blend in flour, salt and pepper. Add broth gradually, stirring constantly until mixture boils. Boil and stir 1 minute. Stir in spinach; cook over low heat 15 minutes. Stir in cream and nutmeg. Serve piping hot. Garnish each serving with 1 lemon slice and a sprinkle of sieved egg yolk.

8 TO 10 SERVINGS.

From the recipe repertoire of the Swedish Village comes this robust blend of favorite ingredients. Head cook, Therese Hennemann, suggests balancing the heartiness with a tossed green salad.

Potato-Cheddar Soup

10	cups soup stock or 10 cups water and 10 teaspoons instant bouillon
2	cups shredded raw potatoes or frozen hash browns
2 to	4 ounces (½ to 1 cup) shredded Cheddar cheese
1	tablespoon flour
	White pepper to taste
1	cup cream or milk
¼	cup butter
	Snipped fresh parsley

Heat stock to boiling. In another large soup kettle, combine potatoes, cheese, flour and pepper; add enough cream to make a thick paste. Gradually add boiling liquid and butter, stirring constantly until thoroughly blended; simmer slowly about 10 minutes. Ladle into individual soup bowls; garnish with parsley.

10 TO 12 SERVINGS.

This dill-sparked soup with an unexpected but appealing crunch provided by the cucumber addition is from the Language Village German cookbook. Tester LuAnn Haugen, Fargo, ND., rated it "excellent" and timed preparation to only 30 minutes.

German Potato Soup

6	medium red potatoes, peeled, cut into ½-inch pieces
3	cups chicken stock
1½	teaspoons salt
¼	teaspoon white pepper
1	medium cucumber
1	tablespoon chopped onion
2	cups half & half
1	teaspoon fresh or dried dill weed

Combine potatoes, chicken stock, salt and pepper in 2-quart saucepan. Heat to boiling. Reduce heat and simmer until potatoes are soft. Meanwhile peel cucumber; halve lengthwise. Scoop out seeds and discard. Cut cucumber into ¼-inch pieces; set aside. Cook onion until soft in just enough chicken stock to cover onion; set aside. Remove potatoes from stock; reserve stock. Rice or mash potatoes and return to stock. Stir in cucumber, onion, half & half and dill weed. Simmer over low heat about 5 minutes or until thoroughly heated.

6 TO 8 SERVINGS.

A favorite wintertime supper for Beverly Deeds, Edina, MN., is this warming soup accompanied by slices of Swedish limpa bread and brick cheese. Tester Lisa Riddle, Minneapolis, MN., found it as delicious as it is easy to make.

Norwegian Pea Soup

1	pound green or yellow split peas
2	quarts boiling water
¼	pound lean salt pork (in one piece)
1	large carrot, diced
1	large stalk celery, including leaves, diced
5	green onions, including tops, sliced
2	teaspoons salt (varies with saltiness of pork)
¼	teaspoon pepper

Sort peas. Place in boiling water in large heavy kettle over moderate heat; add salt pork. Cover and simmer about 1½ hours. Add remaining ingredients; cover and simmer, stirring occasionally, 1 to 1½ hours or until quite thick (about the consistency of gravy). Add salt if desired.

6 SERVINGS.

"This is heaven-sent for our hot Baton Rouge, LA., days," says Ann deLeon. Tester Mrs. Ancel Keys, Minneapolis, MN., suggests serving it Spanish style by adding a little crushed ice to each cup or bowl just before serving.

Gazpacho

2   (16-ounce) cans peeled tomatoes, undrained, chopped*

½   cucumber, peeled, chopped

¼   cup chopped green bell pepper

¼   cup vegetable oil

2   tablespoons wine vinegar

1   tablespoon grated onion

2   cups tomato juice

1   tablespoon Worcestershire sauce

Salt and pepper to taste

4   drops Tabasco

Combine all ingredients. Cover and refrigerate until thoroughly chilled. Serve in chilled demitasse cups or small glasses. **8 SERVINGS.**

*Tip: *Six large fresh tomatoes, chopped, can be substituted for the canned tomatoes.*

Another version of the Spanish-inspired soup featuring all tomato juice rather than tomatoes. Arrange garnish selections artfully on a plate or pass in individual bowls.

Blender Gazpacho

2   cloves garlic

2   slices white bread

1   cup water

¼   cup olive oil

1   teaspoon salt

1   tablespoon vinegar

1   (48-ounce) can tomato juice

½   teaspoon whole cumin seed, if desired

Chopped onion, cucumber, green pepper and cooked egg white for garnish

Combine all ingredients except garnishes in blender. (There is enough for 2 blender containers.) Blend until smooth. Refrigerate. Serve in soup bowls. Pass garnishes on a separate plate.

12 SERVINGS.

When Kay Kallos, Atlanta, GA., lived in Kassel, Germany, she became accustomed to "heavy soups and stews served in the school cafeteria. I clearly understood the custom of a post-lunch nap after eating such weighty fare," she recalls. This stew is a bit lighter and one Kay has adapted from a German cookbook.

Lentil Stew

¾   cup uncooked lentils, soaked overnight, drained and rinsed

4   medium red potatoes

1   carrot, sliced

1   leek, sliced

1   medium yellow onion, chopped

1   bay leaf

3   whole cloves

2   cups vegetable, chicken or beef stock

Salt and pepper to taste

Yogurt

Chopped fresh parsley

Bacon or ham bits, if desired

Place lentils, potatoes, carrot, leek, onion, bay leaf, cloves, stock, salt and pepper in large soup kettle and cover with water. Heat to boiling; reduce heat and simmer 30 minutes. After lentils have nearly doubled in volume, add water to cover, if necessary, and heat to boiling again. Reduce heat and simmer 30 minutes longer. Remove bay leaf. Serve topped with yogurt, chopped fresh parsley and bacon or ham bits.

6 SERVINGS.

Because this caviar of grains was a staple of northern Minnesota Native Americans, it is only fitting that this soup is frequently served at the Minnesota Governor's residence. Although wild rice closely resembles other forms of rice, it is actually an aquatic grain-like seed that is protein-rich and low in fat.

Minnesota Wild Rice Soup

¼	cup butter or margarine
1	medium onion, finely chopped
1	teaspoon salt
1	teaspoon curry powder
½	teaspoon dry mustard
1	teaspoon dried chervil leaves
½	teaspoon white pepper
8	ounces fresh mushrooms, sliced
½	cup thinly-sliced celery
½	cup all-purpose flour
6	cups chicken broth
2	cups cooked wild rice
2	cups half & half
⅔	cup dry sherry
	Snipped fresh parsley or chives

In large saucepan, melt butter over medium heat. Add onion and seasonings. Cook and stir about 5 minutes or until golden. Add mushrooms and celery; cook and stir 2 minutes. Stir in flour. Gradually add broth, stirring constantly 5 to 8 minutes until slightly thickened. Stir in wild rice and reduce heat to low. Stir in half & half and sherry. Heat to simmer, stirring occasionally. Ladle hot soup into individual bowls; garnish with parsley.

ABOUT 12 SERVINGS (3 QUARTS).

Soup for breakfast? Yes, in Japan where it is typical. Miso is a paste commonly composed of fermented soybeans, rice malt and salt. You will find it and dashi at Asian food markets.

Miso Soup

½	(14-ounce) block tofu
4	fresh Chinese black or other mushrooms
4	cups dashi (fish stock)
3 to 4	tablespoons miso

Cut tofu into small cubes. Remove stems from mushrooms and cut tops into ½-inch strips. Heat mushrooms and dashi to boiling. Boil 1 minute; add tofu. Gradually stir miso into soup, making sure to remove all lumps. Heat to boiling; turn off heat. (Do not overcook the miso.)

3 TO 4 SERVINGS.

Just visualize this innovative soup and the serving "bowl" as a centerpiece of your next harvest-time gathering! The recipe is a favorite of Philip Brunelle, Minneapolis, founder and Musical Director of the Plymouth Music Series of Minnesota. Added to his many honors are the distinctions of having appeared as a guest on the first Prairie Home Companion radio show and frequently teaming with Garrison Keillor in sold-out performances across the country. "Be very careful when serving this soup not to pierce the pumpkin sides or your tureen may spring a leak," cautions Philip.

Pumpkin Soup in a Pumpkin Shell

Large pumpkin to serve as a tureen
Soft butter
Salt

SOUP

2	tablespoons butter
¼	cup finely-chopped onion
4	cups cooked/canned pumpkin
5	cups chicken stock
5	cups milk
¼	teaspoon ground cloves
1	teaspoon sugar
2	teaspoons lemon juice
4 to	6 drops Tabasco
1	teaspoon salt
1	cup coarsely shredded Swiss cheese
½	cup heavy cream

About 2 hours before serving, cut 4 to 5-inch lid from top of pumpkin. Heat oven to 400°. Scoop out seeds and stringy portion from inside of pumpkin, using ice cream scoop or grapefruit spoon with serrated edges. Rub inside of pumpkin with soft butter and sprinkle with salt. Place pumpkin in shallow pan. Bake 1 to 1½ hours or until barely tender. (If you err, err on the side of hardness.) To retain orange color of shell, wrap shell in foil after about 30 minutes of baking.

In Dutch oven, melt 2 tablespoons butter over medium heat until it foams. Add onion and cook 3 minutes, stirring until transparent. Add pumpkin, stock, milk, cloves, sugar, lemon juice, Tabasco and 1 teaspoon salt. Stir to blend; heat to boiling. Reduce heat to lowest point and cook soup, stirring occasionally, 20 minutes. Put soup through a sieve or food mill. (Do not use a food processor or blender as the soup should have texture.) Stir in cheese and cream. Return to Dutch oven; heat thoroughly but do not boil. When shell is ready, transfer to platter and fill with hot soup; replace lid. To serve, ladle hot soup into serving bowls and using long-handled spoon scrape some flesh from sides of pumpkin to add to soup.

10 TO 12 SERVINGS.

Charlie Boone, prominent Minneapolis media personality, discovered this "marvelous soup in Tuscany while touring Italy." In addition to using fresh, fully ripe tomatoes, Charlie comments, "You can't go wrong with this recipe if you make sure basil is fresh, the bread stale and the garlic lavish. It isn't called 'peasant soup' for nothing!" He has found it appealing served hot, chilled or at room temperature.

Tomato and Bread Soup

1   cup very good olive oil

3 to   4 cloves garlic, crushed

1   medium leek, finely chopped

1   pound 2 ounces fresh tomatoes, peeled, chopped

8   fresh basil leaves (or more)

4½   cups stock

    Salt and pepper

1   pound 2 ounces whole wheat bread, stale, torn into small pieces

1   cup olive oil

    Freshly grated Parmesan cheese

Heat 1 cup olive oil in deep pan; sauté garlic and leek until soft. Add tomatoes and basil; heat to boiling. Boil 5 to 10 minutes. Add stock, salt and pepper. When soup returns to boiling, add bread; cook 2 minutes. Remove from heat; cover and let stand 1 hour. Mix well; pour on some olive oil and serve with cheese.

Home Economist, Star Tribune food writer and owner of Park Row Bed and Breakfast in St. Peter, MN., Ann Burckhardt, prepared this soup for a March of Dimes benefit in Minneapolis, where local celebrities were asked to showcase favorite recipes. A festive fall offering for a first course or meal.

Pumpkin-Wild Rice Soup

2   tablespoons butter or margarine

1   cup chopped onion

4   cups chicken broth

1   (16-ounce) can pumpkin (2 cups)

1⅓   cups cooked wild rice

⅛   teaspoon white pepper

1   cup heavy cream

    Snipped fresh chives or parsley

Melt butter in large saucepan. Add onion and cook until light brown. Stir in broth and pumpkin. Cook 10 to 15 minutes, stirring occasionally. Add wild rice and pepper; cook 10 minutes longer.* Stir in cream; heat to boiling. Serve garnished with chives.

8 SERVINGS.

Tips: *At this point the soup can be
covered and kept over low heat until
served.
Squash Wild Rice Soup: Two cups
cooked/leftover buttercup or
butternut squash can be substituted
for the pumpkin.

*A unique bouquet of spices gives this chill-chaser special flavor and aroma. A sprinkle of
almonds and paprika crowns each savory serving of this recipe from Patricia Meyers,
Edina, MN.*

Spiced Wild Rice Mushroom Soup

⅔ cup uncooked wild rice

4 cups water

1 (2½-ounce) package slivered
   almonds

¼ cup butter or margarine

8 ounces fresh mushrooms, sliced

1 stalk celery, thinly sliced

⅓ cup flour

3 (10½-ounce) cans chicken broth

½ teaspoon curry powder

½ teaspoon dry mustard

1 teaspoon Worcestershire sauce

¼ teaspoon pepper
   Generous shake of Tabasco

¼ to ½ teaspoon cinnamon

2 cups half & half
   Paprika

Heat wild rice and water to boiling;
reduce heat, cover and simmer 30 minutes, stirring occasionally. Turn off heat
and allow to remain on burner 25 minutes longer. Drain and set aside. Cook
and stir almonds in small pan over low
heat until light brown; set aside. Heat
butter in large kettle; sauté mushrooms
and celery about 2 minutes. Sprinkle flour
over mixture; cook and stir 1 minute.
Gradually add chicken broth, stirring until
mixture is somewhat thickened. Stir in
remaining ingredients except almonds and
paprika. Heat thoroughly. Sprinkle with
almonds and paprika just before serving.

8 SERVINGS.

Let your microwave and blender or food processor do most of the work suggests home economist, Janet Sadlack, Burnsville, MN. Here a traditional French favorite is enlivened with the addition of colorful fresh carrots.

Golden Vichyssoise

4	leeks, sliced (white portion only)
½	cup sliced celery
1	clove garlic, minced
3	medium potatoes, peeled, sliced (about 3 cups)
4	carrots, sliced
1	(14½-ounce) can chicken broth
1	teaspoon salt
1½	cups half & half
2	teaspoons snipped chives

Combine leeks, celery, garlic, potatoes, carrots, chicken broth and salt in 2-quart microwave-safe dish. Cover with plastic wrap. Microwave on HIGH for 16 to 18 minutes or until vegetables are tender, stirring once. Let stand 10 minutes. Pour mixture into food processor or blender. Cover and process at medium speed until smooth. Return to dish. Cool. Stir in half & half and chives. Cover and refrigerate until chilled. Garnish each serving with additional chives, if desired.

5 TO 6 SERVINGS.

A streamlined approach with elegant results. You will find this just as satisfying but less rich than some versions since cream is not used. Garnish with freshly snipped chives.

Blender Vichyssoise

1	large potato, chopped
1	large Bermuda onion, chopped
½	cup butter
¼	cup dry white wine
1	tablespoon lemon juice
2 to 3	chicken bouillon cubes

Combine all ingredients in large saucepan with just enough water to cover. Cook until potatoes and onions are tender. Place mixture in blender or food processor. Process until creamy. Refrigerate until chilled. Serve garnished with snipped fresh chives or parsley, if desired.

4 SERVINGS.

This heirloom recipe for Sviske Suppe from Cora Stahn, Sauk Rapids, MN., is a 100-year-old family favorite brought by Cora's mother from Norway. Tester Linda Johnson, Edina, MN., reminisced as she sampled, "Tasting this brought back fond memories of my grandma's kitchen on the farm."

Holiday Fruit Soup

8 to	10 whole cloves
16	ounces prunes
16	ounces raisins
2	(3-inch) cinnamon sticks
½	cup quick-cooking tapioca
2½	cups water
1	cup sugar
2	cups grape juice

Place cloves in small square of cheesecloth and tie securely with string. Combine cloves with prunes, raisins and cinnamon sticks with water to cover in saucepan. Heat to boiling; reduce heat and simmer 15 to 20 minutes. Combine tapioca and 2½ cups water in small saucepan; let stand 5 minutes. Heat to boiling; cook and stir until tapioca is transparent. Add tapioca to fruit mixture. Stir in sugar and grape juice. Simmer slowly, stirring frequently for 15 minutes. (Mixture will thicken as it cools; more water can be added as desired for thinner mixture.) Remove cinnamon sticks and cloves. Serve warm or cold.

20 TO 24 SERVINGS.

Hege Herfindahl, Benson, MN., explains that this recipe for Norwegian Sotsuppe was "traditionally offered to new mothers to help them regain their strength." Today it is a wintertime treat that has the bonus of "making the house smell wonderful as it simmers."

Sweet Soup

1	cup prunes
1	cup raisins
1	cup chopped apple
1	orange, cut into small pieces
4	cups water
1½	teaspoons lemon juice
½	cup sugar
2	(3-inch) cinnamon sticks
¼	teaspoon salt
2	tablespoons quick-cooking tapioca
1	(10-ounce) package frozen raspberries, thawed
½	cup whipping cream
2	tablespoons sugar

In large kettle, combine prunes, raisins, apple, orange, water, lemon juice, ½ cup sugar, cinnamon sticks and salt. Heat to boiling; reduce heat and simmer slowly, uncovered, for 1 hour. Add tapioca; stir carefully until it is transparent. Add raspberries and simmer for 5 minutes. Remove cinnamon sticks. Whip cream with 2 tablespoons sugar. Serve soup warm, topped with whipped cream.

10 SERVINGS.

The recipe for this traditional Swedish family dish is shared by Birgit Hemberg of Sweden. She is the editor of **Allt om Mat**, *the country's leading food and entertaining magazine and is considered a foremost authority on Scandinavian cuisine. Her husband, composer Eskil Hemberg, has performed with the Plymouth Music Series of Minnesota.*

Pea Soup with Pork

18   ounces dried yellow peas*

7½   cups water

1   (1⅔ to 2¼-pound) pork knuckle or 1 (scant pound) pork shoulder**, lightly salted

1   onion, sliced

½ to 1 teaspoon thyme and/or marjoram

Soak peas in cold water to cover (1 tablespoon salt per 4¼ cups water) about 12 hours. In soup kettle, combine 7½ cups water and pork knuckle; heat to boiling. Skim. Add onion to meat. Cover; simmer over low heat about 60 minutes. Drain peas and add to soup. Cover and boil until meat is tender and peas are soft, 1 to 1½ hours. Remove meat; cut into slices or dice. Return to soup. Season soup with thyme and salt, if needed. Serve with mustard.

4 TO 6 SERVINGS.

*Tips: *Dried green peas can be substututed for yellow peas.*
*   **If pork shoulder is used, put on at the same time as the peas as it needs less cooking time than the pork knuckle.*

Another soup from the recipe files of Sweden's Birgit Hemberg features kale, a green vegetable cousin to cabbage and rich in vitamin A. Kale is usually prepared like spinach and should be used when leaves are dark blue-green with no suggestion of yellowing or wilting. When the Scandinavian spring weather produces nettles, the young shoots are sometimes substituted for kale.

Kale Soup

1   head of fresh kale or 1 (about 13-ounce) package frozen kale

4½   cups stock

2   tablespoons butter

3   tablespoons flour

¾   cup cream

      Salt and white or black pepper

      Hard-cooked egg halves

Rinse kale thoroughly; remove any tough stalks. Heat stock to boiling; add kale. Boil about 15 minutes. Drain kale; reserve cooking liquid. Finely chop kale. Melt butter in saucepan; blend in flour. Thin with stock and cream. Add kale (if frozen kale is used, thawing is not necessary). Boil some minutes. Season with salt and pepper. Serve with hard-cooked egg halves.

4 SERVINGS.

Booths, counter stools and chrome-legged tables contribute to the 50s ambiance of The Ediner Restaurant in The Galleria shopping complex, Edina, MN. You can listen to the juke box while you order the "blue plate special," a hamburger, fries and shake or this very popular menu item, their signature soup.

Ediner's Chicken Noodle Soup

1½   gallons water

¼   cup chicken bouillon granules

½   teaspoon dried basil leaves

1¾   pounds chicken

2   bay leaves

4   cups diced carrots

4   cups diced celery

4   cups chopped onions

4   ounces thick home-made style noodles

      Salt and pepper to taste

Combine water, chicken bouillon, basil, chicken and bay leaves in stock pot. Heat to boiling; reduce heat and simmer until chicken is tender. Remove chicken; cool. Add carrots, celery and onions; cook until vegetables are tender. Bone chicken; cut into ½ to ¾-inch pieces. Cook noodles as directed on package; drain. Add chicken and noodles to soup. Simmer until thoroughly heated. Season to taste with salt and pepper and additional basil, if desired. Remove bay leaves.

8 TO 10 SERVINGS.

EGGS & CHEESE

Song An important part of all cultures, music is also an integral component of the Language Villages. Singing enables participants to become familiar with the sound of a language, develop greater understanding of the culture, and learn new vocabulary. These staff members teach a Finnish song to their learning group.

Ski season guests at Jim and Mary Richards' Maplelag Resort in Callaway, MN., are greeted by this, the first dish on the Sunday morning smörgåsbord. It must be assembled, covered and refrigerated the night before serving. For home entertaining, offer with sliced baked ham or Canadian bacon, miniature sweet rolls and a fruit compote.

Sunrise Egg Soufflé

8	ounces (2 cups) shredded Cheddar cheese
12	eggs, slightly beaten
¼	cup butter, cut up
½	teaspoon salt
	Dash of pepper
2	teaspoons dry mustard
1	cup half & half

Sprinkle cheese in 13x9x2-inch pan. Pour eggs over cheese; dot with butter. Combine seasonings with half & half; pour over eggs. Cover and refrigerate overnight. Heat oven to 325°. Bake 35 to 45 minutes or until top is light brown and eggs are set.

12 SERVINGS.

Satisfy hearty appetites with this recipe from the German Village Cookbook. Known as "hoppelpoppel" in the working class section of Berlin, the recipe adapts well to the addition of leftover cooked vegetables. Add just before pouring egg mixture into the pan.

Farmer's Omelette

4	slices bacon
⅓	cup finely-diced onion
4	eggs
½	teaspoon salt
	Pepper to taste
½	teaspoon dried basil leaves
2	medium potatoes, boiled, thinly sliced

Cook bacon in medium skillet until crisp; remove and drain, reserving drippings in skillet. Beat eggs, salt, pepper and basil together in small bowl until well blended. Heat bacon drippings over medium heat. Place potato slices in skillet; cook just until potatoes begin to brown. Sprinkle with onion; place bacon over onion.

Pour egg mixture over all and gently tip skillet from side to side to spread eggs evenly. Reduce heat to low and cook without stirring 5 to 6 minutes, shaking pan gently to prevent eggs from sticking. Omelette is done when eggs are set but still slightly moist. Slide omelette onto plate. Serve at once.

2 SERVINGS.

A rise and shine make-ahead from Illinois Senator Paul Simon. Layer ingredients the night before baking, cover and refrigerate. Ready for breakfast or brunch in less than an hour.

Sausage Soufflé

6	slices white bread
1	pound pork sausage
8	eggs
2	cups milk
1	teaspoon salt
1	teaspoon dry mustard
4	ounces (1 cup) shredded mild Cheddar cheese

Grease 13x9x2-inch glass baking dish. Cut crusts from bread; cut bread into cubes. In skillet, cook sausage until brown; drain. Arrange bread cubes in greased baking dish; sprinkle with sausage. In bowl, beat eggs, milk, salt and mustard together; pour over bread. Top with cheese. Cover with plastic wrap; refrigerate overnight. Heat oven to 350°. Remove plastic wrap. Bake about 45 minutes.

8 SERVINGS.

While vacationing in Tenerife, Diana Gulden and her husband, José, savored this "tropical rendition of the classic Spanish omelet." The setting was ideal — "a tiny hotel dining room overlooking the ocean and surrounded by fields of banana trees." In Spain this is called "tortilla de plátano" — the Spanish word tortilla refers to an egg dish rather than a flat bread like the Mexican tortilla.

Tenerife Banana Omelet

2	eggs
¼	teaspoon salt
	Dash of sugar
1	medium banana, ripe but firm
1	tablespoon olive oil

Beat eggs, salt and sugar. Thinly slice banana; carefully mix with eggs. Heat oil in small nonstick skillet. Pour in egg mixture; reduce heat. Cook until bottom of tortilla has browned. Invert a dinner plate over skillet and turn tortilla onto the plate. Slide tortilla off plate back into skillet (cooked, brown side will be up). Continue cooking until bottom is brown. Slide out of skillet onto serving plate. DO NOT FOLD.

1 SERVING.

Tip: Recipe can easily be doubled and cooked in a large skillet.

The Hotel Sofitel is famous for this recipe. If you wish to make it a specialty of your house, you may want to invest in an authentic French egg poacher for beautiful shaping and to ensure poaching instead of steaming. Be sure cooked egg is well drained before transferring to Canadian bacon and muffin.

Eggs Benedict

HOLLANDAISE SAUCE

3   cups butter

¾   of juice of 1 lemon and equal amount of water

5   egg yolks

     Salt and pepper

     Tabasco

EGGS

2   quarts water

2   teaspoons white vinegar

8   eggs

4   English muffins

2   tablespoons butter

8   slices Canadian bacon

2   tablespoons butter

     Ripe olives or truffles, minced

Clarify* 3 cups butter in double boiler over very low heat. Strain lemon juice; combine with equal amount of water in another double boiler or heavy saucepan. Add egg yolks to lemon mixture and over very low heat, whip until smooth and thick. Add clarified butter a little at a time, whipping constantly until thick. Season with salt, pepper, Tabasco and remaining lemon juice.

Heat water and vinegar to a slow boil. Break each egg separately into a custard cup and gently slide egg into water. Cook eggs 3 minutes without boiling; remove from water with slotted spoon. Place on cloth to drain.

While eggs are cooking, sauté English muffin halves in 2 tablespoons butter until crispy and browned. Sauté Canadian bacon in 2 tablespoons butter. Place 1 slice Canadian bacon on each muffin half; top with 1 egg; pour Hollandaise sauce over and top with olives or truffles.

8 SERVINGS.

Tip: *To clarify butter, melt very slowly without stirring to evaporate most of water and separate out milk solids (which sink to the bottom of the pan). Skim off any foam that forms on the surface. Pour off golden liquid, which is the clarified butter.*

Mary and Jim Dickson, Northfield, MN., sampled this Mexican eye-opener many times during a summertime trip to Mexico City. When they returned home to a garden overflowing with tomatoes, they created their own version to rekindle colorful memories. Tester Gail Tsuboi, Moraga, CA., enjoyed it for a festive brunch, particularly when accompanied by corn tortillas.

Huevos Rancheros

3 tablespoons vegetable oil

1 cup finely-chopped onions

½ teaspoon finely-chopped garlic

5 medium tomatoes, peeled, seeded, finely chopped or 2⅔ cups chopped drained canned Italian plum tomatoes

3 canned serrano chiles, rinsed in cold water, drained, finely chopped

1 teaspoon salt

½ teaspoon sugar

Freshly-ground pepper

2 tablespoons finely-chopped fresh cilantro, if desired

½ cup vegetable oil

12 tortillas

6 tablespoons butter

12 eggs

Salt and pepper

1 tablespoon water

8 ounces (2 cups) shredded Monterey jack cheese

1 large avocado, peeled, sliced

In heavy 2 to 3-quart saucepan, heat 3 tablespoons oil over medium heat until a light haze forms above it. Add onions and garlic; cook, stirring frequently, 4 to 5 minutes or until onions are soft and transparent but not brown. Stir in tomatoes, chiles, salt, sugar and ground pepper. Heat mixture to boiling; reduce heat and simmer uncovered, stirring occasionally 15 minutes or until most of the tomato juices have evaporated and the sauce becomes a thick purée. Add cilantro, turn off heat and cover to keep warm.

In small skillet, heat ½ cup oil. Holding tortillas with tongs, dip one at a time into hot oil for 10 seconds or until limp. Line two 10x6x2-inch baking dishes with tortillas; keep warm. In a large skillet, heat butter carefully. Break eggs into the skillet; sprinkle with salt and pepper. When egg whites are set and edges cooked, add 1 tablespoon water. Cover skillet and cook eggs to desired doneness. Carefully arrange cooked eggs on tortillas. Spoon sauce around eggs in baking dishes. Sprinkle with cheese. Place under broiler 1 to 2 minutes or until cheese is melted. Garnish with avocado slices.

6 TO 12 SERVINGS.

Onion fanciers in particular will relish this German-style quiche. Tester Marsha Burt, Eagan, MN., served it with pleasing results to her visiting parents and notes that "the flavor reminds me of grilled onions, which I love." A mild onion like Vidalia is especially suitable.

Onion Pie

	Pastry for 9-inch 1-crust pie
2	pounds onions, thinly sliced
1¾	ounces diced bacon
2	tablespoons butter
2	eggs
1	tablespoon cornstarch
¾	cup dairy sour cream
	Salt and pepper to taste
	Nutmeg to taste
½	teaspoon caraway seed
	Butter flakes

Heat oven to 450°. Butter 9-inch pie pan; line with crust; flute edge. Cook onions and bacon in butter until onion is soft. Spread over crust. Beat eggs, cornstarch and sour cream; season and pour over onions. Sprinkle with butter flakes. Bake about 40 minutes.

6 SERVINGS.

In Bavaria, where this is a specialty, boxed mixes that include all necessary ingredients are available on grocers' shelves. Restaurants often serve it attractively garnished with fried parsley, which you can make at home while the cheese is draining and the oil is still hot. Recipe contributor Gary Tucker, Ogden, UT., suggests cranberry preserves as an alternate to the wild currant. Serve as an appetizer or main dish with the toast wedges and fresh fruit.

Camembert Bavarian

1	egg
1	teaspoon water
4	small camembert cheese rounds
1	cup fine dry bread crumbs
	Vegetable oil for deep frying
	White toast wedges
	Parsley
	Wild currant preserves

Beat egg and water together. Dip each cheese round into egg mixture, then in bread crumbs to coat heavily. Heat ½ inch of oil in electric fry pan or stovetop skillet to 400°. Fry cheese in hot oil, turning once, until golden brown. Remove from heat, drain and serve at once. Flavor of the cheese intensifies with cooking and the rounds will be runny. Serve on toast wedges garnished with parsley or preserves.

4 SERVINGS.

"My father is from Germany and as a child, I ate this at least once a week," recalls Ceil Manchester, Homer, AK. *"Now I prepare it often for family and friends who have grown very fond of the flavors."* Remember to reserve time for chilling dough before adding filling. For a less robust flavor, trim amount of onion.

Zwiebelkuchen

CRUST

¾	cup milk
2	tablespoons shortening
2	packages active dry yeast
¾	cup warm water (105 to 115°)
1	teaspoon salt
1	teaspoon sugar
1	egg, beaten
3	cups all-purpose flour

FILLING

3 to 4	white onions, sliced
2 to 3	tablespoons butter
3	eggs
1	(16-ounce) carton dairy sour cream
	Salt and pepper to taste
8	slices bacon, diced
	Poppy seed

Heat milk and shortening to scalding; cool. Dissolve yeast in warm water. Add salt, sugar, 1 egg and yeast mixture to milk; stir until well blended. Stir in enough flour to make a soft workable dough. Wrap in plastic wrap; refrigerate about 1 hour for easier handling.

Heat oven to 350°. Sauté onions in butter. Beat 3 eggs; stir in sour cream, salt, pepper and onions. Meanwhile, pat crust out in greased 15x10x1-inch pan or large cookie sheet with sides. Pour filling over crust; sprinkle with bacon and poppy seed. Bake 45 to 50 minutes or until light brown and filling is set.

4 TO 6 SERVINGS.

From the Hotel Sofitel, Edina, MN., the site of many Language Village award dinners, comes a specialty they serve in-house and also have available for take-out. Note that pastry portion should be prepared several hours before rolling into crust.

Sofitel Quiche Lorraine

PASTRY

1	cup all-purpose flour
½	cup butter, softened
1	egg yolk
	Dash of salt
5	tablespoons water

FILLING

2	ounces (½ cup) shredded Swiss cheese
½	cup diced cooked ham or bacon, crisply cooked, crumbled
1	cup milk
1	cup cream
2	eggs
2	egg yolks
	Salt
	Cayenne pepper
	Nutmeg

Two and a half to three hours ahead of baking, prepare pastry. Thoroughly mix pastry ingredients together with an electric mixer armed with a hoop. If dough is sticky, add flour until it becomes smooth. Refrigerate 2 hours. Heat oven to 400°. Grease bottom of 10-inch quiche or pie pan. On lightly-floured surface, roll out pastry into circle slightly larger than the pan; fold in half, then quarters. Unfold in pie pan and crimp edges with water-wetted fingertips. Sprinkle cheese and ham in pastry shell. In bowl, combine milk, cream, 2 eggs and 2 yolks and seasonings. Pour over cheese in pastry shell. Bake about 30 minutes or until filling is set and lightly browned.

8 SERVINGS.

Cheddar and Swiss cheeses share the spotlight in this heirloom dish from Carey Benson, Roswell, GA. Her great-great grandmother was born in the French province of Lorraine and passed this traditional recipe along to be enjoyed by future generations.

Mixed Cheese Quiche

3	eggs, beaten
1	cup light sour cream
1	teaspoon Worcestershire sauce
6 to 8	slices bacon, crisply cooked, crumbled
1	small onion, sautéed until soft
2	ounces (½ cup) shredded Cheddar cheese
2	ounces (½ cup) shredded Swiss cheese
1	(8 or 9-inch) unbaked pie shell

Heat oven to 350°. Combine all ingredients except pie shell; mix well. Pour into pie shell. Bake about 45 minutes until filling is set. Garnish with parsley, chervil, crumbled bacon or yellow cheese triangles, if desired.

4 TO 6 SERVINGS.

This version of the Mexican classic — "stuffed chiles," — is baked rather than deep fried. Kathy Uvaas, Fergus Falls, MN., brought it back from California and finds it as appealing to Midwest palates as it is to West Coast tastes. "It's a big hit at potlucks," she adds. Sour cream, chopped cilantro and/or ripe olives make complementary garnishes.

Chiles Rellenos Casserole

16	ounces (4 cups) shredded Monterey jack cheese
16	ounces (4 cups) shredded Cheddar cheese
3	(4-ounce) cans whole green chiles
3	eggs
3	tablespoons flour
1	(5-ounce) can evaporated milk
1	(15-ounce) can tomato sauce

Heat oven to 350°. Combine cheeses; layer half in 13x9x2-inch baking dish. Rinse and seed chiles; pat dry with paper towel. Layer half of chiles over cheeses. Reserve 1 cup cheeses; layer remaining cheeses and remaining chiles in baking dish. Beat eggs, flour and milk together; pour over cheeses and chiles. Bake 30 minutes. Spread tomato sauce over top. Sprinkle with reserved cheeses. Bake 15 minutes longer.

8 TO 10 SERVINGS.

Hold the pepperoni and other usual pizza ingredients. Testers gave this unique variation on the usual theme blue ribbon status. Contributor, Andrea Schulze, Ellsworth, WI., serves it as an entrée. However, it could be cut into small pieces for an appetizer as well.

Greek Pizza

8	ounces filo pastry leaves
6	tablespoons butter, melted
3	tablespoons olive oil
1	cup chopped onions
3	large cloves garlic, crushed
¼	teaspoon salt
2	tablespoons olive oil
½	teaspoon dried basil leaves
½	teaspoon dried oregano leaves
4	teaspoons lemon juice
14	ounces fresh spinach, stemmed and chopped or 1 (10-ounce) package frozen chopped spinach, thawed, drained
	Freshly-ground black pepper
½	cup sliced pitted ripe olives
¼	cup crumbled feta cheese
12	ounces (3 cups) shredded mozzarella cheese
2	medium tomatoes, sliced

Follow package directions for thawing and using filo dough. Heat oven to 400°. Combine melted butter and 3 tablespoons olive oil. Sauté onions and garlic with salt in 2 tablespoons olive oil until onion is clear and soft. Add herbs, lemon juice, spinach and pepper. Cook and stir over medium high heat until spinach is limp and liquid has evaporated. On large greased cookie sheet with sides, or 15x10x1-inch jelly roll pan, begin layering leaves of filo dough, brushing each with butter-olive oil mixture with pastry brush. Continue layering until leaves and butter all are used. With slotted spoon, transfer spinach mixture to top of stack of filo. Spread mixture evenly over surface, leaving ½-inch border of pastry. Sprinkle with olives, feta cheese and half of mozzarella cheese. Arrange tomatoes on top; sprinkle remaining mozzarella over all. Bake about 25 minutes or until cheese is browned.

4 TO 6 SERVINGS.

The average American consumes seven and a half pizzas a year. Probably few are as tasty or innovative as this vegetable-topped, cornmeal crust version. Margaret Schulze, Walker, MN., knows she will be asked to share the recipe whenever she serves it. Vary toppings to suit your tastes and garden's bounty.

Gardener's Pizza

CRUST

1¼	cups all-purpose flour
⅔	cup yellow cornmeal
1	teaspoon baking powder
1	teaspoon salt
⅔	cup milk
¼	cup vegetable oil

TOPPING

1	(8-ounce) can pizza sauce
1	medium green bell pepper, cut into rings
1	medium onion, thinly sliced, separated into rings
1	medium zucchini, thinly sliced
8	ounces (2 cups) shredded mozzarella cheese
¼	cup grated Parmesan cheese

Heat oven to 425°. Combine flour, cornmeal, baking powder and salt; stir in milk and oil. Stir with large spoon until mixture forms a ball. Turn out into greased 14-inch round pizza pan; let stand 2 to 3 minutes. With back of large spoon or hands, press dough into pan. Shape edge to form rim. Bake about 15 minutes. Remove from oven. Spread pizza sauce over partially baked crust; top with vegetables and cheeses. Bake 15 to 20 minutes longer or until golden brown.

4 SERVINGS.

Cindy Kryda, Marshfield, WI., sampled this at a party 20 years ago and it has been a favorite from then on. "It has an easy-to-serve, pudding-like consistency and goes nicely with buttery croissants and a fresh fruit medley," she says. Assemble the night before, then bake and enjoy the next morning.

Scrambled Eggs Supreme

18	eggs
½	cup butter or margarine, melted
½	cup half & half
1	(10¾-ounce) can condensed cream of mushroom soup
¼	cup dry sherry
16	ounces fresh mushrooms, sliced
2	tablespoons butter
8	ounces (2 cups) shredded Cheddar cheese

Beat eggs, melted butter and half & half together. In skillet, scramble egg mixture until firm, but still wet. Spoon eggs in 10x8-inch baking dish. Combine soup and sherry; pour evenly over eggs. Sauté mushrooms in 2 tablespoons butter. Arrange over soup layer. Sprinkle with shredded cheese. Cover and refrigerate overnight. Heat oven to 250°. Bake 50 to 60 minutes.

10 SERVINGS.

High school French teacher, Carol Nasby, Fairmont, MN., has ample opportunity to experience European cuisine when she leads student groups in trips abroad every other year. And, she is fortunate enough to have restauranteur friends in the Alps. Swiss cheese can be substituted for the traditional Emmenthaler and pieces of apple and/or cauliflower and broccoli florettes can be used as "dippers" for variety.

Fondue Suisse

1	clove garlic, cut in half
1	cup dry white wine
½	teaspoon lemon juice
8	ounces (2 cups) shredded Gruyère cheese
8	ounces (2 cups) shredded Emmenthaler or Swiss cheese
1	tablespoon cornstarch
2	tablespoons kirsch
	Pepper and nutmeg to taste
	Cubed French bread

Rub interior of fondue pot with cut garlic. Heat wine and lemon juice to boiling. Stir in cheeses, little by little, while pot is over low heat. Stir continuously until melted. Combine cornstarch with kirsch; stir into cheese mixture. Stir 2 to 3 minutes over heat until mixture thickens. Stir in pepper and nutmeg. Place over low flame and serve with bread.

4 TO 6 SERVINGS.

Nancy Thorson, Red Wing, MN., obtained this Cheddar creation from a resident of Alsace Lorraine. "In France, quiche is often eaten for supper and leftovers such as beans or bits of ham are added," says Nancy. Tester Keri Ricks, Appleton, WI., sprinkled on the cheese before baking and liked the results.

Cheddar Quiche

Pastry for 9-inch one-crust pie
½ pound bacon, crisply cooked, crumbled
2 eggs
1½ cups milk
4 ounces (1 cup) shredded Cheddar cheese

Heat oven to 375°. Line 9-inch pie pan with pastry; flute edge. Sprinkle bacon over crust. Beat eggs with milk; pour into pie crust. Bake 45 to 60 minutes or until golden brown and custard has set. Sprinkle with shredded cheese. (Cheese can be added before baking.)

6 SERVINGS.

This elegant French-inspired brunch dish can be assembled the night before serving, with the exception of the crumb topping. Add that just before baking to preserve crisp texture. Just the right amount of cheese is included to be distinctive but not overpowering.

Bleu Cheese-Egg Bake

16 ounces fresh mushrooms, sliced
2 tablespoons butter
12 eggs, hard-cooked, quartered lengthwise
6 tablespoons butter or margarine
⅓ cup flour
½ teaspoon salt
¼ teaspoon white pepper
3 cups whole milk
2 ounces bleu cheese, crumbled (½ cup)
½ cup finely-chopped celery
¼ cup chopped canned pimento
⅓ cup finely-crushed saltine crackers
1 tablespoon butter, melted

Heat oven to 375°. Sauté mushrooms in 2 tablespoons butter; set aside. Arrange eggs in 11x7x2-inch baking dish. Melt 6 tablespoons butter; blend in flour, salt and pepper. Add milk; cook and stir until thickened and bubbly. Stir in cheese, celery, pimento and mushrooms. Pour sauce over eggs. Just before baking, combine cracker crumbs with melted butter; sprinkle over top of casserole. Bake about 45 minutes or until bubbly in center. Cover with foil if it begins to get too brown.

6 TO 8 SERVINGS.

Each village has its own kitchen staff working to make each meal flavorful and authentic. Their work is cut out for them as they research the target culture's recipes, ingredients and cooking techniques.

Dedicated not only to creating culinary masterpieces, Language Villages cooks are dedicated to the Language Villages program—some have been on staff for more than 10 years!

This chef serves *paella*, a popular meal from Spain's Valencia region, to the Spanish Village.

From Vie de France Restaurant in the Galleria of Edina, MN., comes this specialty of their house for you to prepare in your own kitchen. Their chef suggests serving it with colorful fresh vegetables and spinach or regular fettuccine topped with freshly-grated Parmesan. Use frozen raspberries, thawed and drained, when fresh are unavailable.

Chicken Breasts with Raspberry Wine Sauce

½   cup butter
1   tablespoon raspberry vinegar
¼   cup white wine
¼   cup sugar
½ to ¾ pint fresh raspberries
6   chicken breast halves, skinned, boned
     Salt
     White pepper

In small saucepan, melt butter; stir in vinegar and white wine. Cook until mixture begins to thicken. Stir in sugar; gently stir in raspberries. Season chicken breasts with salt and pepper; sauté in butter until chicken is done. Serve chicken topped with sauce.

6 SERVINGS.

Peter Randall, Edina, MN., finds that guests appreciate the imaginative rich and piquant mustard sauce that enlivens boneless chicken breasts. Mustard seeds have been adding spiciness to dishes for thousands of years. Ancient Egyptians and Romans nibbled on them as a snack and used them as a food preservative.

Chicken Breasts Moutarde

     Salt and pepper
8   boneless skinless chicken breast halves
3   tablespoons butter
2   tablespoons finely-chopped shallots
½   cup dry white wine
1   cup heavy cream
3   tablespoons whole-grain mustard
3   tablespoons snipped fresh parsley

Salt and pepper chicken breasts on both sides. Lightly brown in butter in heavy large skillet over medium heat, 3 to 4 minutes on each side.

Transfer chicken to a platter. Cook shallots in skillet about 30 seconds. Add wine; cook and stir about 1 minute. Stir in cream and cook until sauce is reduced to about ¾ cup. Stir in mustard. Return chicken to sauce and heat until sauce is bubbling and chicken is done. Arrange chicken on serving platter; top with sauce and sprinkle with parsley.

8 SERVINGS.

This popular Norwegian Village entrée features sweet-flavored gjetost cheese. "A wonderful new way to serve chicken," comments tester Cynthia Anderson, Barrington, IL. Before poultry became economical, it was considered special occasion fare throughout Scandinavia.

Chicken in Gjetost Sauce

6	large chicken breast halves, skinned, boned
2 to 3	tablespoons butter
	Salt and pepper to taste
2	cups dairy sour cream
4	ounces (1 cup) shredded gjetost cheese

Place chicken breasts well apart on waxed paper; cover with another sheet of waxed paper. Pound with a flat-surfaced mallet until uniformly about ½-inch thick.

Melt half of the butter in a large skillet over medium-high heat. Add chicken, without crowding; cook just until color turns light throughout, turning once. Add remaining butter as required. Keep hot on serving platter until all is cooked. Season with salt and pepper. When all chicken is cooked, drain any juices from platter back into skillet; reduce heat to low. Stir sour cream and cheese into drippings just until cheese melts (do not boil). Pour sauce over chicken.

6 SERVINGS.

A marvelous use for leftover cooked chicken or turkey that takes only minutes to prepare after rice-cooking step. Team with your favorite apple salad and pass with crisp bread sticks.

Chicken Sauerkraut

½	cup uncooked regular rice
3	tablespoons butter
½	cup condensed tomato soup
1	cup chicken stock
2	cups drained sauerkraut
1	cup bite-sized pieces cooked chicken
	Seasoning to taste

Cook rice according to package directions; drain if necessary. Melt butter in saucepan. Stir in rice; cook 3 minutes. Stir in soup, stock, sauerkraut and chicken; cook 5 minutes. Season to taste.

4 SERVINGS.

From James Mead, head cook at the German Village, comes chicken breasts bathed in a rich, creamy sauce. To avoid harsh flavor, use a high quality sweet Hungarian paprika. Its mild flavor complements the delicate flavors of both poultry and sour cream. Tester Charla Beukema, Marquette, MI., suggests spinach noodles as a colorful accompaniment.

Chicken Paprika

½	cup finely-diced onion
1	cup butter
6	chicken breast halves
5	tablespoons paprika
1	cube chicken stock (base)
¼	cup all-purpose flour
1	cup dairy sour cream

Sauté onion in butter over low heat until it turns yellow; do not brown. Add chicken breasts and sauté on both sides until done; do not brown. Sprinkle chicken and onion with paprika and stir to coat thoroughly. Remove chicken and keep warm. Add chicken stock to onion. Stir flour into sour cream; blend until smooth. Stir into onion; heat to boiling, stirring frequently, until mixture becomes a smooth, slightly-thickened sauce. Serve sauce over chicken; accompany with rice or noodles and a colorful vegetable, if desired.

6 SERVINGS.

This popular entrée from The Green Mill, Too in Minneapolis makes one serving, but is easily increased. Mind the warning about adding the wine carefully so you don't have unexpected flames. Marsala is superb in veal dishes as well as with poultry.

Chicken Marsala

6	ounces skinless chicken breast
1	tablespoon butter
2	tablespoons flour
3	fresh mushrooms, sliced
1	green onion, sliced
⅓	cup Marsala wine
1	tablespoon heavy cream

Pound chicken breast to ¼-inch thickness. Heat butter in skillet over medium heat. Dredge chicken in flour; place in skillet. Cook 2 minutes; turn chicken over. Add mushrooms and green onion; cook 2 minutes longer. Add wine; be careful, wine might ignite. Add cream; let it reduce 1 minute. Place chicken on plate; top with mushroom mixture.

1 SERVING.

The Italian translation means "hunter style" although poultry rather than game is usually featured. And, it certainly would satisfy the hearty appetites of hunters, particularly when served with an abundant pasta side dish. The recipe comes from James Mead, head cook for the German Village.

Chicken Cacciatore

4	chicken breast halves
½	cup flour
1	teaspoon salt
½	cup butter
¼	cup chopped onion
1	clove garlic, finely chopped
¼	cup chopped carrot
3	sprigs parsley
1	sprig fresh basil or 1 bay leaf
4	cups diced tomatoes
1	teaspoon salt
	Dash of pepper
¼	cup sherry

Dredge chicken in flour; sprinkle with salt and brown in butter until golden on all sides. Place in covered dish in warm place. Brown onion, garlic, carrot, parsley and basil or bay leaf in drippings left in skillet. Strain tomatoes (should be 2 cups). Add tomato pulp to browned vegetables in skillet. Add salt and pepper; heat to boiling. Add chicken and sherry; simmer about 45 minutes or until chicken is tender. Remove bay leaf.

4 SERVINGS.

Catsup and cayenne add zest to a brandy-laced sauce for this new addition to the French Village recipe repertoire. "It was given to the kitchen by a program staff member," explains Judy Bahr, head cook. "This is just one example of the cooperation existing between the kitchen and the rest of the program."

Poulet Parisienne

3   boneless skinless chicken breast halves

2   tablespoons butter or margarine

1   tablespoon brandy

2   fresh mushrooms, thinly sliced

1   tablespoon finely-chopped onion

⅛   teaspoon finely-chopped garlic

1   tablespoon flour

½   teaspoon catsup
     Dash of salt
     Dash of cayenne

¾   cup chicken broth

¼   cup whipping cream

1   teaspoon tarragon vinegar

In skillet, brown chicken in butter, about 4 minutes on each side. Add brandy. Remove chicken. Add mushrooms, onion and garlic; cook over low heat 2 to 3 minutes. Stir in flour, catsup, salt and cayenne until well blended. Gradually stir in chicken broth and cream; heat to boiling, stirring constantly. Return chicken to skillet. Add vinegar; cover and simmer 25 to 30 minutes or until chicken is tender and thoroughly cooked.

3 SERVINGS.

Choose your favorite cuts of poultry and marinate overnight in this rum-infused sauce. Jennifer Teichmann, head cook for the Spanish Village, finds this traditional dish well received by all ages. "The rum really offers a unique flavor," observes tester Barbara Wang, Shoreview, MN.

Dominican Chicken

1	cup soy sauce
1	cup lemon juice
½	cup rum
6 to	8 chicken pieces (legs, thighs, breasts)
½	cup all-purpose flour
½	cup nonfat dry skim milk
¼	teaspoon pepper
¼	teaspoon paprika

Combine soy sauce, lemon juice and rum; pour over chicken pieces in shallow dish or zipper closure food storage bag. Marinate several hours or overnight, turning pieces or bag occasionally. Heat oven to 350°. Combine flour, dry milk, pepper and paprika; dredge chicken in mixture. Place chicken on well-greased shallow baking pan. Bake 25 to 30 minutes (thighs and breasts may take longer) or until tender and thoroughly cooked.

6 TO 8 SERVINGS.

Sylvia Hansen, Hillsboro, ND., shares a recipe she savored "while living in the Philippines with the International Farm Youth Exchange." Since vinegar has a starring role, select one of high quality. We suggest a white wine vinegar or one with a mild herb flavor like tarragon or basil. Sherry vinegar, frequently used by French chefs, is also delicious in poultry dishes.

Chicken Adobo

1	(2½ to 3-pound) frying chicken
2	cups water
½	cup vinegar
1	clove garlic, minced
	Salt to taste
	Pepper to taste
½	bay leaf
1 to	1½ tablespoons oil or melted lard

Cut chicken into pieces. Place chicken in large saucepan or Dutch oven with remaining ingredients except oil. Cover and simmer until chicken is tender and liquid has nearly evaporated. Add oil; fry chicken until browned. Serve hot or cold.

4 TO 6 SERVINGS.

This recipe from Claudia McGrath, Bismarck, ND., begins the night before serving with an important marinating step. Tester Jane Gillam, Eden Prairie, MN., feels the marinade is as versatile as it is tasty and would complement other grilled favorites. She agreed with Claudia that this is a wonderfully easy summer entrée.

Grilled Lime Chicken   7 pts. ww.

6 skinless boneless chicken breast halves

MARINADE

3 medium cloves garlic, crushed

½ teaspoon salt

½ cup packed brown sugar

3 tablespoons Dijon mustard

¼ cup cider vinegar
 Juice of 1 lime (2 to 3 tablespoons)
 Juice of ½ large lemon (1 to 2 tablespoons)

6 tablespoons olive oil
 Pepper to taste

Place chicken in shallow dish. Combine all marinade ingredients; pour over chicken. Cover and refrigerate several hours or overnight, turning chicken pieces once or twice. Heat grill. Cook chicken over medium coals until tender and thoroughly cooked. Brush with marinade during cooking.

6 SERVINGS.

½ c
Reeds German Potatoe Salad - 2pts

119

Transplanted Fresno, Californian, Donna Jesperson, Minnetonka, MN., grew up with four sisters who took turns cooking. "This was one of our favorite supper dishes and leftovers taste even better as the chile flavor becomes more intense." Although Donna misses the freshly-made tortillas available in West Coast markets, she still makes this using the variety from the refrigerator case. Sliced avocado and tomato make colorful garnishes. Refried beans and a green or fruit salad complete a delicious menu.

California Chicken

3   whole chicken breasts, skinned, boned, halved

4 to 6 green onions, chopped

1   (4-ounce) can chopped green chile peppers, drained

2   (10¾-ounce) cans condensed cream of chicken soup

1   (16-ounce) carton dairy sour cream

12   corn tortillas, quartered

8 to 12 ounces (1 to 1½ cups) shredded Cheddar cheese

Place chicken in large saucepan; cover with water. Heat to boiling; reduce heat to medium; cover and cook about 15 minutes or until chicken is done. Heat oven to 350°. Combine onions, peppers, soup and sour cream. Drain chicken; cut into bite-sized pieces. Add chicken to soup mixture. Line ungreased 13x9x2-inch baking dish with half of tortillas; spread half of soup mixture evenly over tortillas. Cover with half of cheese. Repeat layers of soup mixture and tortillas; top with cheese. Bake about 35 minutes or until bubbly. Let stand 5 minutes before serving.

6 SERVINGS.

A sumptuous and saucy casserole — perfect for party presentation. Cindy Kryda, Marshfield, WI., says this is "a specialty of my mother-in-law's and a favorite of my husband's family." Garnish with peach halves filled with cranberry preserves.

Chicken-Broccoli Deluxe

1   (2½ to 3-pound) frying chicken, cut up, or 4 chicken breast halves
1   bunch fresh broccoli

SAUCE

⅓   cup butter or margarine
½   cup all-purpose flour
     Salt and pepper to taste
½   cup heavy cream or half & half
2¼ cups chicken broth

8   ounces fresh mushrooms, sliced
1   cup grated Parmesan cheese

Cook chicken in microwave or simmer until tender and thoroughly cooked. Remove meat from bones and cut into bite-size pieces. Heat oven to 350°. Cook broccoli until crisp-tender. Cut into small pieces. Butter large casserole dish (10x10-inches). Place broccoli pieces in casserole. Melt butter; stir in flour, salt and pepper. Combine cream and chicken broth; whisk into flour mixture. Heat to simmering, stirring constantly. Mixture will thicken in 3 to 4 minutes. Pour half of sauce over broccoli; add mushrooms, then layer of chicken pieces. Cover with remaining sauce. Sprinkle generously with Parmesan cheese. Bake about 30 minutes.

10 SERVINGS.

After a trip to the Basque country, Pam Fredericksen, Davenport, IA., dished this up to "a group of friends from graduate school. It made such a hit, the menu was reported in the local newspaper." Tester Mary Meyer, Plymouth, MN., enjoyed this with rice and feels it is tailor-made for larger dinner parties and buffets.

Basque Country Chicken

2	(2½ to 3-pound) frying chickens, cut up
½	cup all-purpose flour
⅓	cup butter or vegetable oil
¾	cup chopped onion
1	clove garlic, mashed
8	ounces fresh mushrooms, sliced
1	(28-ounce) can tomatoes, undrained, cut up
1	cup dry vermouth
1	teaspoon salt
¼	teaspoon pepper
1	bay leaf
½	teaspoon dried basil leaves
½	teaspoon dried thyme leaves
	Hot cooked rice

Coat chicken with flour. Brown in butter in skillet. Remove chicken; brown onion, garlic and mushrooms in drippings. Return chicken to skillet; add tomatoes, vermouth and seasonings. Cover and simmer 1 hour or until tender. Remove bay leaf. Thicken sauce and serve over rice.

6 TO 8 SERVINGS.

Nuts about cashews? Try teaming them with bite-sized pieces of chicken for this "family favorite" from Carol Lowell, Burnsville, MN. Allow 30 minutes for marinating step before cooking. Cashews, particularly popular in South America, India and Asia, are a frequent addition to Asian main dishes.

Cashew Chicken

4	teaspoons dry white wine
1	tablespoon soy sauce
1	egg white
2	teaspoons cornstarch
2 to 3	tablespoons vegetable oil
2	whole chicken breasts, skinned, boned, cut into small pieces
1 to 2	tablespoons vegetable oil
1	large green bell pepper, cut into ½-inch pieces
1	(6 to 8-ounce) package cashews
1	(8-ounce) can sliced water chestnuts, drained
1	tablespoon cornstarch
⅔	cup water
1	teaspoon dry white wine
	Hot cooked rice

Combine 4 teaspoons white wine with soy sauce, egg white and 2 teaspoons cornstarch. Marinate chicken in this mixture 30 minutes. Heat 2 to 3 tablespoons oil in wok over high heat. Stir-fry chicken 3 to 4 minutes or until no longer pink; remove from wok. Heat 1 to 2 tablespoons oil in wok; stir-fry green pepper 2 to 3 minutes. Add cashews and water chestnuts; stir-fry 1 minute. Add chicken, stir-fry 1 to 2 minutes. Combine 1 tablespoon cornstarch with water and 1 teaspoon wine; pour over chicken. Stir-fry, stirring constantly, 1 minute. Serve with rice.

4 SERVINGS.

"On my first visit to Hong Kong, the Hilton Hotel chef told me how to make lemon chicken and it remains one of my favorite recipes," comments Eleanor Ostman, food writer for the St. Paul Pioneer Press. "Hong Kong is my favorite place in the world. In fact, I just returned from my fifth visit there and my fourth trip to China." This entrée goes together quickly and is delightful with a side of fried or plain rice.

Chicken in Lemon Sauce

1	pound chicken meat (2 small whole chicken breasts, skinned, boned)
¼	teaspoon salt
1	egg yolk
7	tablespoons cornstarch
	Vegetable oil for deep frying
1	lemon
2	tablespoons white vinegar
3	tablespoons sugar
½	teaspoon salt
¾	cup water
1	teaspoon cornstarch
1	tablespoon vegetable oil

Cut chicken into 12 pieces. Combine ¼ teaspoon salt, egg yolk, 1 tablespoon cornstarch; stir well. Toss with chicken to coat well. Dredge chicken pieces in 6 tablespoons cornstarch. Heat oil in wok or deep pan. Add chicken and deep fry until golden brown; remove and drain.

Meanwhile, slice lemon and combine with vinegar, sugar, ½ teaspoon salt and water. Dissolve 1 teaspoon cornstarch in 1 tablespoon oil. Stir until slightly thickened; pour over chicken. Serve garnished with tomato and cucumber slices atop rice, if desired.

4 SERVINGS.

"This colorful dish is from the Basque area of France — the region in the Pyrenees mountains just on the Spanish border," says contributor Christine Schulze. She has prepared it often for guests since 1978 when a hospitable French family parted with the recipe. You will want to serve it with rice to absorb every last drop of the exceptional sauce.

Poulet Basquaise

2	tablespoons peanut oil
4	pounds chicken pieces
¾	cup dry white wine
	Salt and pepper
½	teaspoon dried thyme leaves
1	bay leaf
4	sprigs fresh parsley
2	tablespoons peanut oil
16	ounces green/red bell pepper, cut into large julienne slices
16	ounces onions, sliced
16	ounces tomatoes, peeled, seeded, chopped
1	clove garlic, minced
	Dash of sugar

Heat oven to 325°. Heat 2 tablespoons oil in skillet; brown chicken pieces. Add wine. Season to taste with salt and pepper. Tie thyme, bay leaf and parsley in cheesecloth; add to chicken. Cover and bake about 25 minutes. Heat 2 tablespoons oil in large skillet; add vegetables and garlic. Season with salt, pepper and sugar. Cook briskly until all moisture has evaporated. (Be careful not to overcook.) Add vegetables to chicken; set aside. Forty-five minutes before serving, return oven temperature to 325°. Cover and bake about 40 minutes longer. Remove cheesecloth bag.

6 SERVINGS.

*Fresh tarragon harmonizes beautifully with many mildly-flavored dishes and poultry is no exception. Heidi Hollonbeck, Davenport, IA., developed this dish in response to an assignment for a French cooking unit of French class. Her family gave it an **A** and have enjoyed it ever since.*

Tarragon Chicken

6 to 8 skinless, boneless chicken breast halves

1 cup chicken broth or bouillon

3 medium carrots, thinly sliced

2 stalks celery, thinly sliced

1 medium onion, thinly sliced

4 ounces fresh mushrooms, thinly sliced

1 teaspoon dried tarragon leaves

½ teaspoon salt

¼ teaspoon pepper

1 bay leaf

1 egg yolk

½ cup half & half

½ cup dry white wine

3 tablespoons flour

Hot cooked egg noodles

In 12-inch skillet, heat chicken, chicken broth, carrots, celery, onion, mushrooms, tarragon, salt, pepper and bay leaf to boiling. Cover; reduce heat and simmer about 25 minutes or until chicken shows no pink when thickest part is slashed, and vegetables are tender. Remove chicken and vegetables to serving dish; keep warm. In small bowl, stir egg yolk and half & half together with wire whisk. Blend in wine and flour. Mix until smooth. Stir about ¼ cup of the hot pan liquid into the mixture; slowly stir back into simmering liquid in pan. Cook sauce over medium-low heat, stirring constantly, until smooth and thickened. Return chicken and vegetables to pan, stirring gently to combine. Remove bay leaf. Serve over noodles.

6 TO 8 SERVINGS.

*"Almost everyone loves this light and healthy Chinese classic," says staffer Jill Fischer.
"Coating the chicken with cornstarch helps keep it tender during cooking," she adds. For a
spicier version, Jill suggests adding a dash of chili sauce.*

Chinese Village Stir-Fried Chicken

2	whole boneless, skinless chicken breasts
1	scallion
1	teaspoon shredded gingerroot*
1	tablespoon minced garlic
1	tablespoon cornstarch
1	tablespoon sherry
2	tablespoons water
½	teaspoon salt
3	tablespoons peanut oil
1	carrot, cut into julienne strips
1	(8-ounce) can sliced water chestnuts, drained
1	cup sliced bok choy
1	cup sliced celery
1	(8-ounce) can bamboo shoots, drained
¾	cup cashews
1	tablespoon soy sauce
	Dash of sugar
	Dash of wine vinegar
½	cup chicken stock
3	drops sesame oil

Cut chicken into long, thin strips. Mince scallion; combine with gingerroot, garlic, cornstarch, sherry, water and salt. Add to chicken; toss to coat. Let stand 15 to 20 minutes, turning occasionally. Heat oil in wok or skillet. Add chicken mixture; stir-fry until it begins to brown, 2 to 3 minutes. Remove from wok. Add a little more oil if necessary to coat vegetables with oil; stir-fry 2 minutes. Sprinkle with soy sauce, sugar and vinegar. Stir in stock; simmer 1 minute. Stir in chicken and cashews; reheat to blend flavors. Sprinkle with sesame oil; serve immediately.

4 SERVINGS.

*Tip: *Choose firm and heavy pieces of gingerroot (fresh ginger) in supermarket produce department. Store in the refrigerator, wrapped in a paper towel, or freeze in a moisture and vaporproof bag. Grate or cut off what is needed from the refrigerated or frozen unpeeled root.*

An elegant repast for four from Kim Lobert, Grosse Point Park, MI. Raspberry vinegar is available at gourmet and other specialty markets and although it is pricey, its distinctive, delicate flavor makes this dish special.

Poulet au Vinaigre

3   tablespoons vegetable oil

4 to 5 skinless boneless chicken breast halves

1   tablespoon butter

1   medium or 2 small onions, finely minced

2   unpeeled garlic cloves

9   tablespoons raspberry or red wine vinegar

Salt and pepper

In large skillet over medium heat, heat oil. Add chicken breasts and sauté until browned on all sides. Remove to warm platter. Reduce heat to low. Add butter, onion and garlic to same skillet; sauté over medium-low heat 7 to 10 minutes or until onion is golden brown, stirring often. Remove skillet from heat; add 3 tablespoons vinegar, salt and pepper. Return to heat; cover and simmer 10 minutes. Return chicken to skillet; stir in remaining vinegar. Cover and cook over low heat 25 to 30 minutes longer or until fork-tender and thoroughly cooked. Discard garlic; serve sauce over chicken.

4 SERVINGS.

"Delicious and super-moist" best describes this butter-basted entrée says contributor Barbara Des Camps, Casper, WY. Dijon mustard, the featured seasoning, is of medium pungency and gives this dish special character.

Dijon-Style Chicken

⅓   cup butter or margarine

2   tablespoons Dijon Mustard

1½ to 2 cups herb-seasoned stuffing

4   chicken legs with thighs attached

Heat oven to 400°. Melt butter over medium heat. Stir in mustard; blend well. Set aside. Place stuffing mix in a plastic bag and crush to fine crumbs. Roll 1 chicken piece at a time in butter mixture; drain briefly. Coat with crumbs, shaking off excess; place on a rack in a roasting pan, skin side down. Bake 20 minutes. Turn chicken skin side up; drizzle with remaining butter mixture. Bake about 25 minutes longer or until chicken is done.

4 SERVINGS.

Although the translation of "teriyaki" means "grilling or broiling", this recipe can be stir-fried or baked in the oven. Tester Susan Barton, Janesville, WI., calls it "a great party dish" because preparation time is so minimal and results so marvelous. She suggests adding vegetables of choice to boneless chicken pieces. You may also use beef or fish fillets of comparable weight.

Teriyaki Chicken

TERIYAKI SAUCE
1	tablespoon sugar
1	tablespoon sake
¼	cup soy sauce
1	tablespoon mirin (available at most Asian markets)
1½	pounds cut-up skinless, boneless chicken
1	tablespoon vegetable oil

Combine all ingredients for teriyaki sauce; stir until sugar is dissolved. Marinate chicken in sauce until liquid is absorbed, several hours or overnight. Heat skillet until hot; add oil. Sauté meat over medium heat until done. (Be careful that the sugar does not burn.) Or, bake chicken in 300° oven about 20 minutes or until done, turning occasionally.

4 TO 6 SERVINGS.

St. Paul, MN., food writer, Eleanor Ostman, featured this layered dinner-in-a-dish in an article on the cuisine of the Spanish Village. Serve with a fruit salad of papayas and mangos, if available, or other seasonal favorites. Eleanor, who is widely-traveled and well-versed on ethnic fare, has been an enthusiastic booster of the Village programs for many years.

Montezuma's Aztec Pie

2	cups tomatillos (Mexican green tomatoes)
2	cloves garlic, minced
¼	teaspoon sugar
1	(8-ounce) can chopped green chiles
½	onion, chopped
22	corn tortillas
2	cups shredded poached chicken
1	cup dairy sour cream
8	ounces (2 cups) shredded cheese

In blender, process tomatillos with garlic and sugar until smooth. Cook over high heat until mixture has thickened, about 10 minutes. In separate saucepan, sauté onion until limp; stir in green chiles. Cool.

Heat oven to 350°. Spread out 11 tortillas in bottom of ovenproof casserole at least 3½ inches deep. Spread ⅓ each of chicken, chile mixture, tomatillo sauce, sour cream and cheese on tortillas. Repeat layers, finishing with tortillas, sauce, sour cream and cheese. Bake about 25 minutes or until heated through and cheese has melted.

6 SERVINGS.

Carol Rueber, Kanawha, IA., shares a recipe from friends from India "who lived for a time in Cedar Falls, IA." Tester Matthew Scott, Fresno, CA., reported, "There was nothing left with four people at dinner!" He applied the thick marinade with a pastry brush with excellent results.

Chicken Curry Indienne

1   (2½ to 3-pound) chicken (or chicken pieces to equal 1 chicken)

MARINADE
2   tablespoons curry powder
2   tablespoons chili powder
¾   tablespoon freshly-ground or ground coriander
    Salt to taste
½   cup ketchup

1   (1¼-inch) piece gingerroot
1   whole garlic bulb
3   whole cloves
½   onion
1   small cinnamon stick
½   green bell pepper, seeds removed
    Water
1   medium onion, chopped
2   tablespoons butter or margarine
7 or 8 raw cashews, pounded to a paste
2   tablespoons coconut
    Hot cooked brown rice

Cut chicken into small serving-sized pieces.* Combine curry powder, chili powder, coriander and salt; stir into ketchup. Marinate chicken pieces in marinade at least 15 minutes. Peel gingerroot. In blender, process gingerroot, whole garlic, cloves, ½ onion, cinnamon stick, green pepper and small amount of water until smooth. Sauté chopped onion in butter; stir in green pepper mixture and brown slightly. Add chicken; fry a bit until it begins to stick. Add water to about half way up on chicken pieces. Cook 15 to 20 minutes or until chicken is done. Stir in cashews and coconut; cook and stir until thickened. Serve on brown rice.

4 TO 6 SERVINGS.

*Tip: *Cut chicken into very small pieces. In India this dish is eaten with the fingers, so think finger food.*

When a Pakistani student of her husband's visited the home of Judy Torvend Laing, Minneapolis, MN., and offered to make dinner, she recorded each step. The result is this dish the family has "enjoyed for the past 20 years. It makes the house smell wonderful as it's cooking," says Judy. Tester Sue Schiess, Edina, MN., suggests using fresh ginger and garlic and cautions, "Don't be afraid of the spice quantities."

Pakistani Curried Chicken

¼ to ½ cup shortening or vegetable oil
1½   medium onions, sliced
3   teaspoons ground coriander
1   teaspoon turmeric
1   teaspoon cayenne
1½   teaspoons cumin
2   teaspoons ginger
1½   teaspoons garlic powder
1   (3-inch) cinnamon stick
1   (2½ to 3-pound) chicken, cut up*
4 to 5 cups water
1½ to 2 tomatoes, thinly sliced
      Salt to taste
1 to 2 cups dairy sour cream
      Cooked fluffy white rice, if
      desired

In large stove-top casserole or Dutch oven, heat shortening until very hot; brown onions, about 15 minutes. Stir in seasonings. Brown chicken pieces in spice mixture. Add water, cover and cook about 45 minutes or until chicken is done. Remove chicken and set aside. Add tomatoes and cook until sauce-like, about 30 minutes. Add chicken and heat through. Stir in salt and sour cream. Serve with rice; add whole wheat pocket bread, chutney and a yogurt drink, if desired.

6 SERVINGS.

*Tip: *Chicken pieces (thighs, breasts, legs) can be substituted for 1 cut-up chicken. Best flavor when cooked with skin on; remove skin before serving.*

Hillary Rodham Clinton, wife of Arkansas Governor Bill Clinton, contributes a recipe very representative of her state. "Arkansas is the number one producer of rice and chickens in the country," she comments. This dinner-in-a-dish needs few accompaniments. A simple fresh fruit salad and crusty rolls will complete the menu.

Arkansas Chicken and Rice

2   tablespoons chopped green bell pepper

2   tablespoons chopped onion

2   tablespoons butter

2   cups bite-sized cooked chicken pieces

1   (6-ounce) package wild rice, cooked

½   cup mayonnaise

1   (16-ounce) can French-style green beans, drained

1   (10¾-ounce) can condensed cream of celery soup

½   cup sliced water chestnuts

¼   teaspoon salt
     Pepper to taste
     Juice of 1 lemon (2 to 3 tablespoons)

4   ounces (1 cup) shredded Cheddar cheese

Heat oven to 350°. Sauté green pepper and onion in butter. Combine with remaining ingredients except cheese; turn into greased 2-quart casserole. Bake 25 to 30 minutes. Top with cheese; bake 5 minutes longer or until cheese is melted.

8 SERVINGS.

Another favorite recipe from the Arkansas Governor's kitchen is this "capitol" combo which was featured in a collection entitled, **Thirty Years at the Mansion.** *Tester Kathy Cochran, Albertville, AL., rated it "excellent" and commented, "The sauce is the key to this delicious recipe! I am adding this to my favorite and frequent recipe file."*

Chicken Enchiladas

2	(4-ounce) cans whole green chiles
2	tablespoons vegetable oil
1	large clove garlic, minced
1	(28-ounce) can tomatoes
2	cups chopped onions
1	teaspoon salt
½	teaspoon dried oregano leaves
3	cups shredded, cooked chicken
2	cups dairy sour cream
8	ounces (2 cups) shredded Cheddar cheese
1	teaspoon salt
⅓	cup vegetable oil
15	corn tortillas

Remove seeds from chiles; chop chiles. Heat 2 tablespoons oil in large skillet; sauté chiles and garlic. Drain tomatoes, reserving ½ cup juice; break up tomatoes. Add tomatoes, onions, salt, oregano and reserved tomato juice to chiles. Simmer uncovered until thick, about 30 minutes. Remove sauce from skillet; set aside. Heat oven to 350°. Combine chicken, sour cream, cheese and 1 teaspoon salt. Heat ⅓ cup oil in skillet; dip tortillas in oil until they become limp. Drain well on paper towels. Fill tortillas with chicken mixture; roll up and arrange side by side, seam down, in 13x9x2-inch baking dish. Pour sauce over enchiladas. Bake about 20 minutes or until thoroughly heated.

15 ENCHILADAS.

"We've enjoyed this at many a family dinner," says Barbara Francis, Blytheville, AR., who obtained this recipe from her sister-in-law, Susan Francis, Harlingen, TX. Tester Christie Wilson, Los Alamos, NM., comments, "I found that pouring stock over the enchiladas really does keep them moist and I will continue to use that helpful hint. Also the canned tomatoes-chiles combination is a very useful product. My 11-year-old described this recipe as magnificent!"

Chicken-Sour Cream Enchiladas

1	(2½ to 3-pound) frying chicken
1	medium onion, chopped
2	tablespoons margarine
1	(10-ounce) can tomatoes and green chiles (such as Ro-Tel)
4	chicken bouillon cubes
4	cups dairy sour cream
24	corn tortillas
¼	cup margarine
2 to	3 cups chicken stock
8	ounces (2 cups) shredded Monterey jack cheese

Cook chicken; remove bones and cut meat into bite-sized pieces; set aside. Heat oven to 325°. Sauté onion in margarine in large skillet. Add chicken and tomatoes with chiles. Simmer until thoroughly heated. Stir bouillon cubes into sour cream; heat until cubes are dissolved, but do not boil. Lightly fry tortillas, one at a time, in margarine. Place a small amount of chicken mixture on each tortilla; roll up and place seam-side-down in 13x9x2-inch casserole. Pour sour cream sauce over all. Add enough stock so enchiladas are about ⅔ covered. Sprinkle with cheese. Bake about 40 minutes.

8 TO 10 SERVINGS.

Tip: Casserole can be frozen; bake 1½ hours at 325°.

Shareen Connors, Burnsville, MN., received this recipe from "a wonderful Korean couple for whom I worked. It has become a true family favorite and makes a great appetizer as well as entrée." After testing it on her family, Barbara Rottman, Dublin, OH., commented, "This will become a staple for me!"

Korean Chicken Wings

1   (28-ounce) package chicken nibbles

3   carrots, cut into thin diagonal slices

8   green onions, cut into 2-inch pieces

SAUCE

4   teaspoons cornstarch

4   teaspoons water

¼   cup low sodium soy sauce

½   cup packed brown sugar

1   clove garlic, minced

2   tablespoons rice cooking wine or whiskey

2   teaspoons toasted sesame seed, divided

Several small hot chile peppers or crushed red pepper to taste (about ½ teaspoon)

Prepare chicken nibbles according to package directions; when done, keep warm. Steam carrots and onions 1 to 2 minutes in small amount of water in heated wok; push vegetables to side. Dissolve cornstarch in 4 teaspoons water; combine with soy sauce, brown sugar, garlic, cooking wine, 1 teaspoon sesame seed and peppers. Heat to boiling; cook and stir until thickened. Add chicken; stir to coat chicken and vegetables with sauce. Garnish with remaining sesame seed.

4 SERVINGS.

If you haven't experimented with ground turkey, you will want to try this flavorful rendition with Italian overtones. Susan Pfund, St. Paul, MN., who tested the recipe from Donna Nooleen, Edina, MN., said she would definitely make it again and perhaps top it with homemade spaghetti sauce.

Turkey-Stuffed Shells

26	jumbo uncooked pasta shells
2	tablespoons butter
3	tablespoons minced onion
1½	pounds ground turkey
2	(10-ounce) packages frozen chopped spinach, thawed, squeezed dry
¾	cup soft bread crumbs
2	eggs, beaten
½	cup milk
¾	cup grated Parmesan cheese
¾	teaspoon nutmeg
1	teaspoon salt
1	teaspoon dried basil leaves
¼	teaspoon pepper
½	cup water
1	(32-ounce) jar prepared spaghetti sauce
¾	cup grated Parmesan cheese

Cook pasta shells to desired doneness as directed on package; drain and rinse. Heat oven to 350°. Melt butter; sauté onion and turkey until no longer pink. Stir in spinach, bread crumbs, eggs, milk, ¾ cup Parmesan cheese, nutmeg, salt, basil and pepper. Fill each shell with ¼ cup of mixture, pressing firmly into shell. Arrange in greased 13x9x2-inch baking dish. Stir water into spaghetti sauce; pour over filled shells. Sprinkle with ¾ cup Parmesan cheese. Bake about 45 minutes.

8 SERVINGS.

Diners look forward to cosmopolitan cuisine when they visit St. Paul's Quail on the Hill Restaurant. Owner/chef Christian Caille and his wife, Marguerite, share their **signature dish** *since their family name means* **quail** *when translated from French to English. "This is a very popular meal in our restaurant and on our Quail Catering menu, especially during the holidays," comments Marguerite.*

Quail au Frontignan Wine Sauce

4   frozen quail*

STUFFING

3   slices French bread, well toasted
     and crumbled (about 1 cup)
½   cup finely-chopped fresh
     mushrooms
½   cup red or green seedless grapes
¼   cup unsalted butter, melted
½   teaspoon salt
¼   teaspoon freshly-ground white
     pepper

SAUCE

1½   cups chicken stock or canned
     chicken broth
½   teaspoon cornstarch
1   tablespoon water
½   teaspoon salt
½   teaspoon white pepper
2   tablespoons Frontignan,
     California muscat or a sweet
     sherry wine

Thaw quail in refrigerator overnight. Heat oven to 400°. Toss all stuffing ingredients together gently. Spoon ¼ of stuffing into each quail, covering openings at neck and tail by tucking in loose skin. Gently press quail into shape. Roast 20 to 25 minutes. After 15 minutes, baste with drippings accumulated in roasting pan. Baste once or twice more before birds are done. Place quail on platter, cover; keep warm in 160° oven while preparing sauce.

Discard fat from roasting pan. Add chicken stock; boil a few seconds while stirring with spatula to dissolve drippings. Strain mixture into small saucepan. Dissolve cornstarch in water; stir into stock with salt and pepper. Heat to boiling, stirring constantly. At the last minute stir in wine. (Makes about 1 cup sauce.) Coat each quail with sauce; garnish with grapes. Serve with wild rice and vegetables, if desired.

4 SERVINGS.

*Tip: *Buy ready-to-cook quail, if possible;
      get European-style, which are
      partially boned.*

Dinner guests at the home of Gail and Dennis Mathisen, Chanhassen, MN., request this recipe after the first bite. Only brief marinating is required to flavor the mild, meaty fish. Gail suggests using the versatile soy sauce mixture with poultry and other types of fish.

Japanese Grilled Swordfish

4	(1-inch thick) swordfish steaks, about 8 ounces each
½	cup sesame oil
1	cup tamari or regular soy sauce
½	cup lime juice
¼	cup mirin (sweet cooking sake)
2	tablespoons minced garlic
2	tablespoons minced gingerroot
3	tablespoons crushed red pepper flakes
	Vegetable oil

Forty-five minutes before serving, heat grill. Half an hour before serving, place steaks in shallow dish. Combine remaining ingredients except vegetable oil; pour over steaks. Let stand 10 minutes in the marinade. Remove steaks from marinade and lightly dip in oil. Place steaks on grill. Grill 5 to 7 minutes on each side, depending on the thickness and distance from heat; brush with marinade. Garnish with lime slices, if desired.

4 SERVINGS.

Fresh tomatoes and peppers teamed with mild fish fillets translate into an easy, economical entrée. Capers, which act as both condiment and seasoning, are the surprise ingredient.

Mexican-Style Fish Fillets

6 to	8 cod, haddock or halibut fillets
¼	cup lemon juice
	Salt and pepper
¼	cup olive oil
½	cup diced onion
¼	cup diced green bell pepper
½	teaspoon garlic
12	ounces tomatoes
1	teaspoon capers
2	tablespoons sliced stuffed olives

Brush fish with lemon juice; sprinkle with salt and pepper.
Cover and refrigerate. Heat olive oil in saucepan. Stir in onion, green pepper and garlic; cook until onion is soft. Pureé tomatoes in blender; return to saucepan. Stir in onion mixture, capers and olives. Reduce heat and cover. Heat oven to 350°. Bake fish about 20 minutes or until it flakes easily with a fork; serve with sauce.

6 TO 8 SERVINGS.

When Jean VanDeusen, Iowa City, IA., resided in Sweden, she "learned to adjust to a diet featuring fish as the major protein source." Recipes like this from friends made that adjustment quite agreeable. Testers Andrea Schulze and Michael Seifert, Ellsworth, WI., suggest fresh tomato slices to garnish with a bright splash of color.

Swedish Flounder with Spinach

1   (12-ounce) package frozen spinach, thawed.

1   small onion, finely chopped

½   teaspoon salt

Dash of white pepper

Dash of nutmeg

1   teaspoon cornstarch

1   pound flounder or sole fillets

1   cup whipping cream

2 to 3 tablespoons prepared mustard

½   teaspoon salt

½   cup (2 ounces) shredded farmer's cheese

Heat oven to 400°. Place spinach and onion in shallow casserole. Sprinkle with ½ teaspoon salt, pepper, nutmeg and cornstarch. Fold fillets in half; place on top of spinach. Combine whipping cream, mustard and ½ teaspoon salt; pour over fillets. Sprinkle with cheese. Bake about 20 minutes or until fish flakes easily with fork. Serve with potatoes and a salad, if desired.

4 SERVINGS.

No one joining three-time Tour de France winner, Greg LeMond, at his training table could complain about repetitious, bland cuisine. This recipe certainly proves the point. In addition to cycling, LeMond is owner with Chef Scott Kee of a highly-rated restaurant in Edina, MN. Aptly named Tour de France, the eatery displays LeMond's yellow jersey in the dining room. Its menu features international dishes.

Wok-Charred Salmon with Wild Greens

EGG BATTER

1	tablespoon chopped garlic
1	tablespoon chopped shallot
1	tablespoon freshly-grated gingerroot
2	eggs
¼	cup cornstarch
2	tablespoons soy sauce
2	tablespoons Hoisin sauce

VINAIGRETTE

½	tablespoon finely-chopped shallot
½	tablespoon chopped garlic
3	tablespoons cold-pressed peanut oil
1	tablespoon rice wine vinegar
½	tablespoon sesame oil
	Salt and pepper
6	(2-ounce) slices salmon fillet
2	tablespoons peanut oil
5	cups mixed greens

Combine 1 tablespoon garlic, 1 tablespoon shallot and 1 tablespoon gingerroot in food processor; blend until fine. Add remaining batter ingredients and blend. Set aside. Place ½ tablespoon shallot and ½ tablespoon garlic in bowl; slowly whisk in 3 tablespoons peanut oil. Add vinegar and sesame oil to taste. Whisk until well blended. Taste for seasoning. Set aside.

Marinate salmon in egg batter 2 minutes. Put 2 tablespoons peanut oil in a sauté pan over medium heat. When hot, add salmon, one piece at a time. Cook until brown, about 1 minute; turn and cook other side. Remove salmon from pan; place on plate and cover.

Toss greens with vinaigrette and place on plate. Arrange salmon around greens.

2 SERVINGS.

A simple, oregano-sparked mixture marinates salmon overnight or for at least eight hours before grilling. The freshly-grated Parmesan makes a tasty enhancer for the colorful fresh-water fish. Thanks to The Good Earth Restaurant in the Galleria, Edina, MN., for sharing this oft-requested customer favorite.

Marinated Grilled Salmon

½	cup olive oil
¼	teaspoon minced garlic
½	teaspoon salt
¼	cup vinegar
¼	teaspoon dried thyme leaves, crushed
¼	teaspoon dried oregano leaves, crushed
¼	cup white wine
6	(6-ounce) Alaskan King salmon fillets
¾	cup freshly-grated Parmesan cheese

Combine all ingredients except salmon and cheese. Pour over salmon; cover and refrigerate at least 8 hours.

Heat grill. Grill salmon over medium coals for 5 to 7 minutes; turn.

Sprinkle with Parmesan cheese and continue grilling 5 to 7 minutes longer.

6 SERVINGS.

For an enticingly easy lunch or supper, this recipe from Beverly Thorson, Bemidji, MN., is hard to beat. Most ingredients are already on hand for quick combining. Watch carefully during broiling step.

Speedy Shrimp Buns

1	(4½-ounce) can deveined shrimp, drained, rinsed, shredded
1	cup finely-chopped celery
1	tablespoon grated onion
3	tablespoons salad dressing
4 to	5 buns
4	ounces (1 cup) shredded American or Cheddar cheese

Heat broiler. Combine all ingredients except buns and cheese; spread generously on cut sides of buns. Place on broiler pan or cookie sheet. Sprinkle with cheese. Broil until cheese melts and browns.

8 TO 10 OPEN-FACED SANDWICHES.

Kristin Lyons, Kokomo, IN., shares a prize recipe from her Swedish great-grandmother. If fresh dill is available, by all means use it in pattern with the hard-cooked egg slices for an attractive garnish. Kristin suggests serving the salmon with simple additions of boiled new potatoes and peas.

Scalloped Salmon

1	(16-ounce) can salmon, bones and skin removed
16	saltine cracker squares, crushed
¼ to ½	teaspoon salt
⅛	teaspoon pepper
1	cup milk

WHITE SAUCE

¼	cup butter or margarine
¼	cup flour
1	teaspoon salt
¼	teaspoon pepper
2	cups milk
½	teaspoon ground celery seed
½	teaspoon instant onion powder
1	egg, hard-cooked, sliced
	Dried dill weed

Heat oven to 350°. Combine salmon, crumbs, ¼ to ½ teaspoon salt, ⅛ teaspoon pepper and 1 cup milk in bowl. Grease or use nonstick cooking spray on 8x4 or 9x5-inch loaf pan. Pack salmon mixture into pan; dot with butter, if desired. Bake about 30 minutes or until top is lightly browned.

Meanwhile, melt ¼ cup butter over low heat. With wire whisk, stir in remaining white sauce ingredients. Cook until smooth and thick. Serve over salmon loaf. Garnish with egg slices and dill weed.

6 SERVINGS.

*This classic Spanish dish is a favorite entreé of Marie and Richard Lacy, Edina, MN., and this, Marie's special adaptation, was recently featured in a **Good Housekeeping Magazine** article. The word **paella** comes from the traditional two-handled serving dish that shows off the assorted ingredients to perfection.*

Shrimp and Sausage Paella

1	tablespoon olive oil
8	ounces hot Italian sausage, cut into 1/2-inch-thick rounds
1½	cups long grain rice
1	cup chopped onion
1	teaspoon ground turmeric
⅓	cup bottled clam juice
2	cups chicken broth
1	(16-ounce) can stewed tomatoes, undrained
½	cup dry white wine or clam juice
12	fresh raw jumbo shrimp, peeled, deveined
1	cup frozen peas

Heat oil in 4-quart Dutch oven. Add sausage and cook until brown. Remove to a plate. Stir rice, onion and turmeric into pan drippings; cook until onion is tender. Stir in ⅓ cup clam juice, broth, tomatoes and wine. Heat to boiling; reduce heat and simmer 22 minutes. Stir in sausage, shrimp and peas. Cover and simmer 6 to 8 minutes or until rice is tender and most of liquid is absorbed. Remove from heat; cover and let stand 3 minutes or until all liquid is absorbed.

4 SERVINGS.

Named for a Chinese province famous for highly-spiced dishes, this stir-fry is a "quick, low-calorie main dish" contributed by Gail Tsuboi, Moraga, CA. Tester Peter Randall, Edina, MN., who shares Gail's fondness for well-seasoned cuisine, suggests substituting tomato paste for ketchup if a less sweet taste is desired.

Szechwan Prawns

2 tablespoons peanut or vegetable oil

¾ to 1 pound raw prawns, shelled, deveined

½ teaspoon minced garlic

½ teaspoon grated or finely-chopped gingerroot

4 green onions, minced

¼ to ½ teaspoon dried red chile pepper

2 tablespoons dry sherry wine

¼ cup ketchup

Dash of sugar

1 teaspoon cornstarch

2 tablespoons water

Hot cooked rice

Heat oil in wok or skillet until very hot. Add prawns, garlic, gingerroot, onions and pepper; stir-fry until prawns turn pink and white. Quickly stir in sherry, ketchup and sugar. Dissolve cornstarch in water; stir into mixture in wok. Cook and stir until thickened. Serve over rice.

4 SERVINGS.

In truly international style, this recipe is served at the German Village's Italian Night, according to head cook James Mead. Beth Johnson Holod, Village staffer who tested it at a dinner party says, "The guests' immediate reaction was 'Wow'! We had hoped for some leftovers, but no such luck. Four people (and a baby) devoured the entire thing."

Shrimp Buongusto

2	pounds large fresh or frozen shrimp, shelled, deveined
½	cup all-purpose flour
½	cup olive oil
½	cup dry white wine
½	tablespoon tomato paste
¼	cup warm water
½	teaspoon salt
½	teaspoon pepper
	Dash of cayenne pepper
1	tablespoon snipped fresh parsley
1	small scallion, chopped
½	thinly-sliced black truffle, if desired
2	teaspoons lemon juice

Rinse and dry shrimp; roll in flour. Heat oil in large skillet; brown shrimp on both sides. Remove oil from skillet; pour into small saucepan. Add wine to shrimp in skillet; cook until wine has evaporated. To oil in small saucepan, add tomato paste, water, salt, pepper and cayenne; cook 3 to 4 minutes. Pour over shrimp; add parsley, scallion and truffle; cook about 4 minutes. Remove from pan; add lemon juice and serve.

4 TO 6 SERVINGS.

This German Village treat (Krabbentorte) combines shrimp and ham in a quiche-like filling. Serve piping hot with a crisp green salad for lovely luncheon or supper fare.

Shrimp Pie

PASTRY

1 ¼ cups all-purpose flour

1 teaspoon baking powder

Dash of salt

Dash of pepper

4¼ ounces butter

3 to 4 tablespoons water

FILLING

¼ cup butter, melted

7 ounces shrimp

4 ounces (1 cup) shredded mild cheese

4 ounces cooked ham, diced, if desired

1 teaspoon dried thyme leaves

1 medium onion, finely chopped

4 eggs

1 cup milk

Salt and pepper

Heat oven to 400°. Combine pastry ingredients until well mixed. On lightly-floured surface, roll out pastry to fit 9-inch pie pan. Form a high rim around edge. Bake 15 minutes. Combine all filling ingredients. Spread in pie shell. Bake 30 to 40 minutes.

6 TO 8 SERVINGS.

Linda Paulson Norderhaug, Brookfield, WI., who studied both French and Spanish at Concordia College, offers a grilled treat with an Italian accent. Prosciutto, or paper-thin smoked ham, helps prevent the shrimp from toughening during cooking. Linda completes the meal with corn-on-the-cob and a crisp green salad.

Prosciutto-Wrapped Shrimp

Buy 4 to 5 jumbo shrimp per person. Clean and devein shrimp but leave tails on.

Make a marinade of equal parts lemon juice and olive oil. Marinate 1 hour or so — lemon whitens shrimp. Place a fresh basil leaf against the inside curve of each shrimp and wrap around and around with a slice of prosciutto ham. Line up wrapped shrimp on a metal skewer. Grill over high heat about 3 minutes per side, or until tail turns pink and prosciutto changes texture.

Patricia Lund, Edina, MN., an active businesswoman and civic volunteer, highly recommends this streamlined but sophisticated dish for other busy cooks. Border with rice pilaf and add a tossed green salad and hot rolls. Presto — your menu is complete.

Scallop Sauté

1	**pound small scallops**
½	**cup butter**
1	**cup all-purpose flour**
1	**teaspoon finely-chopped garlic**
3	**tablespoons finely-snipped fresh parsley**
	Salt to taste
	Coarsely ground black pepper
	Lemon wedges

Wash scallops and dry thoroughly on paper towels. Roll scallops in flour; put in a sieve and shake vigorously to remove all excess flour. Melt butter, but do not brown. Add scallops, sliding them about in the pan until they are firm but not brown, 2 to 3 minutes. Do not overcook. Add garlic and parsley; heat about 30 seconds longer. Mound on a heated platter and season with salt and pepper. Garnish with lemon wedges; serve at once.

2 TO 3 SERVINGS.

When Ruth Chapman, French Village head cook introduced this to 125 hungry diners, it was an immediate hit! Staffer Linda Erceg has adapted it for family serving and suggests doubling the filling amount if you would like extra to "spoon over the top of the roll." Leftovers store well in the refrigerator and can be reheated in the microwave.

Crab Soufflé

SOUFFLÉ

¼   cup butter

½   cup all-purpose flour

2   cups milk

4   eggs, separated

½   teaspoon salt

    Red pepper

2   teaspoons chopped chives

¼   teaspoon cream of tartar

⅓   cup grated Parmesan cheese

CRABMEAT FILLING

4   green onions, chopped

2   tablespoons butter

12   ounces crabmeat or imitation crab (surimi)

3   ounces cream cheese

⅓   cup half & half

2   tablespoons snipped fresh parsley

    Salt and red pepper to taste

Grease 10x15x1-inch jelly roll pan; line with waxed paper, grease again and flour. Heat oven to 350°. Melt ¼ cup butter in saucepan; stir in flour and cook until bubbling. Stir in milk; boil 1 minute. Beat in egg yolks, one at a time. Stir in ½ teaspoon salt, red pepper and chives. Cool, stirring occasionally. Cover with plastic wrap to prevent film from forming. Beat egg whites and cream of tartar until stiff. Fold whites and Parmesan cheese into mixture. Pour into prepared pan. Bake about 45 minutes.

Meanwhile, prepare filling. Cook onions in butter; stir in remaining filling ingredients; mix well. When soufflé is done, immediately loosen from pan and invert onto cloth towel. Remove waxed paper; spread with filling. Use towel to coax soufflé into a roll. Cut into slices.

10 SERVINGS.

148

This cornerstone of French feasting will have you packing your bags for more of the same in the land of rich sauces and delectable ways with coastal catches. The Hotel Sofitel, Edina, MN., shares their version and suggests serving the rice on the side or placing it in the bottom of the au gratin dish before adding scallops and sauce. Fresh artichoke hearts or steamed broccoli or asparagus spears make a colorful accompaniment.

Coquilles St. Jacques au Gratin

2   cups dry white wine
2 to   2½ pounds fresh bay or sea scallops
2   bay leaves
   Salt and pepper
1   cup water
⅛ to ¼ cup fresh shallots, chopped
⅓   cup butter
⅓   cup flour
   Juice of ½ lemon (1 to 1½ tablespoons)
1   cup cream
6   ounces (1½ cups) shredded Swiss cheese
   Hot cooked rice

Over medium heat, cook wine, scallops, bay leaves, salt, pepper, water and shallots. Cook a few minutes but do not heat to boiling. Remove scallops and bay leaves. Heat remaining liquid to boiling; boil until reduced by one-third. In another saucepan, melt butter; add flour to make a roux. Cook over low heat 10 minutes, stirring so it doesn't brown. Let cool 10 minutes. Add reduced mixture; heat to boiling, stirring constantly to avoid scorching. Simmer 10 minutes. Stir in lemon juice and cream. Season to taste. Place scallops in au gratin dish. Pour sauce over them and top with cheese. Place under broiler until golden brown. Serve with rice.

4 TO 6 SERVINGS.

Tip: When working with roux and stock, remember that one of the two must be hot and the other cold, to avoid lumping when they are combined.

"A terrific low-calorie dish — wonderful for late summer and fall when gardens are prolific," comments Jacquelyn Rosholt, Minneapolis, MN. *Does double duty as a first course for 6 to 8 or a main dish for 4.*

Linguine with Vegetable-Clam Sauce

1   (16-ounce) package uncooked linguine

4   cloves garlic, minced

½   cup chopped onion

2   tablespoons olive oil

3 to 4 zucchini, sliced

3 to 4 tomatoes, chopped

1 to 2 (6½-ounce) cans minced clams, undrained*

5   tablespoons chopped fresh basil

     Salt and pepper to taste

¾   cup (3 ounces) shredded Asiago cheese

     Freshly-grated Parmesan cheese

Cook linguine to desired doneness as directed on package. Rinse and drain. Sauté garlic and onion in olive oil, do not brown. Add zucchini, tomatoes and clams with liquid . Simmer until vegetables are cooked, 15 to 20 minutes. Add basil, salt and pepper during last 5 minutes. Toss linguine with sauce; add Asiago cheese and toss again. Serve with Parmesan cheese.

4 SERVINGS.

*Tip: *One (4½-ounce) can shrimp, rinsed, drained, can be substituted for 1 can of clams.*

Dal Holmberg, Minnetonka, MN., is a "lover of Lake Superior salmon and trout" and created this recipe to add the finishing touch to his catch. He serves as Vice President of the Lake Superior Steelhead Association, an environmental group. Recipe is easily increased to baste more servings.

Lake Superior Marinade

¼   cup butter or margarine, melted

1   tablespoon lemon juice

1   teaspoon seasoned salt

½   teaspoon dill

1   tablespoon steak sauce

Combine all ingredients in a small bowl or pan; keep warm. Heat grill; spray with nonstick cooking spray. Grill fish, skin-side-down about 10 minutes; spoon on sauce. Grill flesh-side-down about 8 minutes. Turn skin-side-down again for 2 minutes; spoon on sauce.

Serve with any remaining sauce.

SAUCE FOR 4 SERVINGS OF FISH.

Once ingredients are readied, this Japanese classic is quickly prepared. If you have a wok, you will find it works beautifully to keep spattering to a minimum. Be sure oil is heated to correct temperature for crisp, golden results. Serve with rice and, of course, have chopsticks available.

Tempura

SAUCE

¼   cup mirin (sweet rice wine)

1   cup soup stock or dashi

¼   cup soy sauce

SEASONINGS

6   tablespoons grated Japanese white radish

1   tablespoon grated gingerroot (or ground ginger)

BATTER

1   egg

½   cup ice water

1   cup all-purpose flour
    Vegetable oil for deep frying

Plan 5½ ounces each seafood and vegetables per person: Shrimp, green bell pepper, carrots, onion, potato, string beans, egg plant, parsley, whatever is available.

Heat mirin to boiling. Add soup stock and soy sauce; simmer. Sieve sauce; set aside.

Prepare ingredients for frying: Remove head, shell and tip of tail of shrimp. Cut beans into 2-inch pieces; gather 2 to 3 beans together for batter. Slice carrots into fine strips, etc. Combine radish and gingerroot.

In wok or large skillet or thick deep pan, heat oil to 370°. In bowl, combine all batter ingredients just until moistened. Mix with chop sticks; do not overmix. Dip pieces of seafood and vegetables into batter. Allow excess batter to drip back into bowl. Fry a few pieces at a time for 2 to 3 minutes, or until crisp. Turn over with chopsticks. (Fry shrimp or fish first, then vegetables.) Drain on paper towels. Serve immediately with sauce and seasonings.

Christmas Eve visitors to the home of Lorraine Amundson, Grand Forks, ND., will find this on the buffet table along with "some good Scandinavian lefse and Swedish meatballs." The accompanying dishes should be colorful with varying textures to enhance the festive spread.

Baked Lutefisk

Choose choice lutefisk; trim. Cut into pieces of equal size. Line pan with foil. Bake lutefisk uncovered at 400 to 425° for 20 to 30 minutes or until it flakes easily with a fork. Serve with melted butter.

Beverly Deeds, Edina, MN., remembers this as one of several courses served by her mother at family Christmas Eve dinners. "My father purchased the lutefisk at a Swedish market so he was certain of high quality," she recalls. "My mother's presentation was beautiful — a border of escarole around the fish, some sauce and seasonings on top and the remaining sauce in a side dish to be passed. This method of cooking keeps the fish nice and moist." Adjust ingredient amounts to suit number of persons being served.

Lutefisk with Cream Sauce

Wash lutefisk with cold water. Place in skillet; cover with cold water to which 1 teaspoon salt has been added. Cook uncovered until water begins to boil. Remove skillet from heat. Place fish on platter and cover with a white sauce made with butter. Sprinkle sauce with allspice and paprika. Garnish with escarole. Spoon some sauce on top and serve the rest on the side.

152

"Spend your time visiting with guests and not in the kitchen cooking," with this make-ahead party entrée from Helen Clark, Arden Hills, MN. "It is deliciously rich and looks festive in a silver chafing dish," she adds. Garnish with fresh chopped parsley or chives. Cooked peas and diced pimento can be added to plain rice to add color plus flavor.

Beef Stroganoff

8	ounces fresh mushrooms, sliced
4	tablespoons butter
2	tablespoons vegetable oil
2	tablespoons dried shredded green onions
2½ to 3	pounds beef tenderloin or sirloin steak*, cut into thin strips
	Salt and pepper
⅓	cup Madeira wine
1	(10½-ounce) can beef bouillon
2 to 3	teaspoons cornstarch
	Hot cooked white rice, wild rice blend or pilaf
1	cup whipping cream or half & half

In large skillet, quickly sauté mushrooms in 2 tablespoons of the butter and 1 tablespoon of the oil, 4 to 5 minutes. Stir in green onions; sauté 1 to 2 minutes longer. Set aside. Drain oil; sauté meat in remaining 2 tablespoons butter and 1 tablespoon oil. (Meat should be browned but rosy-red inside.) Season to taste with salt and pepper. Remove meat from skillet.

Pour wine and bouillon into skillet. Stir into pan drippings and simmer until about 1½ cups remain. Combine cornstarch with 1 tablespoon of the cream; stir cornstarch mixture and remaining cream into wine mixture. Simmer a few minutes; sauce should be slightly thickened. (Add more cornstarch if needed.) Stir in mushrooms and beef until well blended. Serve over rice.

5 TO 6 SERVINGS.

Tip: *Any other very tender cut of meat can be substituted.

Ellen Ylikopsa, Granite City, IL., shares an entrée "served for Sunday dinner and special occasions back home in Germany." Ellen brought this recipe when she immigrated and "although it takes time and love to make it," results are delightful for family or company dinners.

Sunday Dinner Beef Rolls

1   beef flank steak, about ⅓-inch thick, cut into 2 (6x6-inch) pieces
     Salt and pepper to taste
2   slices bacon, finely diced
1   (4-inch) kosher crunchy dill pickle, finely diced
1   small onion, finely diced
     Flour
     Butter or margarine
     Skewers or thread

Rinse meat; dry off with paper towels. Place on flat surface or plate; season with salt and pepper. Place half of bacon, half of pickle and half of onion on one piece of meat; roll up and fasten with skewer or wrap with thread to keep shape. Repeat process with remaining piece of meat, bacon, pickle and onion. Melt butter in heavy skillet; brown meat rolls. Pour in enough water to cover rolls. Cover skillet; simmer 2 hours. Remove rolls; keep warm. Make gravy by mixing flour and water to a paste consistency smooth enough to pour. Slowly add mixture to drippings, stirring constantly until gravy is desired thickness. Pour gravy over unskewered rolls. Serve with mashed potatoes and vegetables, if desired.

2 ROLLS.

"This was introduced to us in 1956 in Germany and has been a family favorite ever since," comments James Schulze, Walker, MN. *"It makes a delicious gravy and can be prepared in advance and reheated,"* he adds. *Carry out the German theme by serving with spätzle.*

Rouladen

8	thin slices beef top round steak, about ⅛-inch thick*
½	cup Dijon mustard
8	slices very lean bacon
4	dill pickles, chopped
1	large onion, finely chopped
	Dried marjoram
	String
8	tablespoons butter or margarine
2	medium carrots
1	medium onion, quartered
6	tablespoons flour
1	quart beef broth, heated
2	bay leaves

Spread each slice of beef with 1 tablespoon mustard; add 1 slice bacon, 1 to 2 tablespoons chopped pickle and 1 tablespoon chopped onion. Sprinkle with marjoram. Roll up and secure with string. In Dutch oven, melt butter and sauté 2 or 3 beef rolls at a time. Transfer to plate. Add carrots and quartered onion; sauté until brown. Whisk in flour and brown lightly. Whisk in broth slowly. Add bay leaves. Heat to boiling; reduce heat and add rouladens. Cover and simmer 1 hour. Heat oven to 350°. Transfer to ovenproof serving dish. Remove strings. Strain gravy and pour over rouladens. Cover and heat in oven about 30 minutes.

4 TO 6 SERVINGS.

Tip: *Beef is best when sliced frozen by butcher.*

These vegetable and egg-stuffed rolls served at the Spanish Village are designed to showcase the excellent beef raised in Argentina. Testers suggest trying another sauce for variation — add a little butter and some red wine to the pan drippings for a gravy-like mixture.

Argentinian Beef Rolls

2	(2-pound) flank steaks
8	(6 to 8-inch) carrots, 1 inch wide, cooked
4	eggs, hard-cooked, sliced
1	large onion, sliced, separated into rings
8	ounces fresh spinach
¼	cup finely-snipped fresh parsley
1	tablespoon salt
	Toothpicks or string
3	cups beef stock
1 to	3 cups cold water
½	cup red wine vinegar
1	teaspoon finely-chopped garlic
1	teaspoon dried thyme

Butterfly each flank steak lengthwise to make a thick flat, almost square piece of meat. (Your butcher may be willing to do this.) Heat oven to 325°. Place half of carrots, eggs, onion, spinach and parsley along the cut surface of each steak; sprinkle with salt. Beginning at wide side, roll up. Secure with string or toothpicks. Place in roasting pan; add stock and water. Roast about 1 hour or until meat thermometer inserted in center of beef roll registers 150°. Meanwhile, heat wine vinegar, garlic and thyme to boiling in saucepan. When beef rolls are done, remove from pan. Allow to stand 5 to 10 minutes; slice into ¾-inch cross-sections. Pour hot vinegar mixture over each slice and serve. Can also be refrigerated immediately after cooking and served cold.

8 TO 10 SERVINGS.

Dana Thome, Grafton, WI., learned to make these from a Honduran friend who explained that the recipe was a dish typical of Zacatecas, Mexico. Although Dana "was not served similar tacos during the two weeks she spent in Zacatecas," she says they are great.

Zacatecas Tacos

¾ to 1 pound beef stew meat or other beef cut into small pieces

1 tablespoon vegetable oil

Garlic salt to taste

Onion powder to taste

Paprika to taste

Dash of Worcestershire sauce

1 or 2 tomatoes

1 medium green bell pepper

1 medium onion

6 to 8 flour tortillas

1 avocado, peeled, sliced

Dairy sour cream

In bowl, combine meat, oil, spices and Worcestershire sauce. Let stand while dicing tomatoes, green pepper and onion. Combine vegetables but do not cook. In skillet, cook meat mixture until done. Warm tortillas; wrap in cloth towel to keep warm. Fill tortillas with meat and tomato mixture. Garnish with avocado and sour cream.

6 TO 8 SERVINGS.

The story goes that old-fashioned dishes like this for "kalops" originated aboard ship where cooks tried to serve satisfying, nutritious fare with limited provisions. Here, cranberry sauce is a surprise ingredient that makes for an unusually tasty sauce. Serve with rice or noodles and a colorful vegetable.

Swedish Callops

3 pounds beef stew meat

1 teaspoon salt

¼ teaspoon black pepper

¼ cup flour

3 tablespoons vegetable oil

2 medium onions, chopped

2 bay leaves

1 (16-ounce) can whole berry cranberry sauce

Sprinkle meat with salt and pepper; dredge with flour. Heat oil in Dutch oven; brown meat on all sides. Add onions, bay leaves and cranberry sauce; stir. Cover and cook over medium heat, stirring occasionally, until meat is tender, about 1½ hours. Remove bay leaves.

6 SERVINGS.

Evelyn Bress, Spencer, IA., first tried this recipe to please "our Japanese AFS student on his birthday." Testing it proved somewhat of a challenge to Carolyn Petterson, Binford, ND., who "had to shop ninety miles away for the ingredients." Did this deter her enthusiasm? Not a whit. "Thank you for giving me the incentive to make this," she said. "The research and shopping was challenging and exciting. This is a great recipe — I'm trying it again soon!"

Sukiyaki

SAUCE

¼ cup Kikkoman soy sauce

2 tablespoons white wine

½ cup water

4 teaspoons sugar

1½ pounds standing rib roast, boned, machine-sliced bacon-thin, cut into small pieces, if desired

4 stalks celery, cut diagonally into ½-inch pieces

2 onions, sliced length-wise

1 bunch green onions, including tops, cut into 2-inch lengths

1 cup sliced fresh mushrooms or 1 (4-ounce) jar sliced mushrooms, drained

8 ounces fresh spinach, slightly steamed or precooked

1 bunch watercress sprigs, if desired

1 (8-ounce) can bamboo shoots, drained

7 ounces water-packed tofu, cut into cubes, if desired

¼ pound beef suet, cut into small pieces (or peanut oil)

Hot cooked sticky rice or other rice

Combine sauce ingredients; set aside. Arrange vegetables, meat and tofu attractively on large platter. (Can be done ahead of time, covered and refrigerated several hours.) Place electric skillet at the table and set at 260°. Melt suet (discard unmelted portion). Add ⅓ of meat to skillet. Pour in a little of the sauce mixture and brown meat. Add vegetables; cook and stir gently 5 to 6 minutes. Add tofu and heat. Cook in 2 more batches, using remaining meat, vegetables, sauce and tofu. Serve with rice.

4 TO 6 SERVINGS.

Variation — Boneless chicken can be substituted for beef to make Chicken Sukiyaki.

Some of the most flavorful "daubes" or French stews originate in the Provençe, although almost every region boasts its own traditional recipe. The main ingredients — meat, poultry, seafood or vegetables in combination, are the focal point of these ragouts rather than the sauce. This particular version, aromatic with garlic and orange zest, will make any dinner party an occasion. Make a day ahead of serving for best flavor. Freezes well.

Daube Provençal

4	pounds beef brisket, trimmed
1	pound lean bacon
	Salt
	Freshly ground pepper
4	large onions, cut into quarters
2	whole garlic heads (20 or more cloves of garlic, depending on size)
2	strips orange peel, diced
1	bay leaf
2	sprigs fresh thyme or 1 teaspoon dried thyme
	Burgundy or other dry red wine

Cut meat into large cubes. In Dutch oven or other heavy deep casserole, cook bacon until crisp. Remove bacon; drain and set aside. Cook meat cubes, a few pieces at a time, in the bacon drippings until meat is golden all over. Sprinkle with salt and pepper. Add onions. Crumble bacon; add to meat mixture. Separate garlic heads; peel and add to meat. Add remaining ingredients with enough red wine to cover. Season with salt and pepper. Cover tightly; simmer over low heat 3 hours or until meat is tender. Keep covered; let cool. Refrigerate, covered. When cold, skim fat from surface. Heat daube to boiling point before serving.

8 OR MORE SERVINGS.

The Allers of Albion, IN., make this the centerpiece of family gatherings served with potato dumplings, boiled potatoes or noodles. Red cabbage is another traditional accompaniment and adds a dash of color to the dinner plate. Marinating begins several days ahead of cooking.

Sauerbraten with Sour Cream Gravy

4 to 5 pound beef pot roast
1 tablespoon salt
1 onion, sliced
10 whole peppercorns
2 bay leaves
3 whole cloves
1 cup cider vinegar
2 cups water
2 ounces salt pork
2 tablespoons vegetable oil
2 tablespoons flour
2 tablespoons sugar
6 gingersnaps, broken
   Salt and pepper to taste
½ cup red wine
½ to 1 cup dairy sour cream

Rub meat with 1 tablespoon salt; put in large bowl. Combine onion, peppercorns, bay leaves, cloves, vinegar and water; heat to boiling. Cool; pour over meat and add enough additional water to cover meat. Cover and refrigerate 36 to 48 hours, turning meat each morning and night. Remove meat from marinade, reserving marinade.

Pierce meat and insert strips of salt pork. Heat oil and brown meat on all sides. Put on rack in roasting pan. Brown flour in oil remaining in pan. Add sugar, gingersnaps, salt and pepper and about 4 cups strained marinade. Cook until smooth and creamy. Pour over meat in roasting pan. Cover and simmer 2½ to 3 hours or until tender, basting about every 30 minutes. Add wine 30 minutes before meat is done. Remove meat. Stir sour cream into gravy just before serving.

6 TO 8 SERVINGS.

A wonderful after-work entrée because no marinating time is involved and after meat is cut, broiling step goes quickly. Remember sauce recipe to use with chicken, pork or fish as well as beef.

Korean Short Ribs

3	pounds beef short ribs	
1¾	cups soy sauce	
5	cloves garlic, minced	
1	teaspoon minced ginger	
¼	cup packed brown sugar	
2	tablespoons sesame oil	
1½	tablespoons sesame seed	
¼	teaspoon pepper	
2	tablespoons chopped green onions	

Cut meat in ½-inch slices, cutting to within 1 inch of bone. (Cut meat should resemble a fan.) Combine remaining ingredients. Heat broiler. Just before broiling, pour sauce over meat. Using hands, work sauce into meat. Place meat on rack of broiler pan; broil 5 inches from heat for 10 minutes. Turn and broil 10 minutes longer.

6 SERVINGS.

"This simmers in the slow cooker while Mom is at work," says Sue Essig, Merriam, KS. The recipe, which originated with Kathy Gold, the German teacher at the high school where Sue teaches, is economical as well as easy. Long, slow simmering tenderizes less-expensive beef cuts like round steak. Serve with a green salad or vegetable.

Slow Cooker German Goulash

2	slices bacon
1½	pounds beef, cubed
1	small onion, chopped
¼	cup Maggi seasoning
2	tablespoons cornstarch
2 to	3 tablespoons water
	Hot cooked noodles

Fry bacon; discard bacon (or save for another use) and save drippings. Brown meat and onion in drippings. Stir in Maggi; place mixture in slow cooker with hot water to cover. Cook on LOW 6 to 8 hours or all day. To thicken cooking liquid, remove meat and keep warm. Pour liquid into saucepan. Dissolve cornstarch in 2 to 3 tablespoons water; stir into cooking liquid. Cook and stir until thickened. Combine meat with thickened liquid; serve over noodles.

6 SERVINGS.

Mardeth Dovre and her husband, Dr. Paul Dovre, President of Concordia College, are particularly fond of this entrée. Traditionally, the family gathers around the fondue pot at holiday time and has a good visit while they enjoy do-it-yourself cooking and dipping into the delectable sauces. Tester Linda Young, Lincoln, NE., and her family were equally enthusiastic. "Our children had never tried fondue before and they loved it! We all ate until we could eat no more."

Oriental Fondue

BURGUNDY SAUCE

1½ cups Burgundy wine

1 (10½-ounce) can beef broth

1 small onion, thinly-sliced

3 sprigs fresh parsley or parsley flakes

1 teaspoon salt

½ teaspoon dried marjoram leaves

⅛ teaspoon pepper

⅛ teaspoon garlic powder

½ bay leaf

HOT AND SWEET SAUCE

1 tablespoon dry mustard

½ teaspoon salt

1 tablespoon lemon juice

¼ cup honey

¼ cup apricot preserves

SOUR CREAM SAUCE

1 cup dairy sour cream

2 teaspoons prepared horseradish

1 teaspoon parsley flakes

½ teaspoon salt

⅛ teaspoon pepper

2 to 3 pounds beef sirloin steak, cut 1-inch thick

Combine all Burgundy Sauce ingredients in saucepan; simmer about 5 minutes. Cover and let stand 2 hours. Combine mustard, ½ teaspoon salt and lemon juice; mix until smooth. Stir in honey and apricot preserves; mix well. Serve hot or at room temperature. Combine all Sour Cream Sauce ingredients; mix well. Refrigerate about 30 minutes before serving.

Cut steak into 1-inch cubes. Heat Burgundy Sauce to boiling; pour into fondue pot. Adjust heat to keep mixture at boiling point. Remove bay leaf. Spear beef cubes with fondue forks and cook in Burgundy sauce 1½ to 2 minutes, depending on desired doneness. Serve with Hot and Sweet Sauce and Sour Cream Sauce.

4 TO 6 SERVINGS.

Lai Ying, a native of Malaysia, shares a favorite recipe of her homeland known as "rendang." Lai suggests preparing a day or so in advance of serving to allow flavors to mellow. "Lemon grass is a fragrant herb used frequently in Vietnamese and southeast Asian cookery. It and other unusual ingredients are available at Asian grocery stores." Lai serves this with rice and "a salad of sliced cucumbers to cool the palate."

Malaysian Beef Curry

3	stalks lemon grass
3	large yellow onions
3	inches (1-inch diameter) gingerroot
8	large cloves garlic
2	tablespoons vegetable oil
1	teaspoon chili powder (or more)
1	tablespoon curry powder
1½	tablespoons galangal powder (laotian powder)
3	pounds beef, cubed
2	(13½-ounce) cans coconut milk

Use only about the top 4 inches of lemon grass. Crush it slightly with knife handle so taste emits during cooking. Process onions, gingerroot and garlic in food processor until finely chopped. Heat oil in Dutch oven; add onion mixture and cook and stir 5 minutes. Add chili powder, curry powder, galangal powder and lemon grass; cook and stir 2 minutes longer. Add meat and coconut milk; heat to boiling. Reduce heat and simmer over medium heat until all liquid has evaporated, stirring frequently. When mixture is almost dry, stir constantly to prevent burning. (Takes about 2½ hours.) (There should be no liquid left in the pan, just a coating covering the meat.) Spoon off any fat before serving.

8 SERVINGS.

This recipe was given to William Snyder, Altoona, IA., when he was stationed in Korea. "It is authentically Korean," he comments, "not an 'Americanized' recipe." Nevertheless, ingredients are readily available and preparation is uncomplicated. Allow several hours for marinating step.

Korean Stir-Fry

½	pound beef, thinly sliced
1	tablespoon sesame oil
1	tablespoon sugar
1½	teaspoons monosodium glutamate (m.s.g.)
1½	teaspoons sesame seed
	Pepper to taste
2 to	2½ tablespoons soy sauce
	Hot cooked rice

Combine beef, sesame oil, sugar, m.s.g., sesame seed and pepper; marinate 3 to 4 hours. Just before cooking, add soy sauce. Stir-fry in lightly greased skillet. Serve with rice.

2 TO 4 SERVINGS.

Daniel Ofstedal, Williston, ND., received this recipe from a Florida friend who prepared it in her native Cuba. Bananas are a surprise ingredient and add interesting flavor and texture.

Cuban Picadillo

2	pounds ground beef
2	onions, cut up
2	green bell peppers, cut up
	Garlic powder, to taste
5	(8-ounce) cans tomato sauce
	Green olives
	Raisins
	Hot cooked rice
	Bananas, sliced

Cook and stir ground beef, onions and green peppers in skillet. Stir in garlic powder. Stir in tomato sauce before beef is completely brown. Stir in desired amount of olives and raisins; simmer. Mixture is done when fat separates from tomato base; drain fat. Serve ground beef mixture over rice and bananas.

8 SERVINGS.

Variation — Finely-chopped potatoes, fried in oil, can be added to ground beef mixture before serving.

Stew meat turns sensational with a day-long marinating process to flavor and tenderize. Do use Burgundy wine in honor of the region of France to which we are indebted for this internationally-renowned repast. Flavors mellow for tasty leftovers and the dish freezes well.

Lac du Bois Bourguignon

1½ to 2 pounds beef stewing meat, cut
    into 2-inch cubes

MARINADE

3   cups Burgundy or other red wine

1   onion, sliced

1   carrot, sliced

    Bouquet garni

1   clove garlic, crushed

6   black peppercorns

2   whole cloves

    Dash of salt

2   tablespoons vegetable oil

¼   cup vegetable oil

6   slices bacon

2   medium onions, sliced

8   ounces fresh mushrooms, sliced

½   cup Burgundy or other red wine

3   tablespoons flour

1   cup broth

    Salt and pepper

    Dash of sugar

    Croutons

    Snipped fresh parsley

Place meat in non-metallic bowl. Cover with wine and other marinade ingredients, pouring 2 tablespoons oil on last. Cover; marinate in refrigerator 2 days, stirring 3 or 4 times. Drain meat, reserving marinade. Reserve sliced onion and carrot. Dry meat thoroughly with paper towels.

Heat half of ¼ cup oil in heavy skillet; brown beef on all sides, a few pieces at a time. Set aside. Cook bacon over fairly high heat until crisp and brown. Remove bacon; drain on paper towels. Add 2 sliced onions; brown. Remove onions; add mushrooms. Cook over medium heat until tender. Set bacon, onions and mushrooms aside. Discard excess fat in pan; add wine. Heat to boiling, stirring to dissolve pan juices.

In casserole, heat remaining oil; add reserved onion and carrot. Cook slowly until soft. Add flour and cook until mixture is rich and brown. Stir in remaining marinade ingredients, wine from skillet, broth, salt and pepper. Return meat to pan and heat to boiling. Cover and bake at 300° for 3 to 4 hours, stirring occasionally until meat is tender.

When meat is done, stir in bacon, onion and mushroom garnish; simmer gently for 15 minutes for flavors to blend. Taste and adjust seasoning if necessary. Serve in individual casseroles with croutons around edges and chopped parsley sprinkled on meat.

6 TO 8 SERVINGS.

Called "piroshki" in Russia and sold by street vendors, these meat-filled turnovers are the perfect accompaniment to a bowl of borscht. They also can be enjoyed as an appetizer or quick lunch. Note one hour chilling step before baking. "Pir" in Russian means "feast" and you're certain to enjoy feasting on these.

Russian Meat Pastries

FILLING

1	medium onion, minced
¼	cup butter
1	pound ground beef
2	tablespoons snipped fresh parsley
1	teaspoon salt
¼	teaspoon pepper
4	drops Tabasco
2	eggs, well-beaten

DOUGH

3½	cups all-purpose flour
1	teaspoon baking powder
½	cup butter
2	eggs, beaten
1	cup dairy sour cream
1	egg, beaten

Cook onion in butter 4 to 5 minutes or until golden. Add ground beef; cook over medium heat, stirring constantly 10 to 12 minutes. Drain fat. Add parsley, salt, pepper, Tabasco and 2 eggs; mix well. Turn mixture into bowl; cover and refrigerate. Remove any fat from surface of chilled meat.

Combine flour and baking powder; with pastry blender or 2 knives, cut in butter until mixture resembles coarse cornmeal. Stir in 2 eggs and sour cream. Knead dough gently on lightly-floured surface until it forms a smooth ball. Wrap dough in waxed paper or plastic wrap and refrigerate 2 to 4 hours.

On well-floured surface, roll out dough to ⅛-inch thickness. Cut dough into rounds 5 inches in diameter. Place 2 tablespoons filling on each round. Brush edges of rounds with beaten egg. Fold dough over filling to make half-moon shapes. Press edges firmly to seal. Place on ungreased cookie sheets. Brush tops with beaten egg. Refrigerate 1 hour. Heat oven to 400°. Bake 25 to 30 minutes or until golden brown.

18 PASTRIES.

A wonderful way to transform simple, economical ground beef into a praise-worthy repast. Here seasonings and high-style rolled presentation make the difference. And, all the work is done the day before serving. Makes an enticing entrée or a unique first course with a meatless main course to follow.

Cuban Beef Rolls

2½	pounds lean ground beef
1½	cups fine cracker crumbs
1	large onion, grated
3	eggs, well beaten
⅓	cup heavy cream
1½	tablespoons salt
½	teaspoon nutmeg
½	teaspoon pepper
¼	teaspoon thyme
¼	teaspoon ground allspice
1	pound bacon

Heat oven to 350°. In large bowl, combine all ingredients except bacon; mix well. Halve mixture and shape each half into an 8-inch roll. On 12-inch piece of waxed paper, arrange ½ pound bacon slices, slightly overlapping so that they measure 8 inches across. Place 1 meat roll across bacon strips, using waxed paper to roll bacon around meat. Peel paper away and wrap roll in foil, twisting ends tightly. Prepare the remaining roll in the same manner. Place rolls in a jelly roll pan; bake about 1 hour and 30 minutes. With a fork, perforate foil on one side of each roll. Let rolls drain on paper towels until they are cool. Refrigerate overnight. Remove foil; cut rolls into slices and serve at room temperature.

10 TO 12 SERVINGS.

This layered rendition of spaghetti comes from Nancy Thorson, Red Wing, MN. "The recipe is from my sister who lives in Boulder, CO., where there are many Hispanics. It's a pleasant change from Italian spaghetti," she adds. Amount of pepper is up to the cook's discretion.

Cuban Spaghetti

2	pounds ground beef
3	large onions, chopped
1	green bell pepper, chopped
½	bunch celery, chopped
2	(10¾-ounce) cans condensed tomato soup
	Salt
	Tabasco sauce
	Cayenne pepper
	Black pepper
1	teaspoon Worcestershire sauce
1	(4-ounce) can mushrooms
1	(8-ounce) package spaghetti, cooked and drained
1	(4¼-ounce) can chopped ripe olives
8	ounces (2 cups) shredded sharp cheese

Heat oven to 350°. Brown ground beef and onions; drain. Stir in green pepper, celery, tomato soup and seasonings to taste. Cook until vegetables are tender. Spread half of meat mixture in a baking dish; layer with half of mushrooms, half of spaghetti, half of olives and half of cheese. Repeat layers. Bake 1 hour or until casserole bubbles.

6 SERVINGS.

An unusual, easy-to-serve presentation for a homey staple of Italian kitchens from Carrie Rocke, Davis, CA. Tester Nanette Rollene, Decorah, IA., offers a most convincing testimonial. "Three hungry boys returning from basketball practice had the pie devoured in 15 minutes."

Spaghetti Pie

1½ to 2 pounds ground beef or sausage

½   cup chopped onion

1 or 2 cloves garlic, crushed

1   (28 to 32-ounce) jar spaghetti sauce

    Basil, if desired

    Rosemary, if desired

    Oregano, if desired

8   ounces uncooked spaghetti, broken in half

2   tablespoons butter

½   cup grated Parmesan cheese

2   eggs, beaten

1   cup cottage cheese

1   egg

6 to 8 ounces (1½ to 2 cups) shredded mozzarella cheese

Heat oven to 350°. Brown ground beef and onion with garlic; drain. Stir in spaghetti sauce, basil, rosemary and oregano. Cook spaghetti to desired doneness; drain. Stir butter, Parmesan cheese and 2 eggs into spaghetti. Press in greased 13x9x2-inch pan to form a crust, working quickly for ease in forming crust. Combine cottage cheese and 1 egg; spread over spaghetti. Spoon meat sauce over cottage cheese.* Bake about 30 minutes; sprinkle with mozzarella cheese and bake 10 minutes longer. Let stand 10 minutes before cutting into squares.

8 SERVINGS.

*Tip: *At this point, pie can be covered and frozen for future use. Thaw before continuing to follow directions.*

"This is really a simplified version of stuffed cabbage," writes contributor Ned Tervola, New York Mills, MN. "The Finnish name is "kaalilaatikko" and we serve this favorite recipe from Grandma with Finnish flat bread."

Finnish Cabbage-Beef Casserole

1	pound ground beef
1	cup chopped onion
1	medium head cabbage, coarsely shredded
¼	cup uncooked regular rice
2	cups stewed tomatoes
1	cup hot water
2	teaspoons salt
¼	teaspoon pepper

Heat oven to 350°. Brown ground beef and onion, cooking until onion is translucent. Combine with remaining ingredients. Place in large greased casserole. Cover and bake about 1½ hours. Serve hot.

6 SERVINGS.

It's stick-to-the ribs fare like this that fuels the Finnish people during their long cold winters. A Finnish woman shared the recipe with Linda Church, Oxford, OH., when she was visiting America. Tester Amy White, Rapid City, SD., served it with a side of cranberry sauce and describes the dish as "very tasty and easy to make."

Finnish Meat-Cabbage Casserole

1	small head cabbage, shredded
2	tablespoons butter
2	tablespoons dark corn syrup
2	teaspoons salt
1	teaspoon ground marjoram
1	pound ground beef
1	cup dry bread crumbs
½	cup milk
2	eggs, beaten

Cook cabbage in boiling water to cover, about 5 minutes or until tender-crisp; drain. Heat oven to 350°. Stir butter, syrup, salt and marjoram into cabbage. In another bowl, mix ground beef, bread crumbs, milk and eggs. Layer cabbage and meat mixture in buttered 2-quart casserole, beginning and ending with cabbage. Cover and bake 45 minutes. Uncover and bake 15 minutes longer. Serve with lingonberries, cranberry sauce or currant jelly and boiled potatoes.

6 SERVINGS.

From a cookbook compiled by students at Jordan (MN.) Elementary School comes a peasant-style dish to quell hearty appetites. Vegetables are important in German cuisine and are frequently combined with pork or beef in robust dishes.

German Sauerkraut Casserole

2	pounds ground beef
2	medium onions, chopped
	Salt and pepper to taste
1	(18-ounce) can tomato juice
2	(10¾-ounce) cans condensed cream of chicken soup
2	cups cooked rice
2	(16-ounce) cans sauerkraut or homemade sauerkraut, drained

Heat oven to 350°. Brown ground beef and onions; drain. Combine with remaining ingredients. Place in large greased casserole. Bake about 1½ hours.

8 SERVINGS

With a mild stroganoff flavor of sour cream sauce, ground beef takes on glamorous overtones for these "bitkis." The oval shaping is traditional. Serve with rice or noodles and a crisp green salad with julienne beet slices added for color.

Russian Beef Patties

4	slices white bread
½	cup milk
1	pound ground beef chuck
	Salt and pepper to taste
¼	teaspoon nutmeg
2	medium onions, thinly sliced
2	tablespoons butter
1	cup dairy sour cream

Soak bread in milk until soggy. Squeeze out milk, crumble and mix with meat. Add salt, pepper and nutmeg; mix thoroughly. Form into oval patties about 2½ inches across. In large heavy skillet, sauté onions slowly in butter. When translucent, remove and place meatballs in pan. Brown on all sides; reduce heat to very low. Spread onions over meatballs. Cook 20 to 25 minutes, turning once. Remove excess fat with bulb baster and stir sour cream into mixture in pan. Heat thoroughly but do not boil.

4 SERVINGS.

Tip: *This dish can be made beforehand by cooking partially and finishing 5 to 10 minutes before serving.*

When Marsha Penti, Hancock, MI., spent time in Finland, she "came to love piirakkas of all kinds." She varies the filling using rice with the beef or substituting a rice/fish combination. "In the fall when I have lots of cabbage, I sauté some with bacon, onion, raisins and shredded apple to add to the filling," she says. Testers Steve and Lynn Holter, Fridley, MN., commented on the marvelous aroma while baking and added, "They taste even better than they smell. Even the kids liked them!"

Finnish Meat Pies

FILLING

2	pounds ground very lean beef
2	tablespoons minced onion
2	teaspoons salt
½	teaspoon pepper
1	egg

CRUST

2	cups all-purpose flour
1	teaspoon salt
¾	cup butter, chilled
1	egg
½	cup dairy sour cream
	Dairy sour cream

Brown ground beef with other filling ingredients. Cool. Heat oven to 350°. Combine flour and salt in bowl. With pastry blender or 2 knives, cut in butter until mixture resembles small crumbs. Combine 1 egg and ½ cup sour cream. Stir into flour mixture, working with fingers to make stiff dough. Divide dough in half. On floured surface, roll each half into 14x6-inch rectangle; place one crust in 15x10x1-inch jelly roll pan. Cover with filling, then top crust; seal edges. Cut vents in top. Bake about 1 hour or until golden. Serve hot with sour cream.

6 TO 8 SERVINGS.

Variation — Add 1 heaping cup cooked rice or substitute rice and cooked salmon for ground beef.

Barbara Eisinger, Morris, MN., fondly recalls this dish as a special treat her father used to make for her and her sisters. "The colors make it an attractive one-dish meal," she says, "and it doubles and triples easily for crowd-sized parties and potlucks." Tester Debbie Trowbridge, Elkhorn, NE., served this with warm flour tortillas and "everyone rolled up the mixture in them to eat. We offered guacamole, chopped tomatoes and sour cream as 'toppers'. It was very, very good."

Taco Casserole

1	pound ground beef
1	medium onion, diced
1	(8-ounce) can tomato sauce
1	(8-ounce) bottle taco sauce, salsa, picante, ketchup or other spiced tomato sauce
½	teaspoon salt
	Pepper to taste
	Tabasco to taste
	Hot chiles to taste
2 to 3	tablespoons cornmeal
1½	cups fresh or frozen whole kernel corn (not canned)
1	cup sliced ripe olives
2	ounces (½ cup) shredded Cheddar cheese or ¼ cup crushed corn chips, for garnish, if desired

Heat oven to 375°. Brown ground beef and onion over medium heat; drain. Stir in tomato sauce, taco or other sauce, salt, pepper, Tabasco, chiles and cornmeal, adjusting for "hot" taste preference and desired thickness. Stir in more cornmeal, if desired. Stir in corn and olives. Transfer mixture to casserole; cover and bake 30 to 40 minutes or until bubbly and heated through. Top with cheese immediately on removing from oven so cheese melts. Garnish with corn chips just before serving to keep them crisp. Serve with a cool fresh vegetable such as cucumber slices, avocado or lettuce leaves, if desired.

4 SERVINGS.

A new twist for an old favorite. If desired, prepare ingredients and layer ahead for later baking. Serve with a guacamole-lettuce salad or a fresh fruit compote and warmed tortillas.

Fiesta Lasagne

1	pound ground beef
1	medium onion, chopped
1	(10-ounce) can tomatoes and green chiles
1	(10-ounce) can stewed tomatoes
1	(8-ounce) can tomato sauce
8	flour tortillas, sliced
1	(8-ounce) carton dairy sour cream
12	ounces Monterey jack cheese, sliced
	Grated Parmesan cheese
1	small jar stuffed olives, drained, sliced

Heat oven to 350°. Brown ground beef and onion; drain. Stir in all tomato ingredients; simmer 30 minutes. Spread half of meat sauce in greased 13x9x2-inch dish. Cover with sliced tortillas. Add Monterey jack cheese, sour cream and remaining sauce mixture in layers. Sprinkle well with Parmesan cheese and olives. Bake about 45 minutes.

8 TO 10 SERVINGS.

Substantial, everyday fare in Sweden is frequented with hearty dishes like "kalpudding." Add some colorful accompaniments like a crisp relish tray, pickled beets and other complementary side dishes for attractive presentation.

Cabbage Pudding

1	(1½-pound) head cabbage
½	pound ground beef
½	pound ground pork
1	tablespoon margarine or butter
½	teaspoon salt
⅛	teaspoon black pepper
1	cup mashed potatoes

Heat oven to 350°. Remove core and chop cabbage into large pieces. Cook cabbage in boiling salted water just until it wilts; drain. Cook beef and pork in margarine. Combine cooked meat, salt, pepper and potatoes. Arrange alternate layers of cabbage, meat and potato mixtures in 2-quart casserole; cover. Bake 45 to 50 minutes.

4 SERVINGS.

With anchovy paste in the meat mixture and lemon juice and capers in the sauce, it is obvious this is no ordinary recipe. With three preparation steps involved, you may wish to double the recipe and refrigerate or freeze half for another meal.

German Meatballs in Lemon Sauce

MEATBALLS

1	tablespoon butter
½	cup chopped onion
½	cup bread crumbs
2	tablespoons cream
½	pound ground beef
½	pound ground pork
1	teaspoon anchovy paste
2	tablespoons snipped fresh parsley
2	eggs
½	teaspoon grated lemon peel
½	teaspoon salt
¼	teaspoon pepper

POACHING LIQUID

2	quarts water
1	medium onion, peeled and studded with a few whole cloves
1	bay leaf
1	teaspoon salt

SAUCE

¼	cup butter
5	tablespoons flour
3	cups strained poaching liquid
3	tablespoons lemon juice
1	tablespoon drained capers
2	egg yolks
2	tablespoons dairy sour cream

Melt 1 tablespoon butter in small skillet over medium heat. Sauté chopped onions until translucent. Set aside. In bowl, combine crumbs and cream; stir in remaining meatball ingredients. Mix with your hands and shape into 8 large meatballs.

Place all poaching liquid ingredients in large kettle or Dutch oven. Heat to boiling over high heat. Reduce heat to low; drop in meatballs. Simmer, uncovered, until meatballs rise to the surface, about 20 minutes. Remove meatballs and strain poaching liquid.

Melt ¼ cup butter in large skillet. Stir in flour; gradually stir in reserved poaching liquid. Heat to boiling, whisking constantly. Sauce will thicken and become smooth. Reduce heat to low; stir in lemon juice and capers. Simmer, uncovered, 15 minutes, stirring occasionally. Meanwhile, stir egg yolks in small bowl. When sauce has simmered, stir a little of it into the yolks, then pour the yolk mixture into the simmering sauce. Whisk in sour cream. Taste for seasoning. Add meatballs; heat thoroughly. Serve sauce over meatballs.

4 SERVINGS.

Julie Bernstein, Grand Blanc, MI., persuaded a Ukrainian friend to instruct her in making this delicious dish. "In Siberia, where it originated, cooks make large batches of Pelmeny and keep them frozen on their rooftops," Julie explains. Tester Linda Young, Lincoln, NE., was so impressed with the recipe she commented, "Our small family finished it off in one sitting. We will definitely use this for the holidays. It takes some practice to fill the thin dough but the results are well worth the effort."

Siberian Dumplings

½   pound ground beef*
½   pound ground pork *
2   medium onions, finely chopped
1   clove garlic, finely minced
    Salt and pepper
2   cups all-purpose flour
1   egg, beaten
¼   cup butter, melted
½   cup cold water
    Dairy sour cream

Combine beef, pork, onions, garlic, salt and pepper; mix well. Place flour in bowl. Add egg, butter and ½ cup cold water; mixing thoroughly until mixture forms smooth dough. Shape dough into ball and place on floured surface. Knead lightly until smooth, about 1 minute. Add additional flour if necessary. Cover with plastic wrap and refrigerate about 1 hour. On floured surface, roll out dough to about 1/16-inch, or half the thickness of pie dough. Using 2½-inch cookie cutter, cut out rounds of dough. In the center of each round, place ½ teaspoonful of meat filling. Fold circle in half to form a crescent, seal edges thoroughly. Fold crescent in half again, pinching edges together. Keep on floured surface. At this point you can freeze them (they freeze well) or boil 10 at a time in boiling water or broth. Boil for only 3 minutes or until they rise to the top. Serve with sour cream.

6 SERVINGS.

Tip: *One pound ground beef can be substituted for ½ pound ground beef and ½ pound ground pork.

A red wine sauce elevates this Norwegian Village favorite from ordinary to extraordinary. Staffer Linda Erceg has a suggestion for hurried cooks — "Form meat mixture into a loaf, bake as you would a regular meatloaf and serve topped with the sauce."

Norwegian Meatballs with Red Wine Sauce

1	pound ground beef
1	pound ground pork
1½	teaspoons salt
½	teaspoon pepper
¼	teaspoon allspice
2	eggs
1	cup milk or broth or water
½	cup all-purpose flour or ½ cup bread crumbs or 1 cup mashed potatoes or ½ to ¾ cup rolled oats
1	medium onion, minced

SAUCE

3	tablespoons pan drippings
3	tablespoons flour
1	(10½-ounce) can beef bouillon
1	cup dry red wine

Combine ground meats, seasonings, eggs, liquid, extender, and onion; mix well. Shape into 1-inch meatballs. Pan or oven fry. Save drippings for sauce. Blend drippings and flour in large saucepan. Rinse baking/frying pan with a little bouillon, scraping free the browned particles. Blend this with remaining bouillon and wine; add to mixture in saucepan. Heat to boiling, stirring constantly. Add meatballs to sauce and simmer at least 10 minutes.

36 MEATBALLS.

When Charlie's Cafe Exceptionale was a cornerstone of fine dining in Minneapolis, this was one specialty that put the restaurant on the gastronomical map. More vegetables can be included if you wish.

Braised Viennese Pork Roast

1	(3-pound) boneless pork loin roast
¼	cup bacon drippings
1	cup chopped onions
1	cup chopped carrots
1	teaspoon paprika
¾	cup chicken broth
2	tablespoons flour
½	cup dairy sour cream
¼	teaspoon caraway seed
1	teaspoon chopped capers
1	tablespoon snipped fresh parsley

In ovenproof skillet or Dutch oven, brown pork roast in bacon drippings; set roast aside. In remaining drippings cook onions and carrots until tender but not brown. Stir in paprika. Place roast atop vegetables; add chicken broth. Cover and roast at 350° for 1½ to 2 hours or until meat thermometer inserted in center registers 170°. Remove roast to serving platter; keep warm.

Strain pan drippings; discard vegetables. Measure pan drippings; skim off excess fat. Add water to drippings if necessary to measure 1⅓ cups. Return to skillet or Dutch oven. Blend flour into sour cream; stir into liquid in pan. Cook and stir until thickened and bubbly. Stir in caraway seed, capers and parsley. Serve with roast.

6 SERVINGS.

Language Village staff member, Jay Richards, shares a Norwegian recipe for fruit-stuffed pork roast. When tester Lois Nehrus, Storden, MN., had difficulty finding dried apples at her grocer, she substituted dried apricots with tasty results. So, suit yourself — both work beautifully.

Stuffed Pork Roast

¼   cup dried apples
10   medium sized prunes
1   medium tart apple, diced
1   (4-pound) lean boneless pork
     roast
     Salt and pepper
3   tablespoons butter

Parboil dried apples, prunes and diced apple for a few minutes; drain. Push thick skewer through center of roast lengthwise. Stuff prunes and apples into opening. Rub roast with salt and pepper. Brown butter, then brown roast evenly. Place meat on rack in roasting pan. Pour in 1 cup boiling water; add more as water evaporates. Roast at 325° for 3 to 4 hours or until meat thermometer inserted in center registers 160 to 170° and juices run clear.

8 to 10 SERVINGS.

"I especially like the fresh tomatoes baked in the rice," comments tester Amy White. This Norwegian entrée also shared by Jay Richards, makes a wonderful winter oven dish. Add a crisp green salad and a simple dessert and your menu is complete.

Tomato Pork Chops

8   large pork chops
¼   cup butter
1   cup uncooked regular rice
3   tomatoes, halved
1   teaspoon paprika
1   teaspoon dried oregano leaves
½   cup ketchup
¼   cup water
     Salt and pepper to taste

Brown pork chops in butter in large skillet; remove chops from skillet. Heat oven to 325°. Brown rice; being careful not to burn. Carefully brown tomatoes. In large heatproof dish, place rice, chops and tomatoes. Combine spices with ketchup and water; pour over chops. Bake 1 hour.

8 SERVINGS.

Only four ingredients are added to this roast for the long, slow cooking. It can be served hot with rice and pea pods or sliced and served cold for a summer buffet.

Japanese-Style Pork Roast

1	(3 to 4-pound) pork roast
½	cup Japanese-style soy sauce
2	tablespoons whiskey
½	cup sugar
½ to 1 teaspoon grated gingerroot or powdered ginger	

Place roast and other ingredients in Dutch oven. Cover and simmer 3 to 4 hours, or until meat thermometer inserted in center registers 160 to 170°, turning several times during cooking.

6 TO 8 SERVINGS.

Rich Speers, Minneapolis, MN., discovered this recipe on a trip to Alsace and since, it has become "a fall/winter favorite for informal evening meals." With assistance from son Kevin, who attended the German Language Village, the Speers translated the recipe and made a few adjustments "with no sacrifice in character."

Alsace-Style Choucroute

2	medium onions
2	tablespoons vegetable oil or equivalent pork fat
1 to 1¼ cups Riesling wine	
2	egg whites and an equal quantity of water or chicken broth
2	thick-cut smoked pork chops
2	cloves garlic, minced
	Pepper
1	bay leaf
4	whole cloves
8	juniper berries
4	pounds sauerkraut, rinsed, drained, pressed in sieve to drain
6 to 8 weisswurst, bratwurst, bockwurst or any combination	

Heat oven to 325°. Slice onions and quarter. Cook onions in oil until golden in 8x10-inch casserole. Add wine and water; beat in egg whites. Add pork chops to casserole. Add garlic, pepper, bay leaf, cloves and juniper berries to 1 pound of the sauerkraut; spread evenly over chops in casserole. Add remaining sauerkraut and tuck in the wurst evenly all around the bed of kraut. Cover loosely with aluminum foil; bake 45 minutes. Uncover and bake 45 minutes longer. Remove bay leaf. Serve immediately.

8 SERVINGS.

Tips: New potatoes, unpeeled and sliced, can be added around edge of casserole just before baking.
Any leftovers can be reheated in microwave.

Jarlsberg, a mild Norwegian cheese, nutty in flavor, melds with onion for a creative stuffing. Jay Richards, Village staffer, devised the recipe as "an innovative way to prepare chops as well as an enterprising use for extra cheese."

Norwegian Pork Chops

6	butterflied pork chops
1	small onion, chopped
4	ounces (1 cup) shredded Jarlsberg or Swiss cheese
½	cup Swedish mustard
2	cups chicken stock

Brown pork chops in skillet. Heat oven to 325°. Combine onion and cheese. Spread mustard on insides of pork chops; fill with onion mixture. Place in baking dish. Pour chicken stock over chops. Bake for about 1 hour or until chops are done.

6 SERVINGS.

"I was a child of the Depression," says Dr. Donald Hoff, Eau Claire, WI., internist. "This was a family breakfast tradition called 'paanast.' Today, it can be served with scrambled eggs and applesauce for breakfast or brunch. Or, it is tasty for supper with a vegetable like broccoli."

German Spareribs

1½	pounds country-style pork spareribs
1	large onion, quartered
1½	teaspoons salt
½	teaspoon pepper
1	teaspoon ground sage
½	teaspoon dried rosemary leaves, crushed
2	cups cornmeal
2	cups cold water or cooled cooking liquid

Place spareribs and onion in Dutch oven or 3-quart saucepan; add water to cover. Cook over medium heat until meat separates from bones, about 30 minutes. Remove meat and onion to a plate to cool. Chill cooking liquid and remove fat. When meat is cool, remove fat and bones and grind or finely chop meat and onion. Heat 2 cups of defatted cooking liquid and add seasonings. Heat to boiling and slowly add cornmeal mixed with cold water. Stir to avoid sticking. Reduce heat and stir in meat mixture. Cover and keep over low heat 10 minutes, stirring occasionally. Pour into greased 9x5x3-inch loaf pan, pressing down with a spoon. Refrigerate, preferably overnight. To serve, cut into ½ to ¾-inch slices. Brown on both sides in lightly oiled skillet.

8 SERVINGS.

"This takes time to prepare, so I usually make a double recipe and freeze part for another meal," explains Nicolle Pata, Danville, CA. *Presentation and textures are inviting and baking instead of deep frying trims calories a bit.*

Chimichangas

2	pounds pork butt, cut into 1-inch pieces
2	cups water, or enough to cover meat
2	cloves garlic, minced
1	onion, chopped
½	teaspoon dried oregano leaves
½	teaspoon ground cumin
2	tablespoons white vinegar
1 to	2 (4-ounce) cans diced green chiles, drained
½	cup butter, melted
8	(8-inch) flour tortillas
	Shredded lettuce
	Guacamole (page 8)
	Ripe olives
	Tomatoes

Place pork in 6-quart kettle. Cover kettle and cook over medium heat until juices have been released, about 10 minutes. Uncover. Turn heat to high and cook, stirring until liquid has evaporated and meat is brown. Pour in water to cover meat. Stir in garlic, onion, oregano and cumin. Cover and simmer over low heat until meat is tender, 1 to 1½ hours. Uncover; increase heat to high and cook until most of liquid is evaporated. Reduce heat; add vinegar and chiles. Stir to release any browned bits stuck on kettle. Shred meat with 2 forks. Heat oven to 500°. Brush butter on both sides of tortillas. Spoon ⅛ of meat mixture onto each tortilla. Fold in sides toward center over meat, then fold lower edge up and roll over to enclose. Place seam-side-down in greased 13x9x2-inch baking dish. Drizzle any remaining butter over top of chimichangas in dish. Bake 8 to 10 minutes or until crisp. Line a platter with lettuce; arrange chimichangas on top. Top with guacamole and garnish with olives and tomatoes.

8 SERVINGS.

Called "thit heo kho" in Vietnamese, this unique dish is a recipe Stewart Herman continues to savor long after living in Vietnam where he taught as a part of a vocational program for relocated residents. The fish sauce is available in Asian markets.

Caramelized Pork

3 pounds boneless pork shoulder*

1 to 2 tablespoons sugar

1 sliver gingerroot, cut into thin lengths

1 medium onion, sliced into thin rounds, separated into rings

1 or 2 cloves garlic, crushed

3 tablespoons soy sauce and nuoc mam (fish sauce), in any combination

6 eggs, hard-cooked

1 tablespoon sugar

1 teaspoon salt

Dash of pepper

Few drops sesame oil

Bean sprouts

Boil pork in Dutch oven or large saucepan about 10 minutes. Remove and cut into bite-sized pieces, including some fat, some lean and some skin in each bite. Sprinkle 1 to 2 tablespoons sugar on bottom of same Dutch oven; heat over high heat until sugar melts to golden brown. Quickly fill with 2 to 3 inches water; put in meat (water should just cover meat).

Add gingerroot, onion, garlic, soy sauce and nuoc mam, eggs, 1 tablespoon sugar, salt and pepper. Heat to boiling; reduce heat and simmer, covered 2 to 3 hours. Serve with bean sprouts sprinkled with sesame oil. To prepare bean sprouts, soak in salted water with a bit of gingerroot overnight, preferably under pressure to help the bean sprouts absorb a salty tang.

6 TO 7 SERVINGS.

Tip: *If you ask for a pork shoulder roast and have it boned by the butcher you can save the bone for soup.*

This white bean stew, a southwestern France staple, begins the day before cooking when the beans are put to soak. Cooking combines stovetop simmering with oven baking, the finished product is an interesting contrast in flavors and textures.

Cassoulet

2	pounds dried white beans
	Salt and pepper to taste
1	(5½-pound) duck
1½	pounds pork loin, cubed
1	pound lamb sausage or other sausage, cubed
10	ounces baby onions
2	pounds tomatoes, diced
2¾	cups white wine
	Dash dried basil leaves
1	clove garlic, chopped
1	tablespoon tomato paste
⅔	cup bread crumbs
1½	quarts reserved bean broth

Soak beans overnight in cold water; drain. Put beans in large kettle or Dutch oven with water to cover generously. Heat to boiling; reduce heat and simmer 25 minutes. Add salt and pepper; continue to cook 25 to 30 minutes longer. Meanwhile, heat oven to 425°. Roast duck 30 minutes. Brown pork loin and lamb sausage in Dutch oven. Add onions, tomatoes, wine, basil and garlic. Let simmer 20 minutes. Add tomato paste and bread crumbs. When duck is done, reduce oven temperature to 350°. Cool duck; cut meat from bones and add meat to cassoulet. Place beans in casserole; pour sauce over beans. Bake about 1 hour, covered, adding reserved bean liquid if necessary.

8 SERVINGS.

"This was our favorite meal when we spent a year in Japan and was one of the few dishes we could master with chopsticks," comments Joelle Snyder, Altoona, IA. "It was also a favorite because we could identify all ingredients and knew what we were eating!" A colorful "quickie" for dinner on the double.

Sweet and Sour Pork

2	tablespoons corn oil
1	pound cooked boneless pork, cut into 1-inch cubes
1	(15¼-ounce) can pineapple chunks
½	cup dark corn syrup
¼	cup vinegar
1	tablespoon ketchup
2	tablespoons soy sauce
2	tablespoons cornstarch
2	tablespoons water
½	cup green pepper pieces
	Hot cooked rice

Heat oil in skillet. Add pork, pineapple chunks, corn syrup, vinegar, ketchup and soy sauce; heat to boiling. Simmer 10 minutes. Combine cornstarch and water; stir into pork mixture with green pepper. Boil 2 minutes, stirring constantly. Serve over rice.

4 TO 6 SERVINGS.

A cornerstone dish of Japanese family dining, this quick and easy stir-fry requires only brief marinating before cooking. Serve with rice or Asian noodles.

Shogayaki

14	ounces thinly-sliced pork (have the butcher slice it)
1	tablespoon sake
3	tablespoons soy sauce
1	teaspoon ginger juice*
3 to 4	cabbage leaves
2	tablespoons vegetable oil
2	teaspoons ginger juice*

Cut pork into 2-inch pieces. Combine sake, soy sauce and 1 teaspoon ginger juice. Marinate pork in this mixture about 10 minutes. Cut cabbage into small squares. Heat skillet; add 1 tablespoon oil and sauté pork over high heat until pork is half-done. Push pork to one side of pan; add 1 tablespoon oil to pan with cabbage and sauté 1 to 2 minutes. Stir in pork, remaining marinade, and 2 teaspoons ginger juice; stir quickly and turn off heat.

3 TO 4 SERVINGS.

*Tip: *To make ginger juice, peel and grate gingerroot; squeeze.*

When Stewart Herman, Fargo, ND., was a teacher for Lutheran World Relief in Vietnam, he particularly enjoyed this "tasty and filling" example of North Vietnamese "home cooking." Back in the States where Stewart is a faculty member of the Concordia College religion department, he impresses dinner guests by serving a selection of Vietnamese dishes accompanied by rice and a vegetable.

Stuffed Bean Curds

½	(2-ounce) package bean threads or glass noodles or vermicelli
4	dried Chinese mushrooms
3	(14-ounce) packages tofu (bean curd), each cut into 16 pieces
	Vegetable oil
½	onion, finely chopped
½	pound ground pork
2	tablespoons nuoc mam (fish sauce)
3	tomatoes, cut into wedges
2	green onions, including green tops, cut into short lengths
	Salt

Soak noodles and mushrooms in water about 30 minutes. Fry tofu in hot oil (sizzling when tofu is added) until golden brown on both sides. Oil should reach past halfway mark on tofu pieces. (The purpose of frying is to strengthen the tofu pieces for the next step.)

Chop soaked bean threads into small lengths; chop soaked mushrooms into tiny pieces; combine with chopped onion, pork and nuoc mam. Mash into a mushy mixture with your fingers. Slice tofu pieces from one corner halfway across in a diagonal fashion. Stuff to overflowing with bean thread filling mixture. Place stuffed tofu on a steamer rack; arrange tomatoes and green onions over tofu. Sprinkle with salt and nuoc mam; steam 20 minutes.

5 TO 6 SERVINGS.

Susan Nepstad Rollins, Loveland, CO., received this unique recipe from a friend whose German-American family made it in the fall using fresh garden produce. "We enjoy it any time of year," says Susan. Testers' comments were unanimously favorable. "This is delicious — it reminded my husband of his German grandmother's cooking," comments Linda Young, Lincoln, NE. LaVonne Williams, Moorhead, MN., agreed. "Easy to make with good flavor from a nice blend of seasonings."

Sausage Green Bean Stew

1   pound German sausage, cut into bite-sized pieces or crumbled

1   medium onion, sliced

¼ to ½ pound new potatoes, cut into pieces

1   cup beef bouillon

1   teaspoon dried sweet basil

1   teaspoon dried summer savory

½   teaspoon seasoned salt

½   teaspoon pepper

1   pound whole green beans, fresh or frozen

8   ounces fresh mushrooms, sliced

In large skillet brown sausage; remove from pan and drain well. In same skillet, cook onion, potatoes, bouillon and seasonings. Simmer about 15 minutes; add sausage, green beans and mushrooms. Continue simmering until potatoes are done.

4 SERVINGS.

Don't despair at long list of ingredients. Preparation is speedy and the dish can be made in advance and reheated although vegetables will lose some of their crisp texture. Mark Anderson, head cook at the Chinese Village, chose this dish to share because "it tastes great and is relatively unusual, highlighting the versatility of eggplant."

Chinese Eggplant with Chopped Meat

2	medium eggplants (about 1 pound each)
8	green onions
7 to 8	cloves garlic
1	(1-inch) piece gingerroot
½	pound ground pork
3	tablespoons soy sauce
1	tablespoon sesame oil
¼	cup corn or peanut oil
2	tablespoons hot pepper paste
1	tablespoon sugar
1½	teaspoons salt
⅔	cup water
	Steamed white rice

Peel eggplants; cut into 1-inch cubes. Cut green and white parts of green onions into ⅛-inch lengths. Mince garlic and gingerroot. Place pork in bowl; stir in soy sauce, sesame oil and half of chopped green onion. Set aside until ready to stir-fry. Heat wok or skillet until very hot; add corn oil and heat again until smoking. Add garlic and gingerroot, stirring constantly 30 seconds. Add hot pepper paste; stir-fry 30 seconds longer. Add pork mixture; stir-fry about 2 minutes until it changes color (maintain high heat under wok). Add eggplants; stir-fry everything over high heat about 4 minutes, gently scooping pieces of eggplant off sides of wok and into middle. Sprinkle sugar and salt over eggplant mixture; stir-fry 2 minutes longer. Add water and remaining green onions. Heat water to boiling; cover pan and without stirring or reducing heat (still on high) let mixture cook about 15 minutes longer. Portions of the dish may appear burned or stuck to the bottom of the wok. Don't be concerned — it's supposed to be that way and that's the best part. Serve with rice.

2 TO 3 SERVINGS.

A hearty skillet supper from the Swedish Language Village. Head cook, Therese Hennemann explains that "traditionally, individual servings are topped with a raw egg yolk or a fried whole egg. Slices of crisp, tart apples make an unusual, but surprisingly suitable accompaniment."

Swedish Hash

3	tablespoons butter or margarine
8 to 10	potatoes, raw or cooked, peeled, cubed
1 to 2	yellow onions, diced
4	ounces cooked ham, diced
4	ounces roast beef or steak, diced
1	teaspoon salt
	Pepper
4	eggs, fried
	Finely chopped fresh parsley

Melt 1½ tablespoons butter in large saucepan over medium-high heat. Add potatoes and cook, stirring frequently, until golden brown, 15 to 20 minutes. Transfer potatoes to bowl. Add remaining butter to saucepan and cook onions over medium-low heat until translucent, about 5 minutes; transfer to bowl with potatoes. Add meat to saucepan; cook until light brown. Return potatoes and onions to saucepan; mix all ingredients over medium heat to heat through. Add salt and pepper to taste. Serve with whole fried egg atop each serving; garnish generously with parsley.

4 SERVINGS.

Eric Peterson, Amherst, WI., "helps Mom mix and shape hundreds of tiny meatballs in early December. We freeze them to serve on Christmas Eve. They are tasty as an appetizer as well as a main dish with carrots, mashed potatoes and lefse."

Norwegian Meatballs

MEATBALLS

5   pounds ground meat (beef, veal, pork; ground 3 times)

2   medium onions, finely ground (save juice)

½   teaspoon nutmeg

½   teaspoon allspice

1   tablespoon salt

½   teaspoon pepper

2   eggs, beaten

½   cup half & half

½   cup cracker meal or matzo meal

4 to   5 beef bouillon cubes or 4 to 5 teaspoons instant beef bouillon

2   teaspoons Kitchen Bouquet
Flour

Heat oven to 350°. Combine all meatball ingredients, knead by hand 5 minutes or more to blend spices into meat. Lightly grease or coat shallow baking pans with no-stick cooking spray. Form small round meat balls; dipping hands into cold water to shape smooth. Bake 10 to 15 minutes. Place meatballs in large kettle; add bouillon cubes, meat drippings from baking pan and water to cover. Stir in Kitchen Bouquet. Heat to boiling; reduce heat and simmer 1 hour. Remove meatballs. Thicken gravy with flour to desired consistency.

ABOUT 120 (1½-INCH) MEATBALLS.

Although there are many different versions of "frikadeller," this is the favorite of Dennis and Carole Johnson, Morris, MN. Recipe is sparked with red and black pepper and meatballs are formed into egg shapes. Danes are said to "have a passion for meatballs."

Zesty Danish Meatballs

2	pounds ground pork
1	tablespoon salt
½	teaspoon red pepper
¼	cup flour
¼	cup dried bread crumbs
1	medium onion, finely chopped
1	teaspoon black pepper
½	teaspoon allspice
3	eggs
¼	cup charged water
	Cream
2	tablespoons butter

Combine all ingredients except cream and butter; mix well. Stir in enough cream to moisten; mix well again. Shape meatballs with a tablespoon; they should be egg-shaped. Fry slowly in butter, turning meatballs as they brown; cook until done.

8 TO 10 SERVINGS.

Milk and cream, used generously in Danish cooking, are included in this recipe for their famous meatballs. If you are planning a traditional menu, complement the entrée with mashed potatoes or potato salad, pickled beets and another vegetable, served hot.

Danish Frikadeller

1	pound pork
1	pound veal
½	cup chopped onion
2	tablespoons butter
¼ to ⅓	cup flour
2	teaspoons salt
1	teaspoon pepper
3	eggs
½	cup light cream
½	cup milk
2	tablespoons butter

Heat oven to 400°. Grind pork and veal together twice. Cook and stir onion in 2 tablespoons butter about 5 minutes. Beat pork and veal together in mixer bowl, slowly. Add flour, salt and pepper. Beat in eggs one at a time. Gradually beat in cream and milk. Blend in onions. Using scoop or tablespoon, form into balls the size of an egg. (If difficult to shape, add a little more flour.) Brown in skillet with 2 tablespoons butter. Bake about 20 minutes.

20 TO 25 MEATBALLS.

When you're cooking for compliments, take time to prepare this elegant stuffed veal roast. Stuffings that include meat are popular in Italian cuisine as are dishes featuring veal. Once roast is ready for baking, preparation is carefree — just bake and serve with a pasta side dish and a light dessert.

Italian Veal with Spinach Dressing

1	tablespoon olive oil
¼	pound ground veal*
¼	pound ground, cooked ham*
3	slices bacon, finely chopped
1	large onion, finely chopped
1	large clove garlic, minced or pressed
1	teaspoon dried basil leaves
1	teaspoon dried tarragon leaves
⅓	cup finely-chopped fresh parsley
8	ounces fresh mushrooms, finely chopped
2	pounds fresh spinach, cooked, chopped, well drained**
3	ounces (¾ cup) shredded Gruyère, Swiss or jack cheese
1	cup soft bread crumbs (2 slices bread)
1	egg
½	teaspoon salt
¼	teaspoon pepper
1	(3½ to 4-pound) veal shoulder or roast, split to form a pocket for stuffing
	Skewers or string
	Vegetable oil or butter
	Dried basil leaves, crumbled
	Dried thyme leaves, crumbled
1	bay leaf

Heat oven to 350°. Heat olive oil in large skillet over medium-high heat; add ground meats and bacon. Cook, stirring until browned. Add onion, garlic, basil, tarragon and parsley; continue cooking, stirring occasionally until onion is soft, about 10 minutes. Remove from heat and combine with mushrooms, spinach, cheese, bread crumbs, egg, salt and pepper; mix well.

Pack stuffing into veal shoulder; fasten opening securely with small skewers or sew with string to hold stuffing inside. Place meat bone-side-down in well-oiled shallow roasting pan. Rub meat with oil. Sprinkle lightly with basil and thyme; add bay leaf. Cover pan and bake 2 to 2¼ hours or until meat is tender when pierced with fork. Remove cover and bake about 15 minutes longer to brown surface. Remove skewers or string and bay leaf; slice between bones to serve.

8 SERVINGS.

Tip: *One-half pound of veal or ham can be substituted for the meat mixture.
**Two (10-ounce) packages frozen chopped spinach, thawed and well-drained can be substituted for fresh spinach.

Leeann Chin, whose sit-down and carry-out Minneapolis and St. Paul restaurants are favorites of Asian food lovers, has authored two cookbooks so some of her trademark dishes can be made at home. Here she shares a sumptuous entrée that can be table-ready in just minutes once cooking begins. Allow a half-hour for refrigeration of veal after it has been cut into strips.

Stir-Fried Veal with Green Onions

1	pound boneless veal steak
1	tablespoon cornstarch
½	teaspoon salt
⅛	teaspoon white pepper
1	bunch green onions with tops
½	teaspoon cornstarch
½	teaspoon sugar
1	tablespoon chicken broth
1	teaspoon light soy sauce
¼	cup vegetable oil
1	tablespoon shredded gingerroot
	Steamed white rice

Trim fat from veal; cut veal lengthwise into 2-inch strips. Cut strips crosswise into ⅛-inch slices. Toss veal, 1 table-spoon cornstarch, salt and white pepper in medium bowl. Cover and refrigerate 30 minutes.

Cut green onions diagonally into 1-inch pieces; mix with ½ teaspoon cornstarch, sugar, broth and soy sauce. Heat wok until very hot. Add oil; tilt wok to coat side. Add veal and gingerroot; stir-fry 2 minutes or until veal turns white. Add green onions; stir-fry 10 seconds. Stir in cornstarch mixture; cook and stir 15 seconds or until well-coated. Serve with rice.

4 SERVINGS.

Eileen Teska, Racine WI., spent a year studying in the south of France and obtained this recipe for Ragout d'Agneau a la Provençal from the woman who cooked for her host family. "Since she didn't measure anything, it took considerable experimenting to get my recipe to taste like hers," says Eileen. "But when I did, every bite brought back the beauties of this region of France."

Lamb Ragout

½ cup cider vinegar

½ cup red wine

1 clove garlic, crushed

3 sprigs fresh rosemary, bruised

2 cups cubed lamb (1½-inch cubes)

¼ cup olive oil

2 teaspoons lemon juice

1 teaspoon finely-chopped garlic

1 teaspoon finely-chopped shallot

1 large green bell pepper, cut into 2-inch squares

4 medium leeks

2 small zucchini, cut into ¾-inch rounds

½ teaspoon salt

Freshly ground pepper

4 medium tomatoes, cut into quarters

Snipped fresh parsley

Combine vinegar, wine, garlic and rosemary. Add lamb; cover and marinate 6 hours or overnight in refrigerator. Drain. Heat oil until almost smoking over high heat. Stir in lamb; brown 2 to 3 minutes, stirring constantly. Reduce heat to medium. Stir in remaining ingredients except tomatoes and parsley. Cover tightly and cook 10 minutes. Stir. Add tomatoes and cook 5 minutes longer. Sprinkle with parsley.

4 SERVINGS.

When Gretchen Calvit, Minneapolis, MN., sampled these on a trip to San Francisco, she couldn't wait to prepare them at home. After experimenting, she feels this version "may be even tastier than the original!" The recipe incorporates favorite mid-Eastern ingredients — lamb, fresh mint, garlic and yogurt. Serve with melon wedges or other seasonal fruit.

Armenian Sandwiches

1	pound ground lamb
1	medium onion, chopped
2	cloves garlic, minced
2	tablespoons snipped fresh mint
2	tablespoons snipped fresh parsley
½	tablespoon dried dill weed
1	(10-ounce) package frozen spinach, thawed, drained
1	cup sautéed fresh mushroom slices, if desired
	Salt and pepper to taste
1	cup water, Burgundy wine or stock

SAUCE

1	cup plain yogurt
½	cucumber, seeded, sliced
4	green onions, chopped
½	teaspoon dill weed
1	package whole wheat pita breads, halved

Brown lamb in heavy skillet; add onion and garlic and cook until onion is soft. Stir in mint, parsley, dill, spinach, mushrooms, salt and pepper. Stir in liquid; heat to boiling. Reduce heat and simmer, uncovered, about 1 hour or until liquid is nearly gone.

Meanwhile, combine all sauce ingredients. Serve lamb mixture in pita bread halves with sauce.

4 TO 6 SERVINGS.

Osaka is famous for its okonomiyaki, or pancakes, which are served with a smorgasbord of toppings to suit every customer's taste and whim. Rather like an Asian version of a burrito or sandwich! For picture-perfect presentation, arrange toppings artfully on a large sectioned platter with sauces in small bowls.

Japanese Pancakes

2 eggs

2½ cups dashi (fish broth)

2 cups all-purpose flour

1½ cups thinly-sliced cabbage

Condiments: bacon, ham, corn, cheese or whatever you like

Sauces: mayonnaise, soy sauce, ketchup, Worcestershire sauce

Heat griddle. Combine eggs, dashi, flour and cabbage in bowl; mix thoroughly. Spoon about ¾-cup of mixture onto lightly-greased griddle; flatten with a spatula. To the uncooked side, add any of the suggested condiments you would like. After about 3 minutes when bottom has browned, flip pancake over. Cook second side 3 minutes longer or until brown. Serve pancakes with suggested sauces.

6 SERVINGS.

An imaginative change-of-pace from the liver and onions combo. Barbara Francis, Blytheville, AR., was not a liver fan until she tried this as a bride. She says the recipe adapts well to making ahead and reheating in a casserole dish. Tester Pamela Kelsey, Bemidji, MN., comments that all diners at her table "enjoyed the flavor."

Mexican-Style Liver

6	slices bacon
¾	cup chopped onion
1	clove garlic, minced
¼	cup flour
1½	teaspoons chili powder
1	teaspoon salt
1½	pounds beef liver
1	(16-ounce) can tomatoes or tomatoes and chiles, cut up
1	(12-ounce) can whole kernel corn, drained
	Hot cooked rice

In large skillet, cook bacon until crisp; drain and crumble. Reserve 3 tablespoons bacon drippings in skillet; cook onion and garlic in drippings until onion is tender but not brown, about 5 minutes. Combine flour, chili powder and salt. Cut liver into thin strips; toss in flour mixture to coat. Remove onions from skillet; set aside. Place liver in skillet; brown quickly on both sides. Stir in onions, bacon, undrained tomatoes and corn. Simmer until mixture is heated through. Serve over rice.

6 SERVINGS.

Tip: Can be made ahead, put into a casserole and refrigerated. Heat in 350° oven 45 to 60 minutes.

Another unusual recipe for liver from Barbara Francis is sparked with sesame seed and sautéed before brief oven heating. Recipe originated with a college roommate's mother and is easily varied with whatever toppings and amounts you choose to use.

Liver con Queso

2	pounds beef liver
¾ to 1 cup sesame seed
¼	cup olive oil
3	large onions, chopped
16	ounces fresh mushrooms, sliced
2	(4-ounce) cans chopped green chiles, drained
3	ounces (¾ cup) shredded Monterey jack cheese
1	avocado, peeled, sliced
1	cup alfalfa sprouts

Heat oven to 325°. Coat liver with sesame seed. Heat 2 tablespoons olive oil in skillet. Sauté liver in oil; remove from skillet and keep warm. Cook onions, mushrooms and chiles in same skillet, adding more oil if necessary, until onions are soft. Place liver in ovenproof dish or shallow casserole; cover with onions, mushrooms and chiles. Sprinkle with cheese; put in oven to melt cheese, about 5 minutes. Garnish with avocado slices and alfalfa sprouts.

4 SERVINGS.

In the "casual-elegant" atmosphere of Ciatti's Restaurant in The Edina, MN., Galleria, pastas and freshly-made sauces are specialties. Hungry customers find both northern and southern Italian dishes offered on the luncheon and dinner menus. Ciatti's culinary staff shares a recipe for one of their most popular items.

Tortellini "Straw and Hay"

6	quarts water
¼	cup vegetable oil
1½	pounds fresh cheese-filled spinach tortellini
1½	pounds fresh meat-filled egg tortellini
1	pound unsalted butter
16	ounces fresh mushrooms, quartered
1	pound prosciutto ham, cut into julienne strips
1	(16-ounce) package frozen green peas, thawed
4	cups heavy whipping cream
1½	pounds freshly-grated Parmesan cheese
6	egg yolks, slightly beaten
½	teaspoon white pepper
½	teaspoon nutmeg

Heat water and oil to boiling in stock pot. Add tortellini; cook 7 to 10 minutes or until desired doneness. Drain; rinse. Melt butter in large skillet; sauté mushrooms about 5 minutes or until limp. Add prosciutto, peas and tortellini; sauté about 5 minutes or until all ingredients are thoroughly heated. Pour cream into mixture; stir gently. Sprinkle cheese over cream and stir mixture until cheese is melted and sauce is smooth. Stir in egg yolks, white pepper and nutmeg until mixture is thickened. Divide evenly among 8 large pasta bowls.

8 SERVINGS.

Eating with chopsticks Villagers at
the Chinese, Japanese and Russian Villages enjoy the authentic foods of the
cultures—sometimes with unfamiliar
tableware. This "villager" enjoys a traditional Japanese breakfast of fish, rice,
soup, fruit and tea.

Although less than one percent of
American students study Chinese, Japanese and Russian, the Concordia Language Villages is committed to exposing
young people to these languages.

Largely because of their non-
Roman alphabets, Chinese, Japanese
and Russian have the reputation of
being extremely difficult to learn.
This myth is forgotten at the Language Villages, where a cultural-
immersion approach to language
teaching actively involves students
in speaking these languages—
immediately.

Wild rice expert, Beth Anderson Erickson, Edina, MN., oversees a wild rice gift and marketing business. Also a home economist and food writer, Beth has developed this meatless main dish with a mid-eastern accent — just one of the gems appearing in her best seller, "Wild Rice for All Seasons."

Mideastern Wild Rice Bake

2 cups cooked wild rice (about ½ cup uncooked)

2 cups finely-chopped leeks

1 cup finely-chopped parsley

1 cup finely-chopped green onions

1 cup finely-chopped fresh spinach or 1 (9 or 10-ounce) package frozen chopped spinach, thawed, well drained

⅓ cup chopped walnuts

1½ tablespoons flour

1½ teaspoons salt

½ teaspoon pepper

8 eggs, lightly beaten

⅓ cup butter or margarine

Plain yogurt or dairy sour cream

Heat oven to 325°. Combine wild rice, leeks, parsley, onions, spinach, walnuts, flour, salt and pepper. Add eggs and mix well. Melt butter in 8x8x2-inch pan. Pour wild rice mixture into pan; bake about 1 hour or until top is crisp and lightly browned. Top each serving with dollop of yogurt.

8 SERVINGS.

A sumptuous side dish to complement your favorite meats and poultry. Gently fold in grapes and raisins before brief final heating so grapes retain their shape.

Wild Rice with Grapes and Raisins

8 ounces uncooked wild rice

3 cups boiling salted water

¼ cup unsalted butter

1 cup diced yellow onion

1 small clove garlic, minced

1 cup seedless red grapes

¼ cup raisins

Salt and pepper

Stir wild rice into boiling water. Cover and simmer about 45 minutes. Uncover and cook off excess moisture. About 10 minutes before wild rice is done, melt butter in skillet; add onion and garlic. Sauté about 10 minutes. Stir in grapes and raisins; sauté about 2 minutes. Combine with wild rice. Salt and pepper to taste.

8 SERVINGS.

Karen Swanson, wife of the Huntmaster at Marsh Lake Hunting Preserve, Chaska, MN., offers an ideal accompaniment for the bounty of the hunt. As sophisticated as it is simple.

Marsh Lake Wild Rice

8	ounces uncooked wild rice
	Chicken broth or bouillon
8	ounces fresh mushrooms, sliced
1	medium onion, chopped
2	tablespoons margarine or butter
1	(8-ounce) can water chestnuts, drained, slivered
½	pound bacon, crisply fried, crumbled
	Salt and pepper
	Seasoned salt

Cook wild rice in water with broth or bouillon added until tender but not mushy; drain if necessary. Sauté mushrooms and onion in margarine in skillet; add to wild rice with water chestnuts and bacon. Toss and season with salt, pepper and seasoned salt.

10 TO 12 SERVINGS.

This congenial Italian rice dish is typical of the many varieties in which rice is permeated with a potpourri of flavors during cooking. Although saffron is pricey, it lends a distinctive flavor and yellow tint to the dish. Purchase the smallest possible quantity since only a pinch is required.

Risotto

1	small onion, minced
½	green bell pepper, chopped
8	medium fresh mushrooms, finely chopped
½	cup butter
1	cup uncooked long-grain rice
2½	cups hot chicken broth
	Dash of saffron
2	tablespoons grated Parmesan cheese
½	teaspoon salt
⅛	teaspoon pepper

Heat oven to 400°. Sauté onion, green pepper and mushrooms in butter. Add rice; cook and stir with fork until light brown. Add chicken broth; heat to boiling. Add saffron, cheese, salt and pepper. Spoon into casserole. Bake about 25 minutes.

4 TO 6 SERVINGS.

Shirley Erickson, Minnetonka, MN., has been featured in several food articles for her expertise in ethnic cuisine. Although foods of her Scandinavian background are probably closest to her heart, she frequently intersperses recipes from other parts of the world in menus for entertaining. This creamy rice bake pepped up with green chiles is ideal with grilled or baked chicken.

Mexicali Rice

1	cup cooked rice
12	ounces (3 cups) shredded Monterey jack cheese
3	zucchini, sliced, cooked
1	large tomato, chopped
1	(4-ounce) can chopped green chiles, drained
2	cups dairy sour cream
¼	cup sliced green onions
¼	cup chopped green bell pepper
1	teaspoon garlic salt
¼	teaspoon dried oregano leaves

Heat oven to 350°. Layer half of rice in casserole. Add half of jack cheese, half of zucchini, half of tomato and half of chiles. Repeat layers, except cheese. Combine sour cream, onion, green pepper, garlic salt and oregano; spread over layers. Top with remaining cheese. Bake 45 to 60 minutes.

4 SERVINGS.

Ideal for today's make-ahead cooking style. Refrigerate or freeze in smaller quantities for family dinners or leave as is for party-perfect serving.

Mashed Potatoes Americana

5	pounds potatoes, peeled
1	cup dairy sour cream
1	teaspoon salt
1	(8-ounce) package cream cheese, softened
2	teaspoons onion salt
2	tablespoons butter
	Paprika

Cook and mash potatoes. Add remaining ingredients except butter and paprika; mix well. Refrigerate. Can be used any time within a week, or can be frozen for up to 3 months. To serve, place in buttered casserole. Dot with butter and sprinkle with paprika. Heat oven to 350°. Bake 30 minutes if refrigerated or 1 hour if frozen.

12 TO 14 SERVINGS.

A side dish inspired by her heritage is shared by Maria Diaz Onheiber, Madison, WI. "The one jalapeño pepper remains intact and imparts flavor to the rice during cooking," she explains. A writer for the **Wisconsin State Journal** *featured Maria and several of her recipes in a recent article. This inviting rice-vegetable combination was described as "an authentic Mexican dish that is a take-off on paella."*

Maria's Mexican Rice

	Olive oil
2 to	3 small onions
½	cup chopped parsley
3 to	4 cloves garlic, minced
2	cups uncooked rice
	Garlic salt
	Pepper
8	ounces fresh mushrooms, sliced
½	cup fresh or frozen green peas
3	large carrots, sliced
1	(9-ounce) package frozen artichoke hearts, thawed
1	jalapeño pepper
1	(28-ounce) can chopped Italian tomatoes
2	bay leaves
4	cups chicken broth

Heat small amount of olive oil in heavy skillet over medium heat until a light haze forms above it. Sauté onions, parsley and garlic, stirring frequently; cook 5 minutes or until soft and transparent but not brown. Add rice, garlic salt and pepper; stir 2 to 3 minutes to coat grains well with oil. Do not let rice brown. Add mushrooms, peas, carrots, artichoke hearts and jalapeño pepper; sauté 3 minutes; add tomatoes and bay leaves. Sauté a few minutes; add chicken broth. Mix thoroughly; bring to a boil. Cover tightly; reduce heat to low. Simmer undisturbed until all liquid has been absorbed and rice is tender but not too soft. Fluff rice with fork before serving; taste for seasoning. If rice must wait, drape pan with a towel and keep warm in a preheated 200° oven.

10 SERVINGS.

When the Lecy family convenes, Amy, of Redwood Falls, MN., says this is a sought-after treat. "It was introduced to my father by his Norwegian grandparents, Bennie and Jensena Lecy." Tester Ingrid Holm, Plymouth, MN., rated them "excellent" on all counts and said her family "kept eating them even after they were full."

Norwegian Potato Dumplings

3	quarts water
4	cups shredded potatoes
2	cups all-purpose flour
1	teaspoon baking powder
1	teaspoon salt
	1-inch cubes of cooked ham
	Melted butter

Heat water to boiling in large saucepan or Dutch oven. Combine all ingredients except ham and butter. Shape into balls about the size of a baseball. Push 1 ham cube into center of each ball. Drop potato balls into boiling water. Cover and simmer 1 hour, stirring occasionally. Serve with melted butter.

4 SERVINGS.

Popular as an entrée or side dish, "chahan" or fried rice can be tailored to use whatever leftover meats, seafood, poultry and bits and pieces of fresh vegetables you have on hand. Rice that has been cooked until barely tender, cooled and refrigerated, retains an appealingly firm texture through the sautéing step.

Fried Rice

5½	tablespoons vegetable oil (divided)
2	eggs, beaten
4	cups cold cooked rice*
4	slices cooked ham, 4 slices bacon or ½ cup shrimp
½	cup chopped green onions
2	green bell peppers, seeded, chopped
½	tablespoon finely chopped gingerroot
½	teaspoon salt
	Dash of pepper
1	tablespoon soy sauce
2	teaspoons sesame oil

Heat 1½ teaspoons of vegetable oil in wok or large skillet. Add eggs and cook until solid. Remove from pan and cut into small pieces. Heat 2 tablespoons vegetable oil in wok; stir-fry rice and eggs. Add meat, vegetables, gingerroot, salt and pepper; cook and stir until well mixed. Add soy sauce; stir to distribute evenly. Sprinkle sesame oil over mixture; stir once before serving.

8 TO 10 SERVINGS.

*Tip: *If rice is cooked a day ahead and refrigerated it is easier to sauté without becoming mushy.*

Jonathan Remund, a native of India, attends the School for Indian Language and Culture in St. Paul, MN. This dish is one he first prepared in Indian cooking class and now makes at home for family dinners. Turmeric, cumin and coriander are frequently used in curries and add distinctive flavors to common ingredients.

Vegetable Pulao

¼   cup vegetable oil
1½   to 2 cups chopped onions
1   teaspoon cumin seed
2   cups rice (Basmati)
1¼   teaspoons salt
1   carrot, chopped
½   cup fresh green beans
½   cup fresh peas
1   teaspoon ground cumin
1   teaspoon ground coriander
½   teaspoon turmeric
½   teaspoon cayenne pepper
    A few whole cloves
    A few bay leaves
4   cups water

Heat oil over medium-high heat in 4 to 6-quart saucepan. Stir in onions and cumin seed; sauté until onions are light brown. Stir in rice and salt; sauté until rice begins to brown. Stir in vegetables; sauté until crisp-tender. Stir in spices and water. Heat to boiling; cook 2 to 3 minutes, stirring constantly. Reduce heat, cover and simmer 15 to 25 minutes. Remove bay leaves.

4 TO 6 SERVINGS.

Jennifer Dean Blair, Rapid City, S.D., dubs this a great "make-and-take dish for potlucks and buffets." Use of nutritious, fiber-rich brown rice adds protein and vitamin E to the mix. You will note that it requires more moisture and cooking time than white rice and offers more volume as well.

Arroz con Queso

1½ cups uncooked brown rice
1   (16-ounce) can black-eyed peas, drained
16   ounces (4 cups) jalapeño Monterey jack cheese, shredded
8   ounces ricotta cheese
½   cup halved, pitted ripe olives
1   large onion, chopped
3   cloves garlic, minced
2   ounces (½ cup) shredded Cheddar cheese

Cook brown rice. Heat oven to 350°. Spray casserole with no-stick butter-flavor cooking spray. Combine rice, peas, jack cheese, ricotta, olives, onion and garlic. Bake about 30 minutes. During last few minutes of baking, sprinkle top with Cheddar cheese.

6 SERVINGS.

Deb Dahlseng, Lowry, MN., carries on the "Rommegrøt tradition for family and friends" with this streamlined variation of the dish she loved as a child. "It's a rich and filling creation Norwegians eat as a side dish, especially during the holidays," she says.

Microwave Rommegrøt

½   cup butter
¼   cup sugar
¾   cup all-purpose flour
     Dash of salt
3   cups milk
1   cup cream

Melt butter in microwave; cool slightly. Stir in sugar, flour and salt. In separate bowl, combine milk and cream. Cover and microwave to almost scalding. Mix a little of milk mixture with butter mixture, making sure there are no lumps. Microwave on HIGH for 3 to 4 minutes. Stir once each minute until thick. Serve warm with a little melted butter and cinnamon and sugar on top, if desired.

10 TO 12 SERVINGS.

When Marie and Dick Lacy, Edina, MN., were on an around-the-world excursion, they clipped this unusual chutney recipe from the Sydney, Australia paper. Marie, who is well-known as an exceptional cook, makes it as a tasty reminder of their travels and to use as hostess gifts. Prepare at least three weeks before serving and use a high-quality vinegar for a mellow, rather than sharp flavor.

Apple and Chili Chutney

3   cups firmly packed brown sugar
1½ teaspoons allspice
1½ teaspoons ground turmeric
1   teaspoon five-spice powder
1   teaspoon salt
½   teaspoon chili powder (or to taste)
½   teaspoon ground cumin
1   bay leaf
1   tablespoon chopped fresh gingerroot
1   tablespoon chopped fresh coriander (cilantro)
2   cups white wine vinegar
4   large green cooking apples, peeled, cored, cut into small pieces
2   cups chopped white onions

Combine brown sugar and seasonings in heavy saucepan; stir in vinegar. Simmer 1¼ hours. Remove bay leaf; stir in apples and onions. Adjust the amount of chili powder, if necessary. Simmer, stirring carefully to keep from mashing the apples, 30 minutes or until chutney is thick. Spoon chutney into sterilized jars. Cool well and seal with wax. Cover with circles of gingham or tie-dyed cotton and tie down with colored ribbons. Label and mark with the bottling date. Chutney will mature in about 3 weeks.

Thirty years ago a chance meeting in Acapulco eventually resulted in the marriage of Sam Onheiber of Madison, WI., and Maria Diaz, a native of Mexico. Over the years, Maria has enjoyed "combining Jewish and Mexican cuisines" while observing the Jewish food mandates in her Madison kitchen. She points out that refried black beans are "high in protein and the broth from boiling the beans makes a wonderful soup stock." Beans should be soaked overnight before cooking.

Refried Black Beans

2	cups dry black beans
4 to	5 quarts water
1	medium onion
4	cloves garlic
1	teaspoon salt
2	tablespoons olive oil
1	small onion, chopped

Wash beans and soak overnight in cold water to cover. Drain. In a stockpot over medium heat, heat beans and 4 to 5 quarts water to boiling. Add whole onion, garlic, salt and olive oil. Boil beans uncovered until soft. Discard onion and garlic.

Heat olive oil in skillet over moderate heat. Add chopped onion and sauté until soft and transparent. Drain beans in colander. Add beans to skillet, mashing with the back of a cooking spoon for about 5 minutes or until the liquid has been absorbed. Taste for seasoning.

6 SERVINGS.

Popular substitutes for potatoes in Scandinavia and a cousin of the turnip, rutabagas often are paraffin-coated to retain moisture content. The waxy surface should be removed before cooking.

Glazed Rutabagas

2	medium rutabagas (about 2 pounds)
¼	cup margarine or butter
2	tablespoons packed brown sugar
1	tablespoon water
1	teaspoon salt

Peel and slice rutabagas; cut into ½-inch cubes. Heat margarine in 10-inch skillet until melted. Add rutabagas; cook over medium heat, stirring frequently, about 10 minutes. Sprinkle with brown sugar, water and salt. Cover and simmer over low heat, stirring occasionally, about 20 minutes or until tender.

6 TO 8 SERVINGS.

Maria Pino, Hinsdale, IL., first tasted this "family specialty" in her grandmother's Cuban kitchen. Accompanied by rice, it becomes a classic Cuban meal. Round out the menu with a refreshing fruit salad.

Cuban Black Beans

16	ounces dry black beans*
¼	teaspoon salt
½	medium onion, chopped
1	tablespoon garlic powder
2	tablespoons olive oil
2	bay leaves
1	sprig fresh coriander (cilantro), if desired
¼	medium green bell pepper, cut into 6 pieces
½	teaspoon ground cumin
¼	teaspoon salt
	Hot cooked long grain white rice

Soak beans overnight in enough water to cover 3 inches over top of beans. Pour beans with water into a large kettle with ¼ teaspoon salt. Cover and cook over medium-high heat for 3 hours or until beans are soft. (If using pressure cooker, cook for 30 minutes.) When beans are soft, add remaining ingredients except rice; mix well. Cover and cook for 20 to 30 minutes longer over medium heat. Remove bay leaves. Serve with rice.

8 SERVINGS.

*Tip: *Beans can be cooked ahead of time; freeze up to 1 month.*

A native of China and India, eggplant adapts beautifully to mid-eastern seasonings. Perfect to pair with leg of lamb or lamb chops. Young, very tender eggplant may be left unpeeled for most dishes.

Eggplant Istanbul

½	cup vegetable oil
1	medium eggplant, peeled, cubed
1	medium onion, finely chopped
2	cloves garlic, crushed
2	tomatoes, peeled, cut into eighths, or 1 (16-ounce) can plum tomatoes, drained
1	(6-ounce) can tomato paste
	Juice of 1 lemon
	Salt and pepper to taste

Combine oil, eggplant and onion in saucepan; cook 10 minutes. Add remaining ingredients except salt and pepper; simmer 15 minutes. Add salt and pepper. If desired, serve with lemon wedges or spoon over hot cooked rice and add an extra squeeze of lemon juice.

6 SERVINGS.

One of the recipes Barbara Francis, Blytheville, AR., cherishes from her mother-in-law is this cheese-topped casserole. To make ahead combine all ingredients except cheese. Cover and refrigerate up to 24 hours.

Bossa Nova Beans

1	(16-ounce) can baked beans
1	(15-ounce) can chili beans
1	(8-ounce) can tomato sauce
½	cup chopped onion
¼	cup packed brown sugar
1	tablespoon ground cumin
¼	teaspoon salt
¼	teaspoon garlic salt
¼	teaspoon pepper
4	ounces (1 cup) shredded Monterey jack cheese

Heat oven to 325°. Combine all ingredients except cheese in 2-quart casserole. Cover and bake about 45 minutes; uncover and bake about 45 minutes longer or until liquid is reduced. Sprinkle cheese over top; serve when cheese is melted.

8 SERVINGS.

This Norwegian specialty enlivens cabbage slices with bacon and that highly-favored Scandinavian herb, dill. By the way, fresh dill freezes well when tightly sealed in plastic bags.

Cabbage with Bacon and Dill

1	small head cabbage
6	slices bacon
1	small onion, thinly sliced
1	teaspoon dill weed or 3 fresh dill leaves, chopped
½	teaspoon salt
¼	teaspoon pepper

Trim and slice cabbage; set aside to drain. Cook bacon in large heavy skillet until crisp. Drain bacon on paper towels; crumble. Reserve some bacon drippings; brown onion. Stir in dill, salt and pepper. Add cabbage; cover and simmer over low heat until cabbage is tender, about 1 hour. Add water, if necessary, during cooking. Spoon cabbage into serving dish; garnish with bacon.

4 TO 6 SERVINGS.

From Phyllis Hanes, food editor of **The Christian Science Monitor,** *comes a leading national dish of Chile which is very much Indian due to indigenous foods used as main ingredients. "If fresh cranberry or shell beans are unavailable," comments Phyllis, "substitute dried cranberry or navy beans." Serve in soup plates so all the sauce is savored.*

Porotos Granados

2	cups fresh cranberry or shell beans
3	tablespoons olive oil
2	tablespoons sweet paprika
1	clove garlic, crushed
1	large onion, finely chopped
	Salt and freshly ground black pepper
1	pound (about 2 cups) butternut squash, peeled, cubed
¾ to 1 cup chicken stock or water
½	cup fresh, frozen or canned whole kernel corn
5	fresh basil leaves

Place fresh, washed beans in soup pot with cold water to cover. Heat to boiling; reduce heat and simmer until tender, about 45 minutes. (Cook dried beans according to package directions.) Reserve bean cooking liquid. Heat olive oil in skillet; stir in paprika until thoroughly mixed. Add garlic and onion; cook over medium heat until soft. Add salt, pepper, squash and chicken stock; cover and simmer gently 10 to 15 minutes or until squash is very soft. (Squash will disintegrate and thicken the sauce.) Add beans, corn, basil and reserved bean liquid. Simmer 5 minutes.

4 TO 6 SERVINGS.

This old-world accompaniment adds color and sweet-sour spark to pork and other entrées. Cabbage should be shredded with a very sharp knife to avoid bruising tender leaves.

Danish-Style Red Cabbage

2½	pounds red cabbage
3	tablespoons butter
1½	tablespoons sugar
2 to 3	tablespoons water
	Juice of ½ lemon or 1 tablespoon vinegar
¾	cup red currant juice or red currant jelly

Trim cabbage and shred. Melt butter and sugar in large heavy saucepan or Dutch oven. Add cabbage and steam 2 to 3 minutes. Add a little of the water and lemon juice. Cover and simmer until tender, 2 to 3 hours, stirring occasionally. Add red currant juice and if necessary more sugar and vinegar to taste.

8 SERVINGS.

Tip: Prepare a day ahead to blend flavors.

Helen Hill, Osseo, MN., found this celebrated East Coast recipe in a 1929 church cookbook. Begin process the night before by soaking beans. Allow plenty of time for boiling and baking steps. Perfect for potlucks, family reunions, block parties and other large gatherings.

Boston Baked Beans

5	cups navy beans
½	teaspoon baking soda
1	pound salt pork, cut up
2	medium onions, chopped
4	cups tomato juice
½	cup ketchup
1	tablespoon molasses
1	cup firmly packed brown sugar
2	teaspoons salt
1	teaspoon paprika
½	teaspoon dry mustard

In large saucepan or Dutch oven, soak beans overnight in water to cover. Drain water; add fresh water to cover, stir in soda. Heat to boiling; skim off bubbles that rise. Simmer 20 minutes. Drain and rinse with cold water. Place beans and salt pork in a bean pot. Combine remaining ingredients; pour over beans until liquid reaches top of beans. Place in 325 to 350° oven; bake 6 to 7 hours, adding extra liquid or water if necessary during baking. Skim off fat as it rises to the surface. Reduce oven temperature to 300° during last 1½ hours of baking.

20 TO 25 SERVINGS

A sensational crowd-pleaser, perfect for a buffet table and terrific teamed with ham, barbecued pork roast and other grilled favorites.

Chile-Cheese Corn Casserole

2	cups milk
3	eggs, beaten
1	cup cornmeal
2	teaspoons garlic salt
1	(4-ounce) can chopped green chiles
2	(16-ounce) cans cream-style corn
3	cups (12 ounces) shredded sharp Cheddar cheese
1	tablespoon vegetable oil

Heat oven to 350°. Combine milk, eggs, cornmeal and garlic salt; add remaining ingredients; mix well. Pour into buttered 13x9x2-inch casserole. Bake 1¼ to 1½ hours or until cooked through and top is golden brown.

10 TO 12 SERVINGS.

A tangy sauce accents the natural flavors of garden-fresh beets and carrots. Janet Sadlack, Burnsville, MN., featured this harvest-time treat in her widely-circulated newsletter, "The Microwave Times."

Beets and Carrots á la Orange

5	medium beets (about 1 pound)*
2	cups sliced carrots (2 to 3 medium)
¼	cup water
2	tablespoons brown sugar
1	tablespoon cornstarch
¾	teaspoon salt
½	cup orange juice
¼	cup butter or margarine
1	tablespoon vinegar

Cut tops from beets, leaving 1-inch stems. Wash beets thoroughly. Place in 2-quart glass casserole. Add water to within ½ inch of top of dish. Cover with casserole lid. Microwave on HIGH 18 to 20 minutes or until beets are just about tender, turning beets over once. Let stand 10 minutes. Drain and rinse in cold water. Slip skins from beets while twisting off stems. Set beets aside.

Combine carrots and ¼ cup water in 1-quart casserole. Cover with casserole lid. Microwave on HIGH for 5 to 6 minutes or until crisp-tender. Let stand 5 minutes. Combine brown sugar, cornstarch, salt and orange juice in 2-cup glass measure; mix well. Microwave on HIGH, uncovered, 2 to 2½ minutes or until mixture boils and thickens. Stir in butter and vinegar. Drain carrots. Slice or cut beets into pieces; add to carrots. Pour sauce over vegetables; mix lightly. Cover. Microwave on HIGH 1½ to 2 minutes or until thoroughly heated.

6 TO 8 SERVINGS.

*Tip: *One (16-ounce) can sliced or quartered beets can be substituted for fresh beets. Add drained beets to cooked carrots; increase last cooking time to 3 to 4 minutes.*

This oft-requested recipe comes from the Montrose, MN., restaurant, Gasthof zur Gemutlichkeit. Chef Sharon Gedeon suggests serving the well-seasoned dish with pork sauerbraten, rouladen and wild game.

Gemutlichkeit Red Cabbage

2	pounds red cabbage
¼	cup fat or lard
1	medium onion
4	whole cloves
3	apples (or 2 cups applesauce)
1⅔	cups red wine vinegar
2	bay leaves
2	teaspoons salt
¼	teaspoon white pepper
½	teaspoon caraway seed
2	tablespoons sugar
1	cup water
2	tablespoons whole cranberries in sauce

Trim cabbage and shred finely. Melt fat in large saucepan or Dutch oven; add cabbage. Peel onion and stick whole cloves into it. Peel and slice apples. Add onion and apples to cabbage. Add vinegar, bay leaves, salt, pepper, caraway seed, sugar and water. Heat to boiling; reduce heat. Add cranberries and stir mixture occasionally. Add more water if necessary to prevent cabbage mixture from sticking to bottom of pan. Cook until cabbage is tender, 45 to 60 minutes. Before serving, remove whole onion and bay leaves.

5 SERVINGS.

Tip: For extra good flavor, add a little red wine toward end of cooking time.

The humble, abundant zucchini is enriched with eggs, cream and cheese for a mild, pleasing side dish. Select zucchini no longer than eight inches for peak flavor.

Zucchini Gratinée

4	pounds zucchini, peeled, sliced
4	eggs
3	cups heavy cream
4	ounces (1 cup) shredded Gruyère cheese
	Dash of nutmeg
	Salt and pepper to taste

Heat oven to 350°. Cook zucchini until soft. Crush cooked zucchini in colander; drain to remove liquid. Place zucchini in 1½-quart casserole. Combine remaining ingredients; pour over zucchini. Bake about 20 minutes.

6 TO 8 SERVINGS.

Peggy Singh, Bloomington, MN., and her husband Amarjit, a native of India, relish recipes of his homeland. As with much Indian cookery, spices take the spotlight to transform common ingredients into exotic treats. Monitor final cooking step to keep vegetables firm and flavorful.

Cauliflower and Potatoes Indienne

2	tablespoons margarine
2	medium potatoes, peeled, cubed
¼	cup vegetable oil
1	teaspoon black mustard seed
½	cup chopped onion
1	teaspoon ground coriander
½	teaspoon ground cumin
½	teaspoon ground turmeric
½	teaspoon paprika
¼	teaspoon ground red pepper
2	tablespoons fresh coriander (cilantro)
2	teaspoons slivered gingerroot
1	teaspoon salt
2	medium heads cauliflower, broken into florets

Melt margarine in skillet over medium heat. Add potatoes and sauté until light brown. Remove from heat. Heat oil in heavy saucepan over high heat; when hot, add mustard seed, shaking pan until it pops. Add onion and brown lightly. Reduce heat; add coriander, cumin, turmeric, paprika and red pepper; blend thoroughly. Add fresh coriander, gingerroot and salt. If mixture seems too dry, add a small amount of water. Add cauliflower and potatoes, turning to coat with spices. Cook over medium heat 25 minutes or until cauliflower and potatoes are tender, yet firm.

4 TO 6 SERVINGS.

This slow-baker, cooked custard-style, comes from Beth Johnson Holod's great grandmother, Molly Ryan. Use of simple, on-hand ingredients endears it to modern cooks.

Escalloped Corn

3	eggs
3	(16-ounce) cans cream-style corn
1	cup cracker crumbs
1	cup evaporated milk
3	tablespoons chopped pimento
¼	teaspoon salt

Heat oven to 250°. Butter 2-quart baking dish. Beat eggs; combine with remaining ingredients; pour into baking dish. Set dish in pan of water on oven rack. Bake about 1½ hours or until set.

12 SERVINGS.

No wonder the popularity of this mild medley of vegetables has grown far beyond the borders of southern France. Christine Schulze, Director of Concordia Language Villages, serves this "in the fall after a trip to the Farmer's Market." She adds an American touch by teaming it with freshly baked corn bread. "Ratatouille is among the many names that still exist from the Old Provençal language," she explains. "Red is the predominant color in Provençe — red-tiled roofs, red soil and red tomatoes used in many dishes."

Ratatouille

1   large onion, cut into thin wedges
2   cloves garlic, minced
¼   cup olive or vegetable oil
1   (14½ or 16-ounce) can whole tomatoes, undrained, cut up or 1 pound fresh tomatoes, peeled, seeded, chopped
1   teaspoon dried thyme leaves, crushed
1   teaspoon dried basil leaves, crushed
1   teaspoon salt
½   teaspoon ground coriander
¼   teaspoon pepper
   Dash of crushed anise seed
1   bay leaf
1   medium unpeeled eggplant
2   medium zucchini, cut into strips
2   green bell peppers, seeded, cut in strips

In Dutch oven, cook onion and garlic in oil until tender. Add tomatoes and seasonings. Cover and simmer 10 minutes. Remove bay leaf. Reserve 2 cups of the sauce mixture. Cut eggplant in half lengthwise, then crosswise into ½-inch slices. Arrange half of vegetables over sauce in pan. Sprinkle with salt and pepper. Cover with 1 cup of the reserved sauce. Arrange remaining vegetables over sauce. Sprinkle with salt and pepper. Pour remaining sauce over vegetables. Cover; simmer about 20 minutes. Uncover; simmer about 15 minutes. Serve hot or at room temperature.
8 TO 10 SERVINGS.

As French as the Eiffel Tower, savory soufflés can be served as a first course, entrée accompaniment or light main dish. Recipe contributor Katherine Bradbury, Edina, MN., suggests beginning with room temperature egg whites for greater volume and beating carefully until they have at least doubled in volume. Like most soufflés, this goes to the table immediately upon removal from the oven.

Mushroom Soufflé

3	tablespoons unsalted butter
8	ounces fresh mushrooms, chopped
3	tablespoons finely chopped white part of scallions
3	tablespoons flour
¼	cup sherry
½	cup milk
¼	teaspoon salt
5	eggs, separated, room temperature

Butter 2-quart soufflé dish. Heat oven to 375°. Melt butter in medium saucepan over medium heat. Add mushrooms and scallions; cook and stir until all liquid has evaporated, 10 to 15 minutes. Stir in flour; gradually blend in sherry, milk and salt. Cook over medium heat until mixture is thickened, 3 to 5 minutes. Remove from heat and carefully beat in egg yolks. In medium bowl, beat egg whites until stiff; stir ¼ of whites into mushroom mixture. Carefully fold in remaining egg whites. Pour mixture into buttered dish. Bake about 40 minutes. Serve at once.

4 SERVINGS.

Called "Zwiebelkuchen" in its homeland, this can be made with a yeast dough or pastry crust. Traditionally served piping hot with a new wine, it can be cut into small wedges for an appetizer or into large wedges as a side dish for meat and poultry entrées.

German Onion Pie

PASTRY

2	cups all-purpose flour
1	teaspoon baking powder
½	teaspoon salt
¾	cup butter
1	medium egg, beaten
1	tablespoon cream, if desired
1	egg white, beaten

FILLING

2	cups chopped onions
2	slices bacon, diced
2	tablespoons butter
¼	teaspoon salt
1	teaspoon caraway seed
½	tablespoon flour
½	cup heavy cream
2	medium eggs, beaten

Heat oven to 375°. Combine flour, baking powder and salt. Cut in butter and work with fingers until mealy. Add egg; blend until consistency of pie dough. Add cream if dough is not sufficiently moist. Work lightly; pat into bottom and up side of 9-inch round layer cake pan. Brush egg white over bottom crust to prevent crust from becoming soggy. Cook and stir onions and bacon in butter until very soft. Add salt and caraway seed. Stir in flour; slowly stir in cream, Remove from heat; add a little of mixture to beaten eggs, then combine the two mixtures. Spoon into pastry-lined pan. Bake about 30 minutes or until pastry is crisp and golden and filling is firm. Serve hot from the oven as a snack with white wine.

8 TO 10 SERVINGS.

Margaret Schulze, Walker, MN., has devised a tasty way to utilize stale French bread and create a party dish at the same time. For mild flavor select Bermuda or Spanish onions that are firm and blemish-free.

French Onion Supreme

CROUTONS
2   tablespoons butter or margarine
1½   cups day-old French bread cubes, crusts removed

CASSEROLE
4   medium onions, sliced
3   tablespoons butter or margarine
2   tablespoons flour
      Dash of pepper
¾   cup beef bouillon
¼   cup dry sherry
2   ounces (½ cup) shredded process Swiss cheese
3   tablespoons grated Parmesan cheese

Heat oven to 250°. Melt 2 tablespoons butter in ovenproof skillet. Add bread cubes and stir well to coat. Place pan in oven for 30 minutes, stirring occasionally. Remove croutons from pan; set aside. Cook onions in 3 tablespoons butter just until tender. Blend in flour and pepper. Add bouillon and sherry; cook and stir until mixture thickens and bubbles. Heat broiler. Turn mixture into 1-quart casserole. Spoon croutons over onion mixture. Sprinkle with cheeses. Broil just until cheese melts, about 1 minute. Serve immediately.

4 TO 6 SERVINGS.

Barbara Francis shares another recipe "passed down in her husband's family — an oft-requested favorite at family reunions." This baked version for rellenos (which means "stuffed") is much easier than the traditional method of deep frying, but offers the same rich flavors. For variety, Cheddar cheese can be substituted or combined with the jack cheese.

Baked Chile Rellenos

6   (4-ounce) cans whole chiles
16   ounces Monterey jack cheese, cut into 3x5-inch strips
2   eggs
2   cups milk
½   cup all-purpose flour
1   teaspoon salt

Heat oven to 350°. Rinse black spots off chiles. Remove seeds; drain chiles on paper towels. Butter 12x8x2-inch casserole. Place 1 cheese strip inside each chile. Place chiles, seam side down, in casserole. Beat eggs with wire whisk; whisk in milk, flour and salt until smooth. Pour mixture over chiles. Bake about 1 hour or until set.

6 SERVINGS.

When peppers are in their prime, enhance your harvest-time table with this upscale side dish from the Swedish Village. Rich in vitamin C, peppers should be of good color and free of soft areas, particularly when prepared this way.

Mushroom-Stuffed Green Peppers

4	cups mushrooms
2	tablespoons butter or margarine
1	yellow onion
3	tablespoons flour
1½	cups cream or milk
	Salt and white pepper
4	green bell peppers
2	ounces (¼ cup) shredded cheese

Rinse and dry mushrooms; dice. Melt butter in large saucepan over medium-low heat. Sauté onion until translucent; remove from pan. Sauté mushrooms until all water cooks out of them. Return onion to saucepan; sprinkle mushroom-onion mixture with flour and gradually add cream, stirring with a wooden spoon. Cook and stir until mixture comes to a boil; boil and stir 1 minute. Reduce heat; simmer gently for a few minutes; season to taste with salt and pepper. Heat oven to 400°. Remove stems and white fibers from green peppers; rinse thoroughly. Parboil peppers for 1 to 2 minutes in lightly salted water; drain. Fill peppers with mushroom mixture and place in lightly greased ovenproof dish. Sprinkle with cheese. Bake 20 to 30 minutes.

4 SERVINGS.

Tip: Can be prepared early in the day and refrigerated until time to bake.

"The only bad thing about these pancakes is you tend to eat too many," explains Nina Jahnke, Homer, AK. The heritage recipe has been savored for several generations by her father's German family. Tester Sem Sutter, Chicago, IL., adds the final accolade — "These are definitely the best potato pancakes we've ever eaten!"

Potato Pancakes

2	pounds potatoes
1	onion
1	tablespoon snipped fresh parsley
2	eggs
2	tablespoons flour
1	teaspoon salt
3	slices bacon, crisply fried, crumbled, if desired
	Vegetable oil
	Applesauce

Peel and shred potatoes and onion. Drain liquid from potatoes. Combine potatoes, onion, parsley, eggs, flour, salt and bacon. Heat thin layer of oil on griddle or in heavy skillet over medium heat. Drop spoonfuls of potato mixture onto pan and shape into patties. Fry 2 to 3 minutes on each side or until lightly browned. Serve with applesauce.

4 to 6 SERVINGS.

A simple, but pleasing recipe with a marvelous aroma. Gail Mathisen, Chanhassen, MN., a patron of the arts, approaches food presentation artistically as well. She finds this recipe complements her other contribution, Japanese Grilled Swordfish, as dinner party favorites.

Potatoes Italian

12	small new potatoes
12	bay leaves
¼	cup olive oil
	Salt
	Sage, if desired

Heat oven to 400°. Make an incision ¾-inch deep into each potato; put bay leaf in each slit. Toss potatoes in baking pan with olive oil and salt. Sprinkle with sage, if desired. Cover pan with foil and bake 1½ hours or until potatoes are done. Remove bay leaves.

6 SERVINGS.

Tip: Pancetta bacon can be wrapped around potatoes.

"This recipe was my great-grandmother's and it's particularly tasty with pot roast or sauerbraten with gravy spooned over," says Eric Peterson, Amherst, WI. Tester Nancy Jordet, St. Peter, MN., used a potato ricer for "easy preparation" and she praises the "dumplings' light texture and unusual, delicious flavor."

German Potato Dumplings

CROUTONS

3	slices day-old bread, cubed
2	tablespoons butter or margarine or bacon drippings

DUMPLINGS

6	medium baking potatoes
2	eggs
½	cup all-purpose flour
2	tablespoons grated onion
1¼	teaspoon salt
½	teaspoon nutmeg

Sauté bread cubes in butter until golden brown; set aside. Cook unpeeled potatoes until tender. Peel, cool and coarsely shred or rice. Stir in remaining dumpling ingredients with a fork until very well mixed. Shape into small balls, putting 1 crouton in the center of each. If potato mixture is too sticky, add small amount of flour. Heat water in large saucepan. Drop dumplings into gently boiling water; cook 10 minutes. Drain; keep cooked dumplings warm in oven while cooking remaining dumplings. Do not crowd dumpling in saucepan.

4 TO 6 SERVINGS.

Carey Benson, Roswell, GA., has adapted the usual calorie-laden French fries to suit a low-cholesterol diet. Tester Karen Tufte, Minneapolis, MN., praised the results remarking, "This recipe is a winner at our house!"

Lowfat Pommes Frites

5	large baking potatoes, peeled
1½	tablespoons vegetable oil
	Salt to taste
1 to 2	tablespoons grated Parmesan cheese, if desired

Place potatoes in large bowl with cold water to cover; let stand 20 minutes. Heat oven to 425°. Cut potatoes into ¼x¼-inch strips. Rinse in cold water. Dry thoroughly. In large bowl, toss with oil. Arrange in single layer on heavy cookie sheet. Bake 20 minutes; turn potatoes and sprinkle with salt. Bake 10 to 15 minutes longer or until golden. Sprinkle with cheese during last 5 minutes of baking.

6 SERVINGS.

Dinner guests of Minnesota Governor Arne Carlson and his wife, Susan, are delighted when this rich, creamy casserole appears on the menu. In fact, many visitors request the recipe, which was developed by chefs at the Governor's residence.

Potatoes Dauphinoise

5   pounds potatoes, peeled and sliced

2   teaspoons minced fresh garlic

    Salt and pepper to taste

1   quart heavy cream

2   cups (8 ounces) shredded Swiss cheese

Heat oven to 375°. Combine potatoes, garlic, salt and pepper. Layer in large baking dish. Pour cream over potatoes; cover with foil.

(Place baking dish on cookie sheet or large flat pan to avoid any spills.) Bake about 60 minutes. Remove foil; sprinkle with cheese and bake 15 minutes longer or until cheese is melted and brown.

10 TO 12 SERVINGS.

Spinach, Japanese style, sparked with toasted sesame seed and dashi, a fish stock available at Asian markets. Serve chilled, at room temperature or hot — and don't forget the chopsticks.

Spinach with Sesame Seed Dressing

2   tablespoons sesame seed

2   tablespoons dashi or water

1½   tablespoons soy sauce

½   teaspoon sugar

10   ounces fresh spinach

Toast sesame seed in dry skillet over medium-high heat, being careful as the seed burns quickly. When seeds begin to pop, put them into a bowl. Reserve 1 teaspoon seed for garnish; grind remaining seed with a mortar and pestle until smooth. Combine with dashi, soy sauce and sugar; mix thoroughly. In large saucepan, heat enough water to cover spinach to boiling. Place spinach in water; let stand 1 minute. Drain and rinse under cold running water; squeeze firmly. Cut spinach into 1-inch pieces. Just before serving, toss spinach with dressing and sprinkle with reserved sesame seed.

2 TO 3 SERVINGS.

When Peter Randall, Edina, MN., presented this cream-topped creation at a potluck dinner party, he received rave reviews and requests to include it in this recipe collection. Peter, a world traveler and former London resident, is an expert at foreign cookery.

French Alpine Potatoes

POTATOES

8 to 10 medium baking potatoes, peeled and thinly sliced*

¼ cup butter

Salt and white pepper

2 cups (8 ounces) shredded Gruyère or Swiss cheese (reserve ¼ cup for topping)

2 medium onions, thinly sliced

1 cup beef stock or bouillon

CREAM TOPPING

1 egg, slightly beaten

½ cup dairy sour cream

½ cup heavy cream

¼ cup reserved cheese

Place potato slices in saucepan of cold water. Heat to boiling; boil gently 8 minutes. Drain immediately; dry in colander or on towel. Heat oven to 425°. In 13x10-inch lasagna pan, arrange overlapping potato slices in several layers. Dot each layer with butter, sprinkle with salt and pepper, thinly scatter with onion rings and sprinkle with cheese. Heat beef stock almost to boiling, pour over potatoes. Bake about 45 minutes or until tender and light brown. (If potatoes brown too quickly, cover loosely with foil.) Combine all topping ingredients; spread over potatoes. Bake about 5 minutes longer or until golden.

6 TO 8 SERVINGS.

Tip: *For the prettiest results, slice potatoes by hand or with a slicing mandolin, rather than a food processor.*

"Even children will eat spinach prepared this way," reports Mary Richards, Callaway, MN. This protein-rich casserole goes together in minutes once the spinach is thawed and drained.

Serbian Spinach

4   cups small curd cottage cheese

¼   cup margarine, cut into small pieces

4   ounces cubed or shredded (1 cup) Cheddar cheese

2   (10-ounce) packages frozen chopped spinach, thawed, drained

3   eggs, well beaten

3   tablespoons flour

¼   teaspoon salt

¼   teaspoon nutmeg

Heat oven to 350°. Combine all ingredients; spoon into well-greased 3-quart baking dish. Bake about 60 minutes or until set.

6 TO 8 SERVINGS.

Tip: Can be assembled early in the day and baked later.

No need to buy a spätzle maker to make these traditional German mini-dumplings. Barbara Rottman, Dublin, OH., finds that a colander works quite well for this wonderful alternative to potatoes or rice.

Spätzle

1   medium onion, finely chopped

2   tablespoons butter

2   cups all-purpose flour

½   teaspoon salt

2   eggs, slightly beaten

1   cup water

Sauté onion in butter until tender and lightly browned; set aside. In bowl, combine flour and salt. In separate bowl, combine eggs and water; stir into flour and salt, mixing thoroughly. Heat a large kettle of salted water to boiling. Transfer spätzle dough to a large colander. Holding colander over kettle of boiling water, force dough through holes with the back of a wooden spoon. Stir spätzle occasionally as they cook; when they rise to the top of the water they are done. Remove with a slotted spoon and toss with sautéed onion. Serve with green beans, if desired.

4 TO 6 SERVINGS.

Easy, excellent and enticing with almost any entrée. Since cilantro is quite perishable, we suggest using when freshly picked or purchased. Store in the refrigerator with water covering stems and leaves, lightly-covered with plastic wrap.

Fettucini Picante

8	ounces uncooked fettucini
3	tablespoons margarine
⅓	cup picante sauce
⅓	cup grated Parmesan cheese
½	cup dairy sour cream
	Salt to taste
¼ to ½	teaspoon snipped fresh coriander (cilantro)
¼	teaspoon freshly ground black pepper

Cook fettucini in saucepan according to package directions; drain. In same saucepan over low heat, combine margarine, picante sauce and cheese. Cook and stir until margarine melts. Remove from heat; stir in sour cream and salt. Add fettucini; toss. Sprinkle with coriander. Serve with additional picante sauce and pepper, if desired.

4 SERVINGS.

These noodles are richer, more flavorful and less likely to break apart during cooking than the store-bought variety. Tester Danielle Mossner, Janesville, WI., found them "delicious, especially with a cheese sauce."

German Village Noodles

2	cups all-purpose flour
2	eggs, well-beaten
2	tablespoons water
½	teaspoon butter, melted
¼	teaspoon salt

Combine all ingredients in bowl; mix well, using buttered hands, if desired. Divide dough into 6 equal parts. On lightly floured surface, roll out each part as thin as possible; let rest 15 minutes. Cut dough into ribbon noodles, ¼ to ½-inch wide. Spread noodles out to dry. To cook, drop noodles into kettle of boiling water (1 tablespoon salt) and cook 12 minutes. Drain and use as recipe requires.

8 TO 10 OUNCES.

St. Paul food writer Eleanor Ostman, "found this recipe on a 1980 trip to Italy" and has made it "countless times" since. It is rich, satisfying and quickly prepared — perfect for impromptu entertaining and after-work enjoyment. Remember — the cooking time for fresh pasta is considerably less than for dried.

Straw and Hay

16	ounces fresh linguini or egg noodles, half plain, half spinach
1	tablespoon vegetable oil
¼	cup butter
1	clove garlic
8	ounces fresh mushrooms, sliced
1½	cups cooked ham, cut into thin strips
1	cup whipping cream
½	cup half & half
1	cup fresh or frozen peas
⅛	teaspoon freshly grated nutmeg
	White pepper to taste
	Freshly grated Parmesan or Asiago cheese

Cook noodles 4 to 6 minutes in about 4 quarts boiling salted water to which 1 tablespoon oil (flavored with garlic clove, if possible) has been added. Meanwhile, rub large skillet with cut piece of garlic; add butter and melt. Sauté mushrooms in garlic butter until lightly brown. Add ham; stir in cream, half & half and peas. Cook until sauce is reduced about ⅓. Stir in nutmeg and pepper to taste. Add cooked pasta and toss lightly with two forks, sprinkling with cheese while mixing. Serve with additional freshly grated cheese.

4 TO 6 SERVINGS.

This unusual and creative combo appeared in the German Village Cookbook published several years ago. Frozen or fresh cooked beans can be substituted.

Green Beans with Pears and Bacon

6	strips bacon
6	canned pear halves, drained
1	(16-ounce) can cut green beans, drained

Fry bacon in large skillet. While it is frying, slice pear halves. When bacon is done, drain on paper towels; set aside. Keep bacon drippings in skillet. Add beans and pears; cook over medium heat just until heated through. Meanwhile, crumble bacon. When beans and pears are hot, add bacon and stir together. Serve hot from skillet.

4 TO 6 SERVINGS.

BREADS

Bahnhof   The Concordia Language Villages is in the process of building an architecturally authentic mini-world. In 1966, the Language Villages purchased an 800-acre wooded site on the shores of Turtle River Lake, near Bemidji, Minn. Construction of the Norwegian Village began in 1969, followed by the German and French Villages. Finnish Village construction began in 1990 and plans for a Spanish Village are in progress.

   Each building is designed for usability and durability in a style found in the target culture. This building at the German Village is reminiscent of train stations found in the Hessen region of Germany.

Sandwiches   Mealtime is a fun part of the village day. "Villagers" visit in the target language and enjoy the culture's food. These "villagers" sample open-faced sandwiches, a typical Danish lunch.

The recipe for these raisin-studded tea table gems was brought back from England by Gretchen Marple Pracht, Edina, MN. Gretchen has been an avid Language Villages supporter since its inception and has hosted many dinners in her home to stimulate interest in all aspects of the program. Scones traditionally are served with jam, honey and/or thick (clotted) cream.

Marple England Scones

2	cups self-rising flour
¼	cup sugar
¼	cup butter or margarine
1	egg, beaten
	About ¼ cup milk
¼	cup raisins or dried currants

Heat oven to 450°. Combine flour and sugar; cut in butter with pastry blender until mixture is the consistency of coarse meal. Stir in egg. Gradually stir in enough milk to make a soft dough. Stir in raisins. Turn onto lightly floured surface and knead about 4 times. Roll out dough ½ inch thick; cut with 2-inch round cutter. Place on greased cookie sheet. Bake about 10 minutes or until light brown.

12 SCONES.

"We love these with butter and syrup or honey," says Carol Lowell, Burnsville, MN. Tester Nancy Thorson found the spice a delightful addition and says her husband felt they were special enough to serve to their gourmet club.

Welsh Cakes

2	cups all-purpose flour
2	teaspoons baking powder
½	teaspoon salt
½	teaspoon pumpkin pie spice, if desired
6	tablespoons lard or butter
⅓	cup sugar
⅓	cup dried currants or raisins
1	egg, beaten
1 to 2	tablespoons milk
	Butter
	Golden syrup or honey

Combine flour, baking powder, salt and pumpkin pie spice. With pastry blender or 2 knives, cut in lard until mixture resembles coarse meal. Stir in sugar and currants. Stir in egg and milk until mixture forms a firm dough. Roll out dough to ¼ to ½ inch thick. Cut into 3-inch rounds with lightly-floured cookie cutter. Cook on hot greased griddle until golden, 5 to 6 minutes on each side. Serve with butter and golden syrup.

15 TO 18 CAKES.

"This old ancestral recipe is traditionally served on special occasions," notes contributor Helen Spencer, Great Falls, MT. Tester Linda Young, Lincoln, NE., found them "easy to make and delicious."

Scottish Oat Cakes

1	cup shortening
1	cup boiling water
4	cups uncooked rolled oats
2	cups all-purpose flour
¼	cup sugar
2	teaspoons baking powder
1	teaspoon salt
½	teaspoon baking soda

Heat oven to 300°. Combine shortening and boiling water until shortening is melted. Combine remaining ingredients in large bowl. Stir shortening mixture into dry ingredients. On floured surface, with floured rolling pin, roll or pat out about 1 cup of dough at a time. Cut into 3-inch wide strips. Place 3 or 4 strips on each cookie sheet. Bake about 30 minutes or just until light brown. Remove from oven; cut strips into 3x3-inch squares. Cut squares diagonally while still hot. Serve warm with butter and marmalade or jam.

5 DOZEN.

Children love watching this puff to perfection as it bakes. Tester Barb Sommer, Helena, MT., substituted two cake pans for the cast iron skillet and found they worked well.

Suomalainen Pannukakkua

2	eggs
2	tablespoons honey
½	teaspoon salt
½	cup milk
½	cup all-purpose flour
¾	cup milk
2	tablespoons butter
	Syrup, honey or jam

Heat oven to 425°. Put cast iron skillet (at least 3 inches deep) in oven for 10 minutes. In bowl, beat eggs; stir in honey, salt and ½ cup milk. Add flour; mix well. Stir in remaining milk. Melt butter in hot skillet; tilt pan to coat bottom and edges. Pour batter into pan. Bake about 25 minutes or until brown and puffy. Cut into wedges; serve immediately with syrup, honey or jam.

2 TO 3 SERVINGS

234

Mia Morrill, San Francisco, CA., looks forward to a once-a-week meal in the Swedish tradition. "Our family enjoys a simple dinner of pea soup and open-faced sandwiches followed by this recipe. We top the pancake with sour cream and jam made from home-grown Italian plums. At harvest we cook the pitted plums with sugar (60/40 fruit to sugar ratio) and then freeze in small containers."

Oven Pancake

2	tablespoons margarine
1	cup milk
2	eggs
⅔	cup all-purpose flour
1	teaspoon sugar
½ to 1	teaspoon ground cardamom
¼	teaspoon salt
	Dairy sour cream or sour half & half
	Plum jam

Grease bottom and side of 9-inch cast iron skillet with margarine. Place skillet in cold oven and turn on to 400°. Blend milk and eggs well in bowl. Combine flour, sugar, cardamom and salt in separate bowl; add all at once to milk mixture. Blend just until smooth (too much blending makes a tough pancake); pour batter into hot skillet. Bake 30 to 35 minutes or until brown and puffy. Cut into wedges and serve immediately with sour cream and plum jam.

6 SERVINGS.

These golden goodies were made by the Swedish grandmother and mother of Susan Hall, Osakis, MN. She likes them hot or at room temperature, rolled up with butter and sugar inside. Yum!

Swedish Pancakes

6	large eggs
4	cups whole milk
2	cups all-purpose flour
⅓	cup sugar
1	teaspoon salt

Heat griddle and grease if necessary. Combine all ingredients; mix well. For each pancake, pour ½ cup batter onto hot well-greased griddle. For very thin pancakes, spread batter with bottom of metal measuring cup. Turn pancakes when edges are dry and bottom is light brown; cook other side until light brown. Serve with butter and syrup.

16 (8-INCH) PANCAKES.

This oven pancake is a favorite for Sunday brunch serving at the Silver Bay, MN., home of Marlis Runnberg. Easy enough for junior cooks to make and appealing to all ages.

Pannukakkua

¼	cup butter or margarine
2	eggs
¼	cup sugar
½	teaspoon salt
2	cups milk
1	cup minus 2 tablespoons all-purpose flour
	Cinnamon-sugar mixture, if desired
	Blueberry, raspberry or other fruit sauce, if desired

Heat oven to 400°. Place butter in 13x9x2-inch pan; put in oven to melt and slightly brown. Meanwhile, beat eggs with electric mixer until slightly foamy. Add sugar, salt, milk and flour; beat well.* Leaving a generous coating of melted butter in the pan; pour most of it into the flour mixture. Beat well. Pour mixture into hot pan. Bake about 45 minutes or until lightly brown and puffy. Cut and serve warm with cinnamon-sugar mixture or blueberry sauce.

6 TO 8 SERVINGS.

*Tip: *Pancake batter can also be made in a food processor.*

Elsa Carlson, Brainerd, MN., shares a specialty of her great grandma, Sally Passi, who operated a restaurant in Ely, MN. Testers Nina and Renee Jahnke, Homer, AK., delighted in the texture, "The eggs make it bubble like mountains and it takes only 5 minutes to prepare."

Great Grandma's Pannukakkua

½	cup butter
2	cups milk
4	eggs, slightly beaten
2	cups all-purpose flour
2	teaspoons sugar
1	teaspoon salt
2	cups milk
¼	cup butter, melted
	Syrup, jam or fruit

Heat oven to 400°. Put ½ cup butter in 13x9x2-inch pan; put in oven to melt. Keep warm until batter is ready. Meanwhile, add 2 cups milk to eggs. Combine flour, sugar and salt; stir into milk and eggs. Add remaining milk and ¼ cup melted butter. Pour mixture into hot pan. Bake about 40 minutes or until brown and puffy. Serve hot with syrup, jam or fruit.

8 SERVINGS.

Janet Dillenburg, Minnetonka, MN., uses freshly picked Harralson apples for this oven pancake. She serves it for breakfast and brunch and sometimes with sausage for supper. Tester Pat Temple, Naperville, IL., liked it hot or cold and said it was "a hit at a ladies' brunch and with college students."

German Apple Pancake

PANCAKE

3	large eggs
¾	cup milk
¾	cup all-purpose flour
½	teaspoon salt
1½	tablespoons butter

FILLING

1	pound (6 to 8) tart apples, peeled, thinly sliced
¼	cup butter
¼	cup sugar
	Dash of cinnamon
	Dash of nutmeg
	Dash of ginger, if desired

Heat oven to 450°. Beat eggs, milk, flour and salt together until very smooth. In a heavy 12-inch cast iron skillet, melt 1½ tablespoons butter. When quite hot, pour batter into skillet and bake 15 minutes. Reduce oven temperature to 350° and bake about 10 minutes longer or until brown. Sauté apple slices lightly in ¼ cup butter; stir in sugar. Season to taste with cinnamon, nutmeg and ginger. Cook apples over medium heat until tender. Place pancake on platter. Spoon half of filling over half of pancake; fold other half of pancake over it. Spoon on remaining filling. If desired, drizzle with 2 tablespoons melted butter and sprinkle with powdered sugar or top with whipped cream.

4 TO 6 SERVINGS.

A unique texture between biscuit and popover and a subtle cheese flavor make this quick-to-fix recipe a boon to busy cooks. Alan Wax, Evergreen Park, IL., suggests serving biscuits piping hot from the oven.

Biscuits au Fromage

¼ cup grated Parmesan cheese
1 cup milk
2 large eggs
1 cup all-purpose flour
1 tablespoon butter, melted
¼ teaspoon salt

Heat oven to 450°. Grease muffin or custard cups and sprinkle with Parmesan cheese; set aside. Combine milk and eggs; stir in flour, butter and salt just until blended. Fill cups ¾ full. Bake 15 minutes; reduce heat to 350°. Do not open oven door. Bake 20 minutes longer. Carefully loosen popovers with spatula and serve immediately.

10 TO 12 POPOVERS.

"My Grandma Johnson was a wonderful Irish-Norwegian cook and these doughnuts were always a special treat," notes Beth Johnson Holod, St. Paul, MN. Extras freeze beautifully.

Grandma's Doughnuts

Vegetable oil for deep frying
2½ cups all-purpose flour
2 teaspoons baking powder
1 teaspoon baking soda
½ teaspoon salt
1 cup sugar
1 cup buttermilk
1 cup hot mashed potatoes
5 tablespoons melted shortening
2 eggs
1 teaspoon vanilla

Heat 2 to 3 inches of oil to 370° in deep fryer or heavy saucepan. Combine flour, baking powder, soda and salt. In separate bowl, combine sugar and buttermilk. Stir in potatoes and shortening; beat until smooth. Add eggs and vanilla; beat thoroughly. Add dry ingredients; beat until blended. On lightly-floured surface, roll out dough, ⅓ at a time to ⅓ inch thickness. Cut with lightly-floured doughnut cutter. Fry each doughnut about 2 minutes on each side. (Be sure to use a deep-frying thermometer.) Drain on paper towels.

30 DOUGHNUTS.

Tip: Recipe can easily be halved.

Sonja Lambach Pavlik, Glendale, WI., combines two favorite German ingredients, potatoes and poppy seed for a "hearty muffin to serve with butter spreads, honey or jam." Great use of left-over mashed potatoes and crumbled day-old bread.

Poppy Seed-Potato Muffins

1	cup vegetable oil
3	eggs
2	cups sugar
2	cups mashed potatoes
1	tablespoon vanilla
2½	cups all-purpose flour*
1	teaspoon salt
2	teaspoons baking soda
½	cup poppy seed

Heat oven to 350°. Line 24 muffin cups with paper baking cups. Combine oil, eggs, sugar, potatoes and vanilla in large bowl. Combine remaining ingredients in separate bowl; stir into potato mixture just until blended. Spoon batter into muffin cups. Bake about 30 minutes or until golden brown.

24 MUFFINS.

*Tip: *One cup dry bread crumbs can be substituted for 1 cup of the flour.*

Another family favorite from Illinois Senator Paul Simon. Tester Mary Theresa Downing, Minneapolis, MN., rated them "excellent" for taste and high fiber content.

Honey Bran Muffins

1	cup boiling water
1	cup raisins or chopped dates
2½	teaspoons baking soda
1	cup sugar or 1½ cups honey
2¾	cups all-purpose flour
½	teaspoon salt
2	eggs
3 to	4 cups hard spring wheat bran or other bran
2	cups buttermilk*
1	teaspoon baking powder
½	cup sunflower or vegetable oil

Pour boiling water over raisins; stir in soda and let cool. Heat oven to 375°. Grease bottoms only of 24 muffin cups or line with paper baking cups. Combine remaining ingredients; stir in raisin mixture just until blended. Spoon into muffin cups. Bake 20 to 25 minutes.

24 MUFFINS.

*Tip: *Two tablespoons lemon juice or vinegar plus milk to equal 2 cups can be substituted for 2 cups buttermilk.*

Now you can make these bakery best sellers in your own kitchen, thanks to Barbara Marick, Bloomington, MN. The distinctive blue-gray poppy seeds, popular in the cuisine of many countries from India to Germany, were first cultivated in fields bordering the Mediterranean.

Lemon-Poppy Seed Muffins

2	cups all-purpose flour
1	tablespoon poppy seed
½	teaspoon baking soda
½	teaspoon salt
1	cup sugar
½	cup unsalted butter, softened
2	eggs
1	teaspoon vanilla
1	teaspoon finely-grated lemon peel
1	cup lemon yogurt

Heat oven to 350°. Line 18 muffin cups with paper baking cups or grease bottoms only. Combine flour, poppy seed, soda and salt; set aside. Beat sugar and butter together until fluffy; mix with eggs, vanilla and lemon peel. Add yogurt alternately with flour mixture, mixing just until ingredients are moistened. Fill muffin cups ⅔ full. Sprinkle with sugar, if desired. Bake about 20 minutes or until golden.

18 MUFFINS.

Variations — Blueberry: Omit poppy seed; gently stir in about 1 cup fresh or thawed, drained, frozen blueberries. Raspberry: Omit poppy seed; gently stir in about 1 cup fresh or frozen whole raspberries. Use raspberry yogurt and sprinkle tops of muffins with cinnamon-sugar.

A rousing "Olé" for this moist variation of the dryer, crumbly type of corn bread. Terrific teamed with chile, taco salad and barbecued entrées.

Mexican Corn Bread

1½	cups yellow cornmeal
1¼	cups buttermilk
¼	cup vegetable oil
1	large egg, beaten
1	small onion, diced
½	cup cream-style corn
6	ounces (1½ cups) shredded Cheddar cheese
¼	cup canned, diced mild chiles

Heat oven to 400°. Combine all ingredients; mix well. Pour into greased 8x8x2-inch pan. Bake about 45 minutes or until toothpick inserted in center comes out clean.

9 TO 12 SERVINGS.

"Much better than the store-bought variety," comments Helen Hill, Osseo, MN. Rusks are unique in that they are twice baked, once in loaf form and then in slices. Good for dunking, by the way.

Orange Rusks

1	cup sugar
½	cup plus 2 tablespoons shortening
2	eggs
½	teaspoon vanilla
2¼	cups all-purpose flour
½	teaspoon cream of tartar
½	teaspoon baking soda
⅛	teaspoon salt
	Grated peel of 1 orange
1	tablespoon orange juice

Heat oven to 350°. Combine all ingredients. Shape into loaf and place in greased 8x4½ or 9x5-inch loaf pan. Bake 45 to 60 minutes or until top of loaf is light brown. Remove from pan and cool 15 to 20 minutes. Reduce oven temperature to 325°. Cut loaf into ½-inch slices. Place on ungreased cookie sheets, cut side down. Bake 20 to 30 minutes or until light golden brown on bottom side. Turn slices over; bake 10 to 15 minutes longer. Cool. Store in airtight container.

15 TO 20 SERVINGS.

Lois Haukebo Swenson, Bismarck, ND., totes these to family reunions and says, "they keep forever in tins." If you prefer a more savory taste, use less sugar.

Roseau County Crackers

4	cups crushed wheat flake cereal
4	cups all-purpose flour
4	cups rolled oats
1	cup sugar
2	teaspoons salt
1½	cups shortening, butter or margarine or combination
1½	cups warm water
2	teaspoons baking soda

Heat oven to 350°. Combine cereal, flour, oats, sugar and salt in large bowl. With pastry blender or 2 knives, cut in shortening. Combine water and baking soda; stir into dry mixture until thoroughly combined. On lightly-floured surface, roll out dough into large rounds (as for flat bread or pie crust) to cracker thinness. Transfer to cookie sheets. Bake about 10 minutes. Cool and break or cut into crackers.*

20 LARGE CRACKERS.

*Tip: *Dough can be cut into small squares before baking and baked as crackers or cookies.*

241

R. Naomi Dahl, Borup, MN., recalls her parents making this together on an old wood-burning kitchen range. Carrying on the tradition, Naomi makes batch after batch to share with friends across the country during the holidays. Allow ample time for chilling step.

Lefse

6	cups riced or mashed russet potatoes
1	teaspoon salt
3	tablespoons margarine or butter
1	tablespoon sugar
2	tablespoons heavy cream or evaporated milk
1½	cups all-purpose flour

Combine all ingredients except flour; refrigerate until thoroughly chilled. Add flour; mix well. Heat lefse or other griddle to 400°. Form dough into long roll and cut into 12 sections. Form each section into a small ball. Roll out very thin with cloth-covered lefse or regular rolling pin on cloth-covered lefse board or other surface. Dust board with flour when turning lefse dough. Bake on ungreased griddle until brown spots appear. Turn and bake other side. Stack lefse between 2 towels to cool. Store in refrigerator in plastic bags; can be frozen.

12 LEFSE.

Chris Mounts, Goddard, KS., recalls his brothers debating whether they wanted pancakes or waffles. His parents settled the discussion by using an electric grill/waffle iron with the grill on the bottom and waffle iron on top. The result? Pan-affles, of course, with an enticing nutty flavor from whole wheat flour.

Pan-affles

¾	cup all-purpose flour
¼	cup whole wheat flour
1	teaspoon baking powder
½	teaspoon baking soda
¼	teaspoon salt
3	tablespoons vegetable oil
1	egg
½	teaspoon vanilla
¾	to 1 cup buttermilk

Heat waffle iron. Blend dry ingredients in a medium bowl. Add remaining ingredients and blend with electric mixer on medium speed until smooth. Grease griddle if necessary. Pour batter into center of griddle. Bake until steaming stops; remove carefully.

4 WAFFLES.

Fruit filling is the center of attention in each square of buttery dough. This recipe comes from a cookbook compiled by students at a Jordan, MN., elementary school.

Bohemian Squares

4	eggs, separated
1	cup plus 2 tablespoons butter, softened
1½	cups granulated sugar
2	cups all-purpose flour
1	tablespoon lemon juice
1	cup cherry or blueberry pie filling
	Powdered sugar

Heat oven to 350°. Beat egg whites until stiff. Cream butter and sugar; gradually stir in egg yolks and flour. Stir in lemon juice and egg whites. Pat dough out on 15x10-inch cookie sheet. Score dough into 3-inch squares. Drop 1 teaspoonful of pie filling onto center of each square. Bake about 45 minutes. Cool. Sift powdered sugar lightly over the top; cut into squares.

ABOUT 15 SQUARES.

Cindy Kryda, Marshfield, WI., learned to make this Czechoslovakian pastry from her father-in-law. Allow ample chilling time for dough and roll quickly while it remains cool and easy to handle.

Kolaches

1	cup butter, softened
1	(8-ounce) package cream cheese, softened
1	tablespoon milk
1	tablespoon sugar
1	egg yolk, beaten
1½	cup all-purpose flour
½	teaspoon baking powder
	Cherry, raspberry, apricot and/or prune filling

Cream butter, cream cheese, milk and sugar. Stir in egg yolk. Combine flour and baking powder; blend into creamed mixture. Cover and refrigerate until dough is thoroughly chilled, at least 4 hours. Heat oven to 400°. Roll or pat out dough on well-floured surface to ¼-inch thickness. Cut into 2-inch rounds with cookie cutter. Place on ungreased cookie sheet and make a depression with thumb or spoon in center of each round. Fill centers with scant teaspoon of filling. Bake 10 to 15 minutes or until light brown. Sprinkle with powdered sugar before serving.

4 DOZEN.

Susan Thompson, Alexandria, MN., obtained this recipe from a Belgian-born cousin. For serving a crowd, she suggests having several griddles going as she did when entertaining a hundred hungry relatives at a family reunion brunch. Whew!

Belgian Waffles

4½ cups all-purpose flour
3⅓ cups lukewarm milk
6 eggs, separated
4 packages active dry yeast
¼ cup lukewarm milk
1 tablespoon sugar
⅞ cup (14 tablespoons) butter, melted

Place flour in very large bowl; make a well in center. Stir in 3⅓ cups milk, then egg yolks. Combine yeast, ¼ cup milk and sugar; stir until yeast is dissolved. In separate bowl, beat egg whites until stiff peaks form. Stir butter and yeast mixture into flour mixture. Fold in egg whites. Let batter rise 45 minutes. (It rises quickly and will be the consistency of pancake batter.) Heat Belgian waffle iron. Spread batter evenly on iron. Bake until steaming stops.

Serve waffles sprinkled with superfine sugar and eaten as finger-food.

Or, top with fresh fruit and whipped cream, chopped pecans and maple syrup, canned pie fillings and whipped cream, or jam.

25 SERVINGS.

This traditional southwestern recipe is one students clamor for at classes offered by the Santa Fe School of Cooking. Heather Randall King brought it home to Edina, MN. Sopapillas are as versatile as they are delicious. Large ones can be stuffed like pita bread; smaller sizes can be used to scoop up rich tangy sauces. Or, they can be served with honey or dusted with a cinnamon-sugar mixture and served for dessert.

Sopapillas

1   cup all-purpose flour
½   teaspoon salt
¾   teaspoon baking powder
¾   tablespoon sugar
½   tablespoon shortening
½   cup milk or ¼ cup milk and ¼ cup heavy cream
    Vegetable oil for deep frying

Combine flour, salt, baking powder and sugar. Cut in shortening with pastry blender or 2 knives until mixture resembles coarse meal. Slowly add milk, working flour with your fingers until it forms a moist dough. Cover dough and let rest for at least 30 minutes. Heat 1 to 2 inches of oil in deep fryer or saucepan to 400°. Divide dough in half; roll into rectangle, trimming edges. Cut into 3x3-inch squares or triangles. Fry in deep fat 30 to 40 seconds, turning sopapillas as they cook until golden brown. Drain on paper towels. Serve hot with honey, if desired.

10 TO 12 SOPAPILLAS.

Ann Lynch, Minneapolis, MN., adapted this recipe from Gunhild Andersson, Delsbo, Sweden. "Gunhild appreciated her history and taught me much about old-time life in rural Sweden. This bread is cooked on top of the stove or over a campfire."

Gunhild's Coal Hoppers

½   cup plain yogurt
½   cup water
⅓   cup light corn syrup
2   cups all-purpose flour
1   cup rye flour
1   teaspoon baking soda
½   teaspoon salt
½   teaspoon anise seed
½   teaspoon fennel seed

Combine yogurt, water and corn syrup in medium bowl. Add remaining ingredients and mix well. Knead a few turns. Divide dough into small balls; roll out on lightly-floured surface. Then roll with textured (kruskavel) rolling pin, if available. Cook in ungreased cast iron skillet over medium heat until light brown. Serve with butter and cheese or gjetost, if desired.

6 TO 10 SERVINGS.

Mary Richards, Callaway, MN., serves this to resort guests at Maplelag and reaps compliments every time. Serve piping hot for best flavor.

Native American Fry Bread

Vegetable oil for deep frying

4 cups all-purpose flour

2 tablespoons baking powder

1 to 2 teaspoons salt

2 tablespoons instant nonfat dry milk

1½ cups warm water

Heat 2 to 3 inches of oil to 375° in deep fryer or heavy saucepan. Combine flour, baking powder, salt and dry milk in bowl. Add warm water and mix with your hands (or dough hook on mixer) until dough is soft. Knead 1 minute on lightly-floured surface. Roll out to about ¼ inch thickness. Cut into 2-inch squares with knife or pizza cutter.

Fry each square until light brown; turn and fry other side. Drain on paper towels.

10 PIECES.

When Christine Schulze, Director of the Language Villages, began counselling at the French Village, she often led the cooking activity. "This is a favorite recipe of the villagers. It's easy and kids enjoy being involved in the process. Crêpes are a traditional meal from the province of Bretagne. My favorite filling is beurre sucre — a little butter and sprinkle of sugar," she adds.

Christine's Crêpes

3 eggs

2 cups all-purpose flour

2 cups milk

2 tablespoons vegetable oil

2 teaspoons vanilla

2 tablespoons sugar

Sugar, jam or chocolate sauce

In large mixing bowl, add one egg at a time to flour, mixing well with whisk. Add milk and mix thoroughly until batter is very smooth. Stir in oil and vanilla; stir in sugar. Oil small skillet with paper towel. Heat until a few drops of water sizzle when sprinkled on pan. Pour a bit of batter onto pan; tilt to cover bottom of pan. Cook crêpe until it begins to brown; turn to cook other side.

To serve, spread crêpes with sugar, jam or chocolate sauce; fold in half and then in half again.

20 CRÊPES.

Orene Docken, Decorah, IA., prepares and chills the dough the night before her grandchildren arrive, knowing this hand-me-down treat is one of their favorite recipes. She suggests shaping all strips on baking sheets at the same time before proceeding to the baking step.

Norwegian Kringle

1	cup buttermilk
1	teaspoon baking soda
½	cup margarine, softened
1	cup sugar
1	egg
1	teaspoon vanilla
3	all-purpose flour
2½	teaspoons baking powder
½	teaspoon salt

Combine buttermilk and soda; set aside. Cream margarine and sugar. Blend in egg and vanilla. Combine flour, baking powder and salt. Add flour mixture and buttermilk alternately to creamed mixture, blending well. Cover bowl; refrigerate 8 hours or overnight.

Heat oven to 425°. On lightly-floured cloth-covered surface, lightly knead dough. Divide into thirds. With hands, roll ⅓ of dough into 15-inch rope. Keep remaining dough refrigerated. Cut rope into 1 to 1½-inch pieces. With hands, roll each piece into pencil-thin strip; shape into figure 8. Place on ungreased cookie sheet. Repeat with remaining pieces. Bake 5 to 6 minutes or until light brown. Cool slightly. Store in tightly-covered container while still warm to keep soft.

3½ TO 4 DOZEN.

Tip: To freeze, place in tightly-covered container. Before serving, thaw and warm briefly in a warm oven.

Head cook, Therese Hennemann, suggests these as "a traditional accompaniment for Swedish yellow pea soup or served as a main dish with a savory filling instead of jam." They are as versatile as they are quick and easy to prepare.

Sjölunden Pancakes

3	eggs
1½	cups milk
1½	cups all-purpose flour
	Dash of salt
1½	cups milk
3	tablespoons shortening or vegetable oil
	Lingonberry jam
	Sugar

In large bowl, beat eggs with wire whisk; add 1½ cups milk and continue beating until blended. Add flour and salt and continue beating to form a smooth batter. Add 1½ cups milk and continue beating until blended. Melt shortening in large crêpe pan; pour into batter, stirring constantly to keep lumps from forming. Batter should be very thin. Pour sufficient batter into hot, lightly greased pan to cover bottom, tilting pan so batter runs slightly up side. Cook over medium-high heat until batter is set. Use spatula to flip pancake, being careful to avoid breaking. Fry second side until golden brown.

Place 1 tablespoon lingonberry jam in center of each pancake; spread over entire surface with back of spoon. Catch side of pancake with fork tines to roll up. Sprinkle lightly with sugar.

3 TO 4 SERVINGS.

Doris Engdahl, Minneapolis, MN., serves these with jam, sugar or syrup as a breakfast or luncheon pastry. Testers Helen Grant and Emily Pye, Minneapolis, MN., suggest eating while still warm the way their families "really liked them." Traditionally, aebleskivers were made in cast iron pans and turned with a knitting needle.

Aebleskiver

3	eggs, separated
2	cups buttermilk
2	teaspoons sugar
½	teaspoon salt
2	cups all-purpose flour
1	tablespoon baking powder
1	teaspoon baking soda

Heat aebleskiver pan. Put 1 teaspoon oil in each hole and fill ¾ full of batter. Cook until slightly crusty on bottom. Add 1 tablespoon applesauce to each hole and top with batter. Turn with pick or fork and cook until brown to form round pastry. Serve with applesauce, jam, sugar or syrup, if desired.

6 SERVINGS.

Patricia Anderson, Montevideo, MN., combines white and whole wheat flour in this version of the popular Scandinavian flat bread. "This is always served at my parents' home at Christmas," says Patricia. She, however, makes it year around because "it is slightly sweet and kids love it as an after-school snack."

Knäckebröd

¾	cup sugar
3½	cups all-purpose flour
2	cups whole wheat flour
2	teaspoons baking powder
1	teaspoon salt
¾	cup vegetable oil
1	teaspoon baking soda
2	cups buttermilk

Heat oven to 300°. Blend sugar, flours, baking powder and salt; cut in oil with pastry blender or 2 knives. Dissolve soda in buttermilk; stir gently into flour mixture until smooth. Do not overbeat. Form into balls about 1½ inches in diameter. On surface lightly-floured with whole wheat flour, roll out like pie crust into desired shapes, about ⅛ inch thick. Prick with a fork or use a notched or patterned rolling pin. Place on lightly-greased cookie sheets. Bake 10 to 12 minutes. Cool. Store in tightly-covered container. Freezes well.

ABOUT 50 ROUNDS.

"My grandma makes these when we visit her at Christmas and other special occasions. My mother is now learning how and she says I'm next," says Conni Ellyn Sloth, Belmond, IA. "They taste like a pancake or doughnut and we enjoy them warm or cold." The Sloths like them so much they keep the dry ingredients ready-mixed for quick access.

Grandma's Aebleskivers

8	eggs, separated
4	cups all-purpose flour
6	tablespoons sugar
8	teaspoons baking powder
1¼	teaspoons salt
2	cups milk
1½	cups cream or half & half

Grease aebleskiver pan with 1½ teaspoon oil. In large bowl, beat egg whites until stiff peaks form. In separate bowl, beat egg yolks; blend in remaining ingredients. Fold egg whites into batter. Heat aebleskiver pan over medium heat. Pour batter into cups, filling ⅔ full. Cook until surface is bubbly and underside is light brown. Turn carefully with fork, skewer or knitting needle. Serve with sugar, syrup, jam or jelly, if desired.

ABOUT 4 DOZEN.

Annie Johnson, Montreal, Canada, perpetuates family tradition by preparing this every Christmas just as she did in her aunt's kitchen while growing up. She advises hiding it from **snitchers** *until serving time or there won't be any left! If you're making it ahead, store in an airtight container where it will keep well for several days.*

Holiday Flatbrød

2	cups boiling water
2	cups cornmeal
¼	cup margarine
¼	cup sugar
1	teaspoon salt
1	cup whole wheat flour

Pour water over cornmeal; add margarine and mix thoroughly but do not over-mix. Cool. Add remaining ingredients, using just enough whole wheat flour to make easy-to-handle dough. Pull off 1-inch ball for each flatbread; roll out as thin as possible. Gently place on ungreased griddle. Bake until edges just start to curl; turn and bake other side. Stack on platter and keep warm in oven. Keeps nicely in airtight container for many days.

2 DOZEN FLAT BREADS.

If you love freshly-baked bread but have little time for making the yeast version, try this savory selection. So easy and so tasty served warm with all manner of ethnic entrées, particularly Italian dishes and paella. Cheese content means leftovers must be stored in the refrigerator; do not freeze.

Cheese-Onion Flat Bread

2	cups self-rising flour
2	tablespoons sugar
1¼	cups hot water
¾	cup (3 ounces) shredded Swiss cheese
3	tablespoons grated Parmesan cheese
½	cup chopped green onions
½	teaspoon dried oregano leaves
2	tablespoons toasted sesame seed, if desired

Heat oven to 350°. Combine all ingredients in large mixer bowl; beat about 1 minute until batter is blended. Place 2 tablespoons vegetable oil in 9-inch round nonstick pan. Spread batter evenly in pan, bringing batter to within ½ inch of edge of pan. Brush top of batter with the little oil that collects on the sides. Bake 40 to 45 minutes or until top is golden brown. Brush with butter. Cool in pan; cut bread with serrated knife. Serve with sweet butter, if desired.

6 SERVINGS.

Tips: Bread should be stored in refrigerator if prepared one day before serving. Do not freeze.

"These loaves won't last long," advises tester, Joy Brown, Blaine, MN. For variety, bread can be flavored with grated orange peel, anise or caraway seed.

Danish Light Rye Bread

1	package active dry yeast
1	tablespoon sugar
4¼	cups warm water (105 to 115°)
½	cup shortening, melted
½ to ¾	cup molasses
½	cup packed brown sugar
4	cups rye flour
8½	cups all-purpose flour

Combine yeast, sugar and ¼ cup of the water; stir until dissolved. Add yeast mixture to remaining warm water in large bowl. Stir in remaining ingredients, using enough all-purpose flour to make a soft dough; mix well. Place in greased bowl; turn greased-side-up. Cover and let rise in warm place (80 to 85°) until double.

Punch down dough. Divide into four parts; shape each into a loaf. Place in greased bread pans; cover and let rise until almost double. Heat oven to 375°. Bake about 1 hour or until loaves sound hollow when lightly tapped.

4 LOAVES.

Former Vice President Walter F. Mondale, Minneapolis, shares his mother's special roll recipe. "Mother, who usually made a six-loaf batch of bread at a time, would pinch off a chunk of the basic dough after the first rising. While waiting for the loaves to rise again, she prepared these delicious cinnamon rolls."

Granny Mondale's Cinnamon Rolls

1	(1-loaf) recipe for white yeast bread
2	eggs, beaten
¼	cup sugar
	Butter or margarine, softened
1	cup sugar-cinnamon mixture

In bowl, combine yeast bread dough with eggs and ¼ cup sugar. On floured surface, knead until smooth, 5 to 10 minutes. Roll or pat dough into rectangle about 10x12 to 16-inches. Spread evenly with butter; sprinkle with sugar-cinnamon mixture. Roll up dough, pinching edges together. Cut into 1-inch slices. Place rolls in 12 to 16 greased muffin cups. Cover and let rise until double. Heat oven to 425°. Bake 15 to 18 minutes.

12 TO 16 ROLLS.

*Linda Poets, Lakeville, MN., usually doubles this recipe "because they go so fast."
Leftovers can be frozen, then warmed before serving.*

Mormor's Cardamom Bread

1	package active dry yeast
¼	cup warm water (105 to 115°)
½	cup butter or margarine
1½	cups milk
¼	cup sugar
½	teaspoon salt
1 to	1½ teaspoons crushed cardamom seed
6	cups all-purpose flour
6	tablespoons butter or margarine, softened
1	cup orange marmalade
1	egg, beaten
1	tablespoon pearl or granulated sugar

In large bowl, dissolve yeast in warm water. Melt butter in small saucepan; stir in milk. Pour lukewarm mixture into yeast. Stir in sugar, salt and cardamom. Gradually stir in flour until dough is well blended. Turn dough onto lightly-floured surface; knead until smooth and elastic, about 8 minutes. Place in large greased bowl; turn greased-side-up. Let rise until light and double, about 2 hours.

Punch down dough. Divide in half. Roll one half into a 12x8-inch rectangle; spread with half of the butter and half of the marmalade. Roll up jelly-roll fashion and cut into 1-inch slices. Put each slice in a greased muffin cup or all slices in greased 12x7-inch baking pan. Repeat with remaining dough, butter and marmalade. Brush each roll with egg and sprinkle with sugar. Let rise until almost double. Heat oven to 350°. Bake about 25 minutes.

2 DOZEN.

Variation — Cinnamon Filling: Combine ½ cup sugar and 1½ teaspoons cinnamon; substitute for marmalade.

This rave-winner comes from the Norwegian Government School for Domestic Science Teachers. Linda Erceg of the Villages staff serves it with brats, cheeses and robust winter soups and keeps extra loaves on hand in the freezer. Multiple testers praised the "fabulous crust and exceptional flavor."

Vørterkake

2   packages active dry yeast
1¼ cups warm milk (105 to 115°)
4   cups all-purpose flour
4   cups rye flour
⅔   cup lukewarm corn syrup
¾   cups vørterøl (dark beer)
½   cup sugar
1   tablespoon salt
¾   teaspoon ground cloves
¾   teaspoon freshly-ground pepper
½   cup raisins

In large bowl, dissolve yeast in milk. Add 2 cups all-purpose flour and stir to make soft dough. Let sit in warm place (80 to 85°) until dough begins to rise. Combine syrup, vørterøl, sugar, salt, cloves and pepper; add to flour mixture. Stir in rye flour, then remaining all-purpose flour, 1 cup at a time until dough becomes supple, but firm enough to hold its shape. (This step is crucial; too firm a dough results in not enough rise; too soft results in a non-stable loaf.) Cover; place in warm draft-free spot and let rise until double.

Punch down dough; turn out onto lightly-floured surface. Fold in raisins and knead a few moments. Divide dough in half; form into 2 round loaves. Place on buttered and floured cookie sheet; cover and let rise until double. Heat oven to 375°. Brush loaves with hot water and prick rather lightly. Bake about 45 minutes or until crust becomes quite shiny and loaves sound hollow when lightly tapped. Cool. Cut into thin slices; serve with butter, marmalade or jam, if desired. Keep refrigerated until served.

2 LOAVES.

Jenna Schieffer, Madison, WI., developed a knack for making bread while living in Switzerland as a foreign exchange student. This is her favorite "because it's easy to make and fun to shape."

Swiss Braid

6 to	7 cups all-purpose flour
2	teaspoons salt
6½	tablespoons margarine, melted
2⅓	cups warm milk (105 to 115°)
3½	tablespoons active dry yeast
⅓	cup warm water (105 to 115°)
1	egg, beaten, or water

Combine flour and salt in large bowl. Combine margarine and milk. Dissolve yeast in warm water; add to milk mixture. Stir into flour mixture; mix well. Turn out onto lightly-floured surface; knead. Let dough rest until double, about 1 hour.

Punch down dough and knead again. Divide dough in half. Roll each half into a long strip; place strips crosswise, one over the other. Turn the 2 strips over each other 4 times. Place on cookie sheet; let rest for 10 minutes. Heat oven to 425°. Brush top and sides of braid with egg for a smooth shine or with water for a crisper crust. Bake on lowest oven rack for 15 to 20 minutes. Reduce heat to 350° and bake about 30 minutes longer.

1 BRAID.

Tip: *One-half cup all-purpose flour can be replaced with ½ cup wheat bran or wheat germ.*

Staffer David Erceg shares his grandmother's recipe which has evolved into a favorite of Villagers "no matter what the language." His wife, Linda, has spied "nine-year-olds devouring three slices at breakfast!"

Grandma Love's Oatmeal Bread

4	cups boiling water
3	cups rolled oats
½	cup packed brown sugar
¼	cup shortening
4	teaspoons salt
2	packages active dry yeast
¼	cup warm water (105 to 115°)
5 to 6	cups unbleached or all-purpose flour

Pour boiling water over oats; cover and let steam 10 minutes. Stir in brown sugar, shortening and salt; let cool to lukewarm. Dissolve yeast in warm water. When oat mixture is lukewarm, stir in yeast, then flour to make a fairly stiff dough. Turn out onto lightly floured surface; knead until elastic, about 10 minutes. Place dough in greased bowl; turn greased-side-up. Cover with damp cloth, let rise in warm place (80 to 85°) until double.

Punch down dough. Divide into 4 equal parts, shape into 4 loaves. Place in greased 9x5x3-inch pans. Let rise until almost double. Heat oven to 350°. Bake 45 to 50 minutes or until loaves sound hollow when lightly tapped.

4 LOAVES.

This *"delicious, popular breakfast bread"* from the French Village recipe files is sumptuous with marmalade or other high-quality preserves. The name is derived from the French word *"bris"*, which means *"to break"* and from *"hacher"*, or to stir. Begin preparation the night before or several hours ahead of baking.

French Village Brioche

1	package active dry yeast
¼	cup warm water (105 to 115°)
½	cup butter, softened
⅓	cup sugar
½	teaspoon salt
½	cup milk, scalded, cooled
3¼	cups all-purpose flour
3	eggs, beaten
1	egg, separated
1	tablespoon sugar

Dissolve yeast in water. Thoroughly cream butter, ⅓ cup sugar and salt. Add milk and 1 cup of the flour; stir together. Add yeast, 3 eggs and egg yolk; beat very well. Add remaining flour and beat 5 to 8 minutes longer. Cover and let rise until double, about 2 hours. Stir down and beat well. Cover with foil and refrigerate 8 hours or overnight. Stir down dough; turn out onto lightly floured surface. Divide dough into 4 equal parts; set one part aside. Cut remaining three pieces in half and form each piece into 4 balls (24 in all). Place balls in well-greased muffin cups. Poke a hole in the top of each ball. Cut reserved dough into 4 wedges; divide each wedge into 6 smaller pieces. Shape each into a small ball and place one on top of each ball in muffin cups. Cover and let rise until double, about 1 hour. Heat oven to 350°. Combine 1 egg white and 1 tablespoon sugar; brush on tops of brioche. Bake about 15 minutes. Serve warm.

2 DOZEN.

From Nancy English, Duluth, MN., comes this holiday hand-me-down from her mother, Kathryn English. "Mother always explained that this is the "real" way Norwegians make this because it contains citron instead of candied fruit."

Jule Kage

2	cups milk, scalded
1	cup sugar
2	teaspoons salt
1	cup butter, melted
2	packages active dry yeast
½	cup warm water (105 to 115°)
8 to 9	cups all-purpose flour
1	cup raisins
½	cup chopped citron
½	cup candied cherries
½	cup chopped almonds
2	eggs, well beaten
1	teaspoon ground cardamom seed

Combine milk, sugar, salt and butter; cool to lukewarm (105 to 115°). Dissolve yeast in lukewarm water; add to milk mixture. Beat in 4 cups flour. Cover and let rise until double. Stir in fruit, nuts, eggs and cardamom; beat well. Stir in remaining flour, reserving ½ cup to flour kneading surface; knead until smooth and elastic. Return dough to greased bowl; turn greased-side-up. Cover and let rise until double.

Punch down dough; form into 3 round loaves. Place on greased cookie sheets. Let rise about 20 minutes or until light. Heat oven to 375°. Bake 35 to 40 minutes or until golden brown and loaves sound hollow when lightly tapped. Remove from cookie sheet. Cool on wire rack.

3 LOAVES.

Ellen Markuson, Minnetonka, MN., cherishes this recipe from a French great-grandmother. It was served with great success at a Girl Scout International Day. Tester Dennis Johnson, Morris, MN., rated it **excellent** *for easy preparation and appearance.*

French Bread

1	package active dry yeast
1½	cups warm water (105 to 115°)
1	tablespoon sugar
1½	teaspoons salt
1	tablespoon shortening
4	cups all-purpose flour

Dissolve yeast in ½ cup of the water. In large bowl, dissolve sugar and salt in remaining water. Add shortening and yeast mixture; mix well. Add flour, a little at a time. Cover bowl and set aside. Stir every 10 minutes, 5 times.* On lightly-floured surface, form into 2 long loaves; place on greased cookie sheet. With knife, make a few diagonal slashes in tops of loaves. Let rise in warm place until light and double.

Heat oven to 400°. Bake 30 to 35 minutes or until brown and crust sounds hollow when lightly tapped. Remove from cookie sheet. Cool on wire rack.

2 LOAVES.

*Tip: *If dough is mixed in food processor, let dough rise in food processor and push button briefly every 10 minutes for 1 hour.*

"This is the classic loaf for both French and Spanish Villages," reports staffer Linda Erceg. "Pay attention to the steaming process because it forms the great outer crispy crust and promotes a moist, soft center," she advises. Leftovers (if there are any) can be made into French toast or garlic crisps.

Baguette

2	packages active dry yeast
2½	cups warm water (105 to 115°)
6	cups unbleached or all-purpose flour
2	teaspoons salt
	Yellow cornmeal
1	egg white

In large bowl, sprinkle yeast over water; stir to dissolve and let stand until foamy. Stir 3 cups of the flour into proofed yeast. Beat until smooth; continue beating vigorously 10 minutes. Beat in salt and as much of the remaining flour as possible. Turn out onto lightly-floured surface. Knead 8 to 10 minutes, adding flour when necessary to reduce stickiness. Form into smooth ball. Place dough in large oiled bowl; turn oiled-side-up. Cover with plastic wrap; let rise in warm place (80 to 85°) at least 2 hours.

Punch down dough, knead 3 to 5 minutes; cover with plastic wrap and let rise until 3 times original size.

Punch down dough, knead briefly and divide in half. Cover with cloth towel and let rest 5 to 10 minutes. Grease large cookie sheet and sprinkle with cornmeal. Form each half of dough into desired shape. Place on prepared cookie sheet; cover and let rise until double.

Twenty minutes before baking, place large shallow pan on lowest shelf of oven; turn on oven to 450° for 15 minutes. Pour 1 to 2 cups cool water into heated pan to produce steam. With razor, slash risen loaves according to shape. Beat egg white and 1 tablespoon water together; brush evenly on loaves. Place cookie sheet containing loaves on center shelf of oven; bake 15 minutes without opening oven door. Remove pan of water from oven and mist loaves with water. Bake an additional 15 minutes, misting bread several times, until crust is golden brown. Remove loaves from cookie sheet and return to oven until bottom has browned. Cool on wire rack.

2 LOAVES.

Senator Paul Simon of Illinois, well known for his support of language education and a strong supporter of the Language Villages, shares this hearty yeast bread recipe. Cottage cheese contributes to a moist, inviting texture and honey provides sweetness.

Honey Whole Grain Bread

3	cups all-purpose flour
2	packages active dry yeast
1½	teaspoons salt
1	cup water
1	cup cottage cheese
¼	cup butter or margarine
½	cup honey
2	eggs
2½	cups whole wheat flour
½	cup rolled oats
⅔	cup chopped walnuts or pecans

In large bowl, combine 2 cups all-purpose flour with yeast and salt. Heat water, cottage cheese, butter and honey until very warm (120 to 130°). Add warm liquid and eggs to flour mixture; mix well. Stir in whole wheat flour, oats and nuts. Stir in remaining all-purpose flour (add more if necessary). Knead on lightly-floured surface until smooth and elastic. Let rise in warm place until double.

Punch down dough; divide into 2 parts. Shape each into a loaf and place in greased 9x5x3-inch pans. Let rise about 1 hour. Heat oven to 350°. Bake 35 to 40 minutes. Remove from pans. Cool on wire rack. Brush tops with butter.

2 LOAVES.

This classic Jewish Sabbath bread comes from Sue Reider, Cedar Rapids, IA. Eggs add richness to the dough and the traditionally braided loaves make an attractive presentation.

Challah

2	packages active dry yeast
2	tablespoons sugar
½	cup warm water (105 to 115°)
12	cups all-purpose flour
½	cup sugar
2	tablespoons salt
4	cups warm water
6	eggs
⅔	cup vegetable oil

Combine yeast, 2 tablespoons sugar and ½ cup water. Combine flour, ½ cup sugar and salt. Put half of flour mixture into large bowl; make a well in center; add yeast mixture and 2 cups warm water. Beat eggs and oil together; add to batter and mix well. Stir in remaining water. Stir in remaining flour mixture; mix well. Knead on lightly-floured surface 8 to 10 minutes. Place dough in greased bowl; turn greased-side-up. Let rise in warm place until double.

Punch down dough. Divide dough in half; divide each half into 3 pieces. Form each piece into 15 to 18-inch rope; place 3 ropes on greased cookie sheet and loosely braid. Pinch ends together; tuck under to seal. Cover; let rise in warm place 30 to 40 minutes or until almost double. Heat oven to 350°. Bake 50 to 60 minutes or until golden brown and loaves sound hollow when lightly tapped. Remove from cookie sheets. Cool on wire racks.

2 LOAVES.

Tip: Large braids can also be baked in greased 9x5x3-inch loaf pans. For smaller braids, divide dough into 5 pieces; divide and form each piece into 3 to make braid. Continue as directed above. Bake small braids 35 to 45 minutes.

Sylvia Fust Hansen, Hillsboro, ND., prizes this recipe from a German-Russian neighbor. Tester Nancy Witt, New York Mills, MN., reports, "My family loved it!"

Frieda's Kuchen

SWEET ROLL DOUGH

1	cake compressed yeast
1	teaspoon sugar
¼	cup warm water
1	cup milk
½	cup shortening (lard, butter or margarine or combination)
½	cup sugar
½	teaspoon salt
3	eggs, beaten
4 to 4½	cups all-purpose flour

FILLING

3	cups cut-up fruit (apples, rhubarb, prunes, apricots, peaches, etc.)
5	eggs, beaten
1¼	cups sugar
1	teaspoon vanilla
1¼	cups cream

TOPPING

1	cup all-purpose flour
1	cup sugar
½	cup butter or margarine
	Cinnamon-sugar mixture

Dissolve yeast and 1 teaspoon sugar in warm water. Heat milk to 105 to 115°. Combine yeast mixture, shortening, ½ cup sugar and salt with milk in large bowl; stir until shortening is melted. Add 3 eggs and 2 cups flour; beat well. Stir in 2 to 2½ cups additional flour until dough pulls away from side of bowl. Let rise in warm place (80 to 85°) until almost double.

Meanwhile, prepare fruit; set aside. In separate bowl, combine remaining filling ingredients; set aside. In separate bowl, combine 1 cup flour, 1 cup sugar and ½ cup butter; set aside. When dough has risen, divide into 6 parts; form into balls. Let rise 10 minutes. Heat oven to 350°. Roll out one ball; pat into 8-inch pie plate. Push up edge on side of plate; prick very well with fork to remove air bubbles. Spread about ½ cup fruit in dough-lined pan; pour ½ cup filling over fruit. Sprinkle topping over filling (sprinkle a little around the edges of the kuchen to keep the filling from getting under the dough). Sprinkle with cinnamon-sugar. Repeat with remaining dough, filling and topping. Bake about 20 minutes or until brown and filling is set.

6 COFFEE CAKES.

Tip: Kuchens freeze well; reheat to serve.

For Jane and Sarah Hollinshead, Rehoboth, MA., "The aroma of these buns rising and baking is a sure sign of Christmas." They feast on this recipe from their Swedish great-grandmother while opening their stockings Christmas morning. Although cardamom can be purchased in powdered form, the freshly-ground seed, available at co-ops, is much preferred.

Swedish Cardamom Buns

4	cups milk
1	cup butter or margarine
1½	cups sugar
12	cardamom seeds, pods removed
1	package active dry yeast
10 to 12	cups all-purpose flour
1¼	cups raisins, if desired
2	egg whites, beaten

Heat milk, butter and sugar over medium-high heat, stirring occasionally, until butter is melted and milk just comes to a boil. Cool to 105 to 115°. Crush cardamom seeds with small mortar and pestle; stir into cooling liquid. Pour into large bowl. Add yeast; stir until dissolved. Stir in flour, 1 cup at a time, until soft dough forms. Stir in raisins. Turn dough out onto lightly floured surface. Let rest 10 minutes. Knead until smooth and elastic, about 5 minutes. Place dough in greased bowl; turn greased-side-up. Cover loosely with cloth towel or waxed paper. Let rise in warm place (80 to 85°) until double (several hours).

Punch down dough. Heat oven to 350°. Divide dough into 36 to 48 pieces; form pieces into ropes; coil into buns. Place buns on nonstick cookie sheets. Cover with waxed paper and let rise until nearly double. Brush with egg whites. Bake about 20 minutes.

3 TO 4 DOZEN.

"These taste wonderful and are good with or without butter," says Dorothea Ofstedal, Williston, ND. *The creative young sons of tester Bonnie Eng, Dassel, MN., added a Mexican accent by using them as* **dippers** *with pizza sauce.*

Swedish Knäkebrod

½   cup margarine
2   cups warm milk (105 to 115°)
1   package active dry yeast
½   cup sugar
5½ to 6 cups all-purpose flour*

Melt margarine in milk. Stir in yeast and sugar to dissolve. Stir in enough flour to make a stiff dough. Knead about 5 minutes on lightly floured surface. Place in greased bowl; turn greased-side-up. Let rise in warm place (80 to 85°) until double. Cut into golf ball-size pieces. Place on ungreased cookie sheets and let rise again. Heat oven to 400°. Cut each ball in half and roll out as thinly as possible with rolling pin on lightly floured surface. Bake on heavy ungreased pan 5 to 6 minutes. Do not turn. Store at room temperature.

70 TO 90 PIECES.

Tip: *Whole wheat flour can be substituted for 1 cup of the all-purpose flour.*

A mouth-watering alternative to blueberry muffins. "This recipe reminds me of Swedish summers when blueberries are plentiful in the pine forests. They make a marvelous breakfast treat and the sweet dough is typically Swedish," says contributor Ann Lynch, Minneapolis. Testers Candace and Courtney Moser, North Oaks, MN., suggest trying other fruits as well, like raspberries and apples.

Fresh Blueberry Cakes

1	cup milk
2	tablespoons butter or margarine
3½	cups all-purpose flour
⅓	cup sugar
1	package active dry yeast
1	pint (or more) fresh blueberries
	Sugar
1	egg, beaten

Heat milk and margarine to 115 to 120° in saucepan. Combine flour, ⅓ cup sugar and yeast; stir in milk mixture until dough forms. Knead on lightly-floured surface. Cover and let rise in warm place (80 to 85°) about 30 minutes. Knead again. Divide into 2 pieces; divide each half into 3 pieces. Roll out each piece into a circle. Place circles of dough on lightly-greased cookie sheets. Place berries on each circle and roll an edge around each cake with fingers. Sprinkle with sugar. Let rise about 30 minutes. Heat oven to 375°. Brush cakes with beaten egg. Bake 15 to 20 minutes.

6 CAKES.

Karen Tufte, Minneapolis, MN., explains that in pre-Christian times, buns with the cross motif represented the four seasons. Later, the marking evolved into an Easter symbol. Karen makes these during Holy Week to serve at family breakfasts. Tester Pamela Kelsey, Bemidji, MN., describes them in one choice word — "Delicious!"

Hot Cross Buns

BUNS

3½ to 4 cups all-purpose or unbleached
    flour

2   packages active dry yeast

1   teaspoon cinnamon

¾   cup milk

½   cup vegetable oil

⅓   cup granulated sugar

¾   teaspoon salt

3   eggs

⅔   cup dried currants

1   egg white, slightly beaten

FROSTING

1½ cups powdered sugar

¼   teaspoon vanilla

    milk

In a mixing bowl, combine 2 cups flour, yeast and cinnamon. In a saucepan, heat milk, oil, sugar and salt until warm (115 to 120°); add to dry ingredients. Add eggs and beat at low speed of electric mixer 1½ minutes. Scrape sides and beat again 3 minutes at high speed. By hand, stir in currants and enough of remaining flour to make a soft dough. Shape dough into a ball. Place in a greased bowl; turn greased-side-up. Cover; let rise in warm place (80 to 85°) until double, 1½ hours. Punch down dough. Cover and let rise 10 minutes. Divide dough into 18 pieces; form into balls. Place on lightly-greased cookie sheet, 1½ inches apart. Cover; let rise until double, about 30 minutes. Heat oven to 375°. Brush buns with egg white (save remaining egg white for frosting, if desired). Bake buns 12 to 15 minutes. Combine powdered sugar, vanilla, remaining egg white, if desired, and enough milk for piping consistency. Cool on wire racks. With a pastry tube, pipe a cross on top of each bun.

18 BUNS.

Dorothea Ofstedal likes to "keep alive Norwegian customs" by baking these traditional rolls each Shrove Tuesday. Tester Lee English, St. Paul, MN., prepared them in only 30 minutes and reports "just great results!"

Fastelavensboller

¼	cup butter or margarine
½	cup sugar
½	teaspoon salt
1	cup milk, scalded, cooled to warm
1	package active dry yeast
¼	cup warm water (105 to 115°)
1	egg, beaten
¾	teaspoon (or more) crushed cardamom
4	cups all-purpose flour
½	cup dried currants
1	egg, beaten

Stir butter, sugar and salt into warm milk. Dissolve yeast in water; stir into butter mixture. Stir in egg, cardamom and flour; mix well. Stir in currants; knead well on lightly-floured surface. Cover and let rise in warm place (80 to 85°) about 1 hour. Punch down dough. Cut dough into 12 pieces; shape into round balls and place on greased cookie sheets about 1 inch apart. Let rise again. Heat oven to 350°. Brush tops of rolls with egg. Bake about 20 minutes.

12 ROLLS.

This Finnish Village favorite was tested by Helen Hill, Osseo, MN., who suggests cutting bread into diamond-shaped pieces and serving with butter and strawberry jam.

Oatmeal Flat Bread

2	cups boiling water
4	cups rolled oats
2	packages active dry yeast
½	cup warm water (105 to 115°)
½	cup sugar
2	tablespoons shortening
1	tablespoon salt
4½	cups all-purpose flour

Pour boiling water over oats; let mixture cool to lukewarm. Dissolve yeast in warm water. Stir sugar, shortening, salt and yeast mixture into oat mixture. Add just enough flour to make a soft dough. Let rise in warm place (80 to 85°) until double. Turn onto well-greased cookie sheet and pat out to cover cookie sheet. Let rest 10 minutes. Heat oven to 350°. Bake about 30 minutes.

A sugar-cinnamon mixture crowns this Mexican sweet bread. Dough can be made the night before serving, covered and refrigerated. Just let rise, shape and bake in the morning. Pop leftovers in the freezer to enjoy another day.

Pan Dulce

BREAD

1	package active dry yeast
¾	cup warm water (105 to 115°)
3½	cups all-purpose flour
¾	cup sugar
¾	teaspoon salt
¼	cup butter, melted
3	eggs, beaten

TOPPING

1	cup sugar
1	cup all-purpose flour
½	cup butter melted
1	egg, beaten
1½	teaspoons cinnamon
¼	teaspoon salt

Dissolve yeast in water. Combine flour, sugar and salt in large bowl. Add yeast mixture, butter and eggs; beat until smooth. Put dough in greased bowl; turn greased-side-up. Cover and let rise until double, about 1 hour. Combine all topping ingredients in separate bowl; mix well. Set aside. Turn dough out onto lightly-floured surface; knead until smooth and elastic, about 5 minutes. Shape dough into 1½-inch balls. Place on greased cookie sheet about 2 inches apart; press each to flatten slightly. Place about 1½ tablespoons topping on each roll. Let rise until double, about 30 minutes. Heat oven to 375°. Bake about 15 minutes. Serve warm.

18 ROLLS.

Tip: Freezes well; thaw and reheat at 400° for 5 minutes

Norwegian Villagers look forward to sampling these butter-basted loaves with a slightly sweet flavor. Wonderful warm from the oven, toasted or as a base for open-faced sandwiches.

Grøv Brød

1	package active dry yeast
¼	cup warm water (105 to 115°)
½	cup molasses
½	cup sugar
1	tablespoon salt
3¾	cups water
½	cup shortening, melted
6	cups all-purpose or unbleached flour
2	cups whole wheat or graham flour

Dissolve yeast in ¼ cup water; let stand 15 minutes to begin to "work." Add molasses, sugar, salt, shortening and remaining 3¾ cups water. Add enough all-purpose flour to make a soft sponge; beat 10 minutes. Stir in whole wheat flour and enough of the remaining all-purpose flour to make a fairly stiff dough. Turn dough out onto lightly-floured surface; knead 5 to 8 minutes. Place in greased bowl; turn greased-side-up. Let rise in warm place (80 to 85°) until double. Knead dough again and let rise. Divide dough into 4 equal parts. Shape into loaves; place in greased 8x4-inch pans and let rise until light. Heat oven to 350°. Bake about 40 minutes or until loaves are brown and sound hollow when lightly tapped. Brush tops with melted butter, if desired.

4 (1½-POUND) LOAVES.

*Cooking for a crowd? Delight your guests with this big-batch recipe for Finnish bread.
Cardamom, a favorite Scandinavian ingredient, is native to India and highly aromatic.
Vary amount used to suit personal preference.*

Pulla

1¼   cups sugar
2   eggs
1½   teaspoons ground cardamom
2½   teaspoons salt
2½   cups warm milk (105 to 115°)
½   cup butter, melted
2½   packages active dry yeast
¼   cup warm water
      About 8 cups all-purpose flour
½   cup butter, softened
      Beaten egg
      Sugar

Combine 1¼ cups sugar and 2 eggs; beat well. Stir in cardamom, salt, milk and melted butter; mix well. Dissolve yeast in water; stir into sugar mixture. Gradually add flour, stirring until well mixed and a soft dough forms. By hand, knead in softened butter until dough comes away from bottom of bowl. Cover and let rise in warm place (80 to 85°) until double.* Punch down dough, divide dough into 4 parts. Divide each part into 3 pieces; roll into long 1-inch wide rolls. Braid 3 strips; place in greased 13x9x2-inch pan. Let rise until dough comes to top of pan. Heat oven to 375°. Brush braids with beaten egg and sprinkle with sugar. Bake 15 minutes; reduce oven temperature to 350° and bake 15 minutes longer or until golden brown. Cool in pan a few minutes; turn out and cool on wire rack.

4 BRAIDS.

*Tip: *If room is cold, place pan of hot
      water in oven with rising dough.*

Swedish bread bakers, of which there are legions, are famous for several types of rye bread. Most loaves are studded with grated orange peel, anise and/or caraway seed. Helen Hill, Osseo, MN., favors this recipe from a long-time friend that features both caraway and anise flavors.

Swedish Rye Bread

2	cups water
½	cup packed brown sugar
1	tablespoon shortening
1	teaspoon salt
1	teaspoon caraway seed
1	teaspoon anise seed
1	cake compressed yeast
3½	cups all-purpose flour
2	cups rye flour
	Butter

Heat water, brown sugar, shortening, salt, caraway seed and anise seed to boiling; reduce heat and simmer 3 minutes. Cool to lukewarm. Add crumbled yeast cake and stir until softened. Stir in all-purpose flour until well mixed. Cover and let rise in warm place (80 to 85°) about 1½ hours. Stir in rye flour to make a stiff dough. Knead on lightly-floured surface. Place in greased bowl; turn greased-side-up. Cover and let rise until double.

Punch down dough; divide in half. Cover and let rise 10 to 15 minutes. Shape into 2 loaves. Place in greased bread pans. Cover and let rise until double. Heat oven to 375°. Bake 35 to 40 minutes or until brown and loaves sound hollow when lightly tapped. Brush tops of loaves with butter.

2 LOAVES.

"Our Grandmother Bird acquired this recipe as a newlywed living in southwestern Wisconsin among the 'Badgers' — Cornish mining families who settled here for the lead mining," explains Ellen Ochs, Menomonie, WI. "Grandmother wrote that in the early 20s this recipe required half of a 35-cent package of Spanish saffron which she obtained at the drugstore." Ellen adds, "You certainly can't buy much saffron for that price now!"

Cornish Saffron Buns

1	rounded teaspoon saffron threads
½	cup boiling water
1	package active dry yeast
½	cup warm water (105 to 115°)
¼	cup shortening
½	cup sugar
1	egg
½	cup golden raisins
½	cup dark raisins
½	cup candied fruit
½	teaspoon salt
3½	cups all-purpose flour

Steep saffron in boiling water several hours or overnight. In large bowl, dissolve yeast in warm water. Stir shortening, sugar and egg together. Stir in yeast and saffron mixture; stir in raisins and candied fruit. Stir in half of the flour; knead in as much of remaining flour as needed to make dough easy to handle. Knead on lightly-floured surface until smooth and elastic. Place in greased bowl; turn greased-side-up. Cover and let rise until double.

Punch down dough; divide in half. Divide each half into 8 pieces and shape into buns. Place on greased cookie sheet. Let rise until double. Heat oven to 375°. Bake until golden brown, about 15 minutes.

16 BUNS.

NOTES

SWEETS

St. Lucia   Young people attending the Language Villages celebrate the traditional holidays of their particular village's culture. St. Lucia Day is celebrated at the Swedish Village where, as in Sweden, the oldest girl wakes the village with the St. Lucia song.

So-called because they contain cereal and certainly could be eaten as a breakfast on the run, these drop cookies are a specialty at the Minneapolis home of sisters Laura and Alaine Tufte. The recipe was devised by their creative mother to entice her daughters to enjoy that important first meal of the day.

Peanut Butter Breakfast Cookies

¾	cup butter or margarine, softened
⅔	cup peanut butter
⅔	cup packed brown sugar
2	eggs
1	teaspoon vanilla
1¾	cups all-purpose flour
1	teaspoon baking soda
¼	teaspoon salt
3	cups Life cereal

Heat oven to 350°. Beat butter, peanut butter and sugar until fluffy. Blend in eggs and vanilla. Combine flour, salt and baking soda. Add to creamed mixture; blend well. Stir in cereal. Drop by heaping tablespoonfuls onto ungreased cookie sheets. Bake 10 to 12 minutes.

3 DOZEN.

Members of First Lutheran Church, Hector, MN., look forward to this sweet treat baked every year by Mary Broderius for the annual Scandinavian smörgåsbord. Of course, she saves some at home, too, for family and friends during the holidays.

Sändbäkkels

1	cup shortening (half butter)
1	cup sugar
1	egg
1	teaspoon almond extract
2½	cups all-purpose flour

Cream shortening; add sugar and cream well. Stir in egg and almond extract. Stir in flour to make a stiff dough. Refrigerate dough for easier handling. Heat oven to 375°. Pinch off a small ball of dough; place in center of sandbakkel tin and with thumb, press dough evenly to thinly cover inside of tin. Place filled tins on cookie sheet. Bake about 15 minutes, watching closely. Cool before removing from tins. To remove from tin, invert and tap gently with a knife.

4 TO 5 DOZEN.

"This was my great-grandmother's recipe which my grandmother, mother and I traditionally make together," says Jeanne Bruder, Winona, MN. "They freeze well and we particularly enjoy them with fresh fruit and whipped cream." Tester Linda Austin, Greensburg, PA., felt results were well worth preparation time. "These are very tasty. My daughter's sixth grade class absolutely loved them!"

Swedish Sändbäkkels

2	cups butter (not margarine or shortening)
2	cups sugar
1	egg, room temperature
1	teaspoon almond extract
	About 5 cups all-purpose flour

Heat oven to 350°. Cream butter and sugar until light and fluffy. Add egg and almond extract; continue beating. Add just enough flour to make a stiff dough; work in with hands on flat surface. Press small balls of dough into sändbäkkel tins as thinly as possible. Bake 5 to 10 minutes or until golden around edge. Watch carefully. Cool slightly; carefully remove from molds. To remove, invert and tap lightly on bottom of tin. Store in tightly covered container.

ABOUT 75 COOKIES.

Tip: Bake a test cookie to determine exact baking time.

Also called "Mexican Wedding Cakes", "These are very popular among the globally-minded young people at Sjölunden." Watch carefully toward end of baking so they don't get too brown on the bottom.

Russian Tea Cakes

1	cup butter or margarine, softened
½	cup powdered sugar
1	teaspoon vanilla
2¾	cups all-purpose flour
¼	teaspoon salt
¾	cup finely-chopped blanched almonds
	Powdered sugar

Heat oven to 400°. Cream butter, ½ cup powdered sugar and vanilla. Add flour, salt and almonds; mix until dough holds together. Shape dough into balls and place on ungreased cookie sheets. Bake 10 to 12 minutes or until set but not brown. Roll in powdered sugar while still warm. Cool; roll in sugar again.

4 DOZEN.

Barbara Francis, Blytheville, AR., remembers her grandmother bringing these cookies every time she came to visit. She suggests a chilling step for the dough so it passes easily through the press. For variety, substitute almond extract for vanilla.

Grandmother's Spritz

1	cup butter or margarine, softened
1	cup sugar
1	egg yolk
1	teaspoon vanilla
2	cups all-purpose flour
	Dash of baking soda

Cream butter and sugar in bowl; stir in egg yolk and vanilla. Combine flour and baking soda; add to creamed mixture, a little at a time, until well mixed. Cover dough and refrigerate about 2 hours or until firm. Heat oven to 350°. Fill cookie press with dough; form desired shapes on ungreased cookie sheets. Bake 10 to 12 minutes.

2 TO 3 DOZEN.

Simple ingredients; sophisticated shaping from special ribbed tins. These delicate French tea cookies are often served with light desserts like sorbets or fruit and frequent elegant European tea tables.

Madeleines

1	cup all-purpose flour
¼	teaspoon salt
4	eggs
2	teaspoons vanilla
2	teaspoons grated lemon peel
⅔	cup sugar
½	cup butter, melted, cooled
	Powdered sugar

Heat oven to 325°. Butter and lightly flour madeleine tins or mini muffin pans. Combine flour and salt. Beat eggs with vanilla and lemon peel until light and lemon colored. Add sugar gradually and continue beating until thick and fluffy. Fold in flour mixture, then butter. Spoon into pans, filling ¾ full. (One-fourth inch deep in muffin pans.) Bake about 15 minutes. Let cool 3 to 5 minutes; remove from tins, shell side up, and cool on wire racks. Sprinkle with powdered sugar just before serving.

4½ DOZEN.

This version, rich with sour cream and buttermilk, comes from the great-great-grandmother of Brett Skaugstad, Iowa City, IA. "Her family still lives on the same farm in Ullensvang, Norway, and I look forward to visiting there some day," says Brett. In the meantime, she enjoys preparing this, her "favorite Norwegian cookie."

Overnight Kringla

2	cups sugar
1½	cups dairy sour cream
1	cup buttermilk
2	eggs
1	teaspoon vanilla
5 to	6 cups all-purpose flour
2	teaspoons baking powder
1	teaspoon baking soda
½	teaspoon salt

Combine sugar and sour cream. Blend in buttermilk, eggs and vanilla. Combine flour, baking powder, baking soda and salt; stir into sugar mixture. Cover and refrigerate several hours or overnight. Heat oven to 400°. On lightly-floured surface, roll out heaping tablespoonfuls of dough into thick pencil-sized rolls; shape into figure "8s." Place on lightly-greased cookie sheets. Bake 6 to 8 minutes or until very light brown.

4 TO 5 DOZEN.

"This Norwegian delicacy, pronounced 'kringlah', was brought to this country by my mother one hundred years ago," explains Cora Stahn, Sauk Rapids, MN. Cora makes them year around and stores them in a tightly-sealed container. "The tricky part," she confides, "is adding just the right amount of flour so the dough is easy to handle — not sticky."

Kringler

½	cup butter or margarine, softened
1½	cups sugar
2	eggs
1	cup buttermilk
1	teaspoon baking soda
5 to	6 cups all-purpose flour

Heat oven to 350°. Cream butter and sugar. Beat in eggs and buttermilk. Combine baking soda and flour; mix 5 cups into butter mixture. Add more if necessary to make a dough that is not sticky. Shape into "logs" about 2 inches in diameter. Cut into ½ to 1-inch thick slices. With hands, roll each slice on flat surface into "pencil" shape. Form into pretzel shapes. Bake on lightly-greased cookie sheets.

5 TO 6 DOZEN.

Alma Shurb, Madison, MN., says with delight, "Everyone likes these!" This would be a fun holiday project to do with a friend or family member. Make plenty and use for gifting. Be sure to roll cookies as soon as they are removed from the iron.

Krumkake

2	eggs
1	cup sugar
1½	cups all-purpose flour
¼	teaspoon salt
1	cup whole milk
½	cup butter, melted
	Vanilla, if desired

Beat eggs; stir in sugar. Combine flour and salt; add alternately with milk to egg mixture, mixing well. Stir in vanilla and melted butter. Heat krumkake iron. Bake 1 soup spoon per kake on hot iron. Turn iron often and roll at once on cone. Cool. Store in tightly covered container.

5 DOZEN.

Allow two hours to chill the dough after combining ingredients in the food processor. Monica Cummings, Long Beach, CA., serves these to her appreciative French class. Tester Kathy Borge, Fargo, ND., found them "very easy to make with good flavor."

French Butter Cookies

1	cup all-purpose flour
½	cup sugar
½	cup butter, cut into 6 pieces
1	egg yolk
1	teaspoon vanilla

In food processor, process flour, sugar and butter until butter is cut into mixture, about 15 seconds. Put egg yolk and vanilla in small dish. With processor running, add through feed tube. Stop processor when dough gathers in a ball, 15 to 20 seconds if butter was soft, 1 to 2 minutes if firm. Place ball of dough on waxed paper. Form into a log 2 inches in diameter, 5 inches long. Roll waxed paper around the log and refrigerate until firm, about 2 hours.

Heat oven to 350°. Cut log in half lengthwise; then slice into ⅛-inch half circles. (For chewier cookies, cut circles about ½-inch thick.) Place on ungreased cookie sheet about ¾ inch apart. Bake about 8 minutes.

ABOUT 3 DOZEN.

"This recipe came from my beloved Norwegian grandmother and evokes wonderful memories from my childhood," says Alma Jean Satran, Golden Valley, MN. "It remains a favorite any time of year with my own family and friends."

Grandma Sandbo's Krumkake

3	eggs
1	cup sugar
½	cup unsalted margarine, melted
½	cup whipping cream
½	teaspoon nutmeg
2	cups all-purpose flour

Beat eggs until very light. Stir in sugar, margarine, whipping cream and nutmeg. Slowly add flour, blending thoroughly with hand beater. Heat krumkake iron. Test batter for easy handling. Place 1 teaspoon of batter on hot iron and bake until light brown, turning iron once. Remove and quickly roll into cone shape. Serve plain or filled with whipped cream and topped with lingonberries.

4 DOZEN.

"This recipe, which has been in my family since about 1850, is a great favorite for kids to make," comments Ingrid Lenz Harrison, Wayzata, MN. Long-time supporters of the Language Village program, the Harrisons highlight these cookies as part of their holiday tradition. Remember to allow an hour for chilling the dough.

German Butter Cookies

3¼	cups all-purpose flour
1	cup sugar
1	cup butter, softened
	Grated peel of 1 lemon
	Dash of salt
2	eggs
3	egg yolks
	Colored sugar or sliced almonds
1	egg white
1	tablespoon water

Tip: Cookie dough can also be mixed in a bowl.

Sift flour directly onto table; make well in center. Pour a little sugar into well, remaining onto the sides. Cut butter into small pieces and place on top of sugar. Add lemon peel and salt. Break eggs and yolks into center. Work with hands, from outside into center. Knead until everything holds together well. Form into ball; refrigerate 1 hour.

Heat oven to 375°. Roll dough to ⅛-inch thickness. Cut cookies; place on lightly-greased cookie sheets. Combine egg white and water; brush on cookies. Sprinkle with colored sugar or almonds. Bake in center of oven about 7 minutes.

4½ TO 5 DOZEN.

"This cookie is part of our family Christmas tradition. All the adult women and some of the children get together and make dozens and dozens of Norwegian cookies for the family and for gifting," says Sandra Hall, Crystal Lake, IL. Although Sandra's grandmother could roll the dough paper thin, Sandra agrees that isn't especially easy and suggests just rolling as thinly as you can for easy transference to cookie sheets.

Havre Kage

3   cups quick-cooking rolled oats

3   cups all-purpose flour

2   cups sugar

     Dash of salt

1   cup butter or margarine

1   cup dairy sour cream

1   teaspoon baking soda

Heat oven to 325°. Combine oats, flour, sugar and salt. Cut in butter as for pie crust. Combine sour cream and soda. Add to crumbly mixture and knead by hand. Dough will feel dry; if too dry add more sour cream. Roll out dough thinly; sprinkle with sugar. Cut into squares or rectangles about 2x2-inches. Place on nonstick or lightly-greased cookie sheets. Bake about 5 minutes.

ABOUT 8 DOZEN.

Jenny McBride, mother of four grown children and grandmother of seven, has had plenty of cookie-making experience. This is one of her favorite recipes which she frequently shares with fortunate neighbors in Wisconsin and Florida. Although you can use standard cookie cutters, Jenny makes them mini-size using canapé cutters.

Scottish Fans

1   cup butter, softened

¾   cup packed brown sugar

2¼ to 2½ cups all-purpose flour

2¼   teaspoons salt

Heat oven to 300°. Cream butter and brown sugar. Stir in 2¼ cups flour and salt. Work dough with hands until well combined. Add more flour if dough is sticky. Roll out or pat dough to ½-inch thickness on lightly-floured surface. Cut with small cookie cutters and place on cookie sheet. (Cookies will not spread.) Bake 30 to 35 minutes until set but not brown.

3 TO 5 DOZEN.

Myrtle Swanson, formerly of Edina, MN., was known for her annual holiday boutique where she offered home-baked goodies and crafts she had fashioned just for the occasion. Neighborhood children would stand three deep waiting to sample these moist no-bake cookies and mothers were most appreciative that Myrtle was willing to share the recipe.

Frying Pan Cookies

1½   cups cut-up dates
1   cup sugar
2   eggs, well beaten
2   tablespoons butter
¼   teaspoon salt
2   cups crispy rice cereal
½   cup chopped pecans
1   teaspoon vanilla
      Shredded coconut

Combine dates, sugar, eggs, butter and salt in large skillet. Cook over low heat until dates are very soft, 15 to 20 minutes, stirring constantly. Remove from heat. Stir in cereal, pecans and vanilla. When cool enough to handle, form into small balls and roll in coconut to cover completely.

ABOUT 4 DOZEN.

For the holidays, Valentine's Day or anytime, try this buttery shortbread recipe. Refrigerating the dough for several hours before rolling makes it easy to handle. Watch carefully during baking so they do not brown beyond the traditional pale golden color.

Scottish Shortbread Hearts

1½   cups butter, softened
1   cup powdered sugar
1   teaspoon vanilla
3   cups all-purpose flour
½   teaspoon salt
      Red colored sugar

Cream butter, powdered sugar and vanilla until light and fluffy. Stir in flour and salt only until blended. Gather dough into 4 balls; cover and refrigerate 1 to 2 hours. Heat oven to 325°. Roll one ball of dough at a time to ⅜-inch thickness on lightly-floured surface. Cut with 2 to 2½-inch heart-shaped cookie cutter. Place on ungreased cookie sheet. Sprinkle with red sugar. Bake about 15 minutes or until cookies barely begin to color but not to brown. Remove to wire rack to cool.

ABOUT 2½ DOZEN.

Tip: Try other cookie cutter shapes and other colored sugars.

Ellie Steffensen, Omaha, NE., remembers her grandmother making this recipe in Denmark and it has been a family favorite ever since. Tester Paulette Malecek, Bloomington, MN., who found preparation easy and results excellent, shared them at a neighborhood picnic. "I expected to have some leftovers for my family, but all were gone in a matter of minutes."

Danish Currant Cookies

1	cup butter, softened
1	cup sugar
2	extra large eggs
2	cups all-purpose flour
½	teaspoon cream of tartar or ½ teaspoon ammonium carbonate (Bakers ammonia)
1	teaspoon lemon extract
	Grated peel of 1 lemon
1	cup blanched, drained dried currants
½	cup sugar

Heat oven to 350°. In large mixing bowl at high speed, cream butter and 1 cup sugar thoroughly. Add eggs one at a time. Stir in flour, cream of tartar, lemon extract and grated peel. Divide dough in half; spread each half in a thin layer on greased 15x10-inch pan. Sprinkle half of currants on each pan; sprinkle each pan with ¼ cup sugar. Pat down lightly with spatula. Bake 12 to 15 minutes or until light brown. Cut into squares immediately after removing from oven. Cool in pan.

8 TO 9 DOZEN.

No shaping required. Just press rich, buttery dough in a pan, bake and cut into bars. "These make a delicious holiday treat and can be made ahead and frozen," says contributor Rebecca Hotvedt, East Grand Forks, MN.

Danish Cinnamon Bars

1	egg
3	cups all-purpose flour
1	cup packed brown sugar
2	tablespoons cinnamon
1¼	cups butter or margarine, melted
2	teaspoons vanilla
	Granulated sugar

Heat oven to 350°. Beat egg; add remaining ingredients except granulated sugar and mix well. (Use your hands if necessary.) Press dough into ungreased 13x9x2-inch pan. Sprinkle granulated sugar evenly over bars. Bake 15 to 20 minutes. Cool slightly; cut into bars. Cool completely; remove from pan and store in airtight container.

20 TO 24 BARS.

"Fantastic with coffee, tea or brandy and well worth the trouble to make," says Miriam Rocke, Davis, CA. "This recipe was given to my great-great-great grandmother in 1885 when she visited her old home in Bergen, Norway. Since then it has been a family tradition to make these for Christmas." Miriam suggests storing for a week or two before serving for better flavor.

Norwegian Fattigmands Bakkelse

10	eggs
2	egg yolks
10	tablespoons very thick whipping cream
13	tablespoons sugar
¼	teaspoon cinnamon
1	teaspoon freshly-ground cardamom
6 to	10 tablespoons French or apricot brandy
8 to	10 cups all-purpose flour
½	cup butter, melted
4	pounds lard for deep frying (or vegetable oil)

Beat eggs, yolks, cream and sugar together about 30 minutes. Stir in cinnamon, cardamom and brandy, to taste. Stir in part of the flour and butter. Stir in and knead in enough flour to make dough smooth and elastic like bread dough. Place in bowl; cover with cloth towel. Refrigerate several hours or overnight.

Divide dough into 8 or more pieces. On lightly-floured surface, roll one piece at a time as thinly as possible. With sharp knife or pizza cutter cut dough into long thin triangles, about 3 to 6 inches long. Make a slash near the point of the triangle and tuck the point through the slash. Roll out all bakkels before frying as they brown quickly.

In heavy Dutch oven, melt lard or heat oil to 370 to 375°. Place bakkels in hot fat. When one side browns and they come to the top, turn and fry until golden brown, being careful not to let them get too dark. (They continue to brown after being removed from hot lard, so allow for that.) Drain on paper towels. Store lightly covered.

10 TO 12 DOZEN.

Melanie Ann Bruder, Winona, MN., received this recipe from her Swedish grandmother who was a home economics teacher. The Bruders carry on the tasty tradition by making it during the holidays. A special treat for all ages with steaming hot chocolate, coffee or tea on a winter day.

Fattigmands

6 egg yolks
¼ cup sugar
⅛ teaspoon salt
6 tablespoons cream
1 tablespoon butter, melted
⅛ teaspoon freshly-ground cardamom
About 1½ cups all-purpose flour
Vegetable oil for deep frying

Beat egg yolks until thick and lemon colored. Beat in sugar, 1 tablespoon at a time. Stir in remaining ingredients with a spoon. Refrigerate about 1 hour. Heat oil to 360 to 380° in deep fryer or heavy saucepan. Divide dough into four parts. Roll out 1 part at a time, very thinly, on lightly-floured surface. Cut into 3-inch diamond shapes. Cut slits in each diamond. If desired, pull one corner of diamond through the slit. Deep fry until light brown. Roll in sugar, if desired.

4 TO 5 DOZEN.

"Unless you're allergic to chocolate, these simple treats are absolutely irresistible!" Therese Hennemann, head cook at the Swedish Village, ought to know because she has watched hungry villagers make them disappear on many an occasion. Perfect for warm days when you don't want to turn on the oven.

No-Bake Chocolate Balls

½ cup butter or margarine
½ cup sugar
2 tablespoons unsweetened cocoa
1 teaspoon vanilla
2 tablespoons strong, brewed coffee
1½ cups rolled oats
Coconut

Cream butter, sugar, cocoa, vanilla and coffee. Add oats and mix with wooden spoon until blended. Shape into bite-sized balls; roll in coconut. Refrigerate to chill; store in refrigerator.

ABOUT 25 COOKIES.

Nine-year-old Jenna Brooke Bratvold, Bagley, MN., shares a well-tested recipe enjoyed by several generations. Jenna's grandmother recalls, "My mother always dipped her rosettes in granulated sugar because her father didn't like white powdery sugar on the bib of his overalls." She adds several helpful hints —"Don't overbeat eggs or rosettes will be blistery. And, instead of washing the iron after use, just wipe it off well and store wrapped in paper toweling."

Grandma's Rosettes

2	eggs
1	teaspoon sugar
¼	teaspoon salt
1	cup milk
1	cup all-purpose flour
	Vegetable oil for deep frying

Beat eggs lightly; add sugar, salt and milk. Gradually stir in flour until smooth. Heat 2 to 3 inches of oil to 365° in deep fryer or heavy saucepan. Place rosette iron in hot oil 30 to 60 seconds or until iron is hot. Drain excess oil from iron on paper towels. Gently dip hot iron into batter. (Do not allow batter to come over top edge of iron.) Fry 25 to 35 seconds. Remove from iron; drain on paper towels. Rosettes will drop from iron when pushed gently with a piece of paper towel or cheese cloth. Cool rosettes; dip into or sprinkle with powdered or granulated sugar. Store in tightly covered container. Can be frozen.

45 TO 50 ROSETTES.

Tip: Rosette batter thickens as you work. If necessary, add milk, 1 tablespoon at a time, several times while frying rosettes. If batter is too thick, rosettes will not be crisp.

Florence Bye, Osseo, MN., introduces her recipe by commenting, "Because we are of German nationality, we didn't know what a rosette iron was until my sister inherited one from her mother-in-law. Since, she has made thousands — for church bazaars, holiday gifts and my daughter's wedding. In fact, she has received many orders to fill for Christmas."

Aunt Annette's Rosettes

2	eggs
¼	teaspoon salt
1	cup whole milk
½	cup all-purpose flour
½	cup cornstarch
2	tablespoons reconstituted lemon juice
1	teaspoon vanilla
2	teaspoons sugar
2	tablespoons vegetable oil
	Sugar for dipping
	Vegetable oil for deep frying

Combine all ingredients except sugar for dipping and oil for frying; mix well. Strain; refrigerate 30 minutes. Meanwhile blend granulated sugar in blender to make super-fine sugar for dipping rosettes after frying. Heat 2 to 3 inches of oil to 350° in deep fryer or heavy saucepan. Place rosette iron in hot oil 30 to 60 seconds or until iron is hot. Drain excess oil from iron on paper towels. Gently dip hot iron into batter. Do not allow batter to run over top of iron. Return iron to hot oil, immersing completely about 1 minute or until rosette is golden brown. Remove rosette while hot; drain on paper towels. Dip both sides in fine sugar. Cool on paper. Store in tightly covered container.

75 ROSETTES.

These sugar-coated, deep-fried treats from E'Lise Christensen, Council Bluffs, IA., originated with her great grandmother, Vilhelmina Jespersen Magnussen. "My grandmother, Vasthi Magnussen Christensen, still makes them for Christmas," says E'Lise. Because they are good **keepers,** *you can prepare them several weeks before the holidays.*

Danish Bowknots

2   tablespoons butter or margarine, softened

1   cup granulated sugar

3   eggs

2   tablespoons evaporated milk or cream

3   cups all-purpose flour
     Vegetable oil for deep frying
     Powdered sugar

Cream butter and sugar; mix in eggs and milk. Add 2½ cups flour gradually, mixing well. Refrigerate several hours or overnight. Roll out very thin on surface floured with remaining ½ cup flour (the thinner, the more delicate and crunchy). Cut into 1-inch strips; then into 4-inch pieces. Make a slit in each piece about ¾-inch long. Pull one end of strip through slit, carefully to form a *knot.* Place on cookie sheet in 2 or 3 layers (too many layers flatten bows), separated with waxed paper. Refrigerate 20 to 30 minutes. Heat 2 to 3 inches of oil to 360° in deep fryer or deep electric skillet. Fry knots, until golden brown, 1 to 2 minutes, turning once or twice. Drain on paper towels. Sprinkle lightly with powdered sugar. Store in tightly-covered metal container in a cool place. Can be frozen.

100 COOKIES.

These biscuit-like cookies from Ann Lynch, Minneapolis, MN., are "not too sweet and great for dunking. The Swedes eat these with butter and cheese or crumbled up in filmjolk (we would use yogurt)," Ann explains. Although preparation begins two days ahead of baking, steps are easy to follow.

Skåne Pepparkakor

1¾ cups light corn syrup*
1¼ cups sugar
6   tablespoons butter
1½ tablespoons cinnamon
1½ tablespoons ginger
2   eggs
2   egg yolks
½   cup milk
9   cups all-purpose flour
1   tablespoon baking powder
2   teaspoons baking soda

Heat corn syrup and sugar to boiling. Pour over butter and spices in large bowl. Stir and cool. Beat eggs, yolks and milk in small bowl. Stir into syrup mixture; refrigerate until cold. Combine a little of the flour with baking powder and baking soda; stir into syrup mixture. Add remaining flour a little at a time until well mixed. Cover; refrigerate 24 hours. Roll dough into 2 or 3 long rolls, 6 to 7 cm. in diameter. Roll in waxed paper; refrigerate several hours or overnight. Heat oven to 325°. Cut into ½-cm. thick slices. Bake on ungreased cookie sheets 10 to 15 minutes. Remove from cookie sheet; cool on rack. Store in closed cookie jar.

7 DOZEN.

*Tip: *Molasses can be substituted for corn syrup for a stronger flavor.*

"Beginning in the 1860s, many Norwegians settled in Lisbon, IL., near Chicago," explains Nancy Thorson, Red Wing, MN. "Letters from America encouraged others to come, including our relatives." It's obvious from this recipe that cooking skills were not left behind. Tester Rebecca Hotvedt, East Grand Forks, MN., used the molasses option and rated them "excellent" on all counts.

Lisbon Church Pepperkakor

1   cup butter, softened
1½   cups sugar
1   egg
1½   tablespoons grated orange or lemon peel
2   tablespoons corn syrup, maple syrup or molasses
1   tablespoon water, orange juice or lemon juice
3¼   cups all-purpose flour
2   teaspoons baking soda
2   teaspoons cinnamon
1   teaspoon ginger
½   teaspoon cloves

Cream butter and sugar; add egg and beat until fluffy. Add peel, syrup and water; mix well. Combine dry ingredients; stir into creamed mixture. Refrigerate until thoroughly chilled. Heat oven to 375°. On lightly floured surface, roll dough to ⅛-inch thickness. Cut in desired shapes with floured cookie cutters. Place 1 inch apart on ungreased cookie sheets. Bake 8 to 10 minutes.
6 DOZEN.

Delphine Aubourg, Granville, OH., maintains close ties with her native France. She was born in Paris and visits relatives in Normandy almost every summer. This unusual tea cookie is a specialty of that area. Tester Linda Church, Oxford, OH., "served these at a picnic and they were well liked by all ages." Be sure to allow time for dough chilling.

French Sables

3	eggs, hard-cooked
2	cups all-purpose flour
¾	cup sugar
	Dash of salt
	Grated zest of 1 orange
1	cup butter, softened

Separate egg whites from yolks. Mash yolks with fork. Combine flour, sugar, salt and orange zest in bowl; mix. Add butter and egg yolks; blend well until mixture forms a ball. If consistency seems too sticky, add flour until dough does not stick to hands. Place ball of dough in bowl; cover with cloth towel. Let rest 1 hour. Heat oven to 400°. Butter and flour cookie sheet. Roll out dough to ¼-inch thickness on lightly-floured surface. Cut out cookies with an inverted drinking glass, about 3 inches in diameter. Place cookies on prepared cookie sheet. Make a cross-shaped indentation on each cookie. Bake 8 to 10 minutes or until lightly browned.

35 COOKIES.

"This is certain to take care of any chocolate cravings," says Marjorie Kugler, North Oaks, MN. "My mother's family came over on the Mayflower and this recipe can be traced back to England." Marjorie, who heads her own interior design company, Interspace, Inc., chaired the Villages' International Family Christmas event and has headed decoration committees for other village galas. The Kugler's daughters attended the Villages and all three served as counselors, as well.

Fudge Square Cake

CAKE

1½   cups all-purpose flour

1   cup sugar

1   teaspoon baking soda

1   teaspoon salt

6   tablespoons unsweetened cocoa

3   tablespoons shortening

1   teaspoon vanilla

1   cup sour milk*

TOPPING

1½   cups packed brown sugar

½   cup unsweetened cocoa

1½   cups boiling water

Sweetened whipped cream

Heat oven to 350°. Grease 8x8x2-inch pan. Combine all cake ingredients until well blended. Pour into greased pan. Blend brown sugar and ½ cup cocoa; sprinkle over batter. Pour boiling water over all. Bake about 30 minutes or until cake springs back when lightly touched. (The cake will be on top and the fudge sauce on the bottom.) Invert cake onto serving plate; serve with whipped cream.

8 TO 12 SERVINGS.

*Tip: *One tablespoon lemon juice plus milk to make 1 cup can be substituted for sour milk.*

This almost flourless cake from Pam Stanoch, Plymouth, MN., originated in France. Tester Maxine Thorkelson, Golden Valley, MN., raved, "This is simply delicious — a wonderful chocolate taste subtly flavored with almond."

French Almond Fudge Cake

½   cup almonds
½   cup butter
7   ounces semi-sweet chocolate chips
½   cup sugar
1   teaspoon vanilla
4   eggs, separated
¼   cup flour

Heat oven to 350°. Totally crush almonds in food processor. Grease 11-inch round cake pan*. Melt butter and chocolate chips together. Stir in sugar, vanilla and egg yolks. Beat egg whites until very stiff peaks form; gently fold into chocolate mixture. Fold in flour and almonds. Bake about 25 minutes. Remove from pan and cool. Sprinkle with powdered sugar, if desired.

12 SERVINGS.

*Tip: *Cake can also be baked in 9-inch round or 11x7-inch baking pan.*

This Lac du Bois classic is frequently served for International Day. The not-too-sweet batter is congenial with rhubarb, apples, bananas, pears, even raspberries. Dust with powdered sugar, if desired, and serve anytime of day.

La Clafoutis aux Cerises

1   pound fresh cherries*
3   eggs
     Dash of salt
1   cup milk
1   teaspoon vanilla
1   cup sugar
1½   cups all-purpose flour
1½   teaspoons baking powder
6   tablespoons butter, melted, cooled

Heat oven to 350°. Grease and flour 12-cup bundt pan or 10-inch springform pan. Pit, dry as much as possible and toss cherries in flour. In mixer bowl, beat eggs and salt. Add milk and vanilla; beat in sugar. Stir in flour, baking powder and butter. Fold in cherries. Pour into pre-pared pan. Bake about 50 minutes or until golden brown.

12 TO 16 SERVINGS.

*Tip: *One large apple, peeled, diced and tossed in cinnamon-sugar mixture, then flour, can be substituted for cherries.*

An old-fashioned made-from-scratch chocolate cake from Linda Norderhaug, Brookfield, WI., to impress guests at any celebration. Add the frosting of your choice — chocolate, caramel, mocha or fluffy white and top with chocolate shavings or curls or chopped nuts.

Minnesota Fudge Cake

1	egg
1	cup sugar
4½	ounces unsweetened chocolate
¾	cup milk
¼	cup butter
½	cup shortening
1½	cups sugar
1½	teaspoons vanilla
½	teaspoon red food color
4	eggs
1	cup milk
1½	teaspoons baking soda
½	teaspoon salt
3	cups all-purpose flour

Beat 1 egg; combine with 1 cup sugar, chocolate and ¾ cup milk. Cook and stir over low heat, until chocolate is melted. Cool to room temperature. Heat oven to 350°. Grease three 9-inch round cake pans. Mix butter and shortening; gradually add 1½ cups sugar. Cream until fluffy. Add vanilla and food color. Add 4 eggs, one at a time, beating well after each addition. Combine dry ingredients; add to butter mixture alternately with 1 cup milk, beating well. Beat until smooth. Blend in chocolate mixture. Pour into greased pans. Bake 25 to 30 minutes or until toothpick inserted in center comes out clean. Cool and frost as desired.

12 SERVINGS.

Definitely a special occasion dessert from the pastry chef at Hotel Sofitel, Edina, MN. Genoise, a light buttery sponge cake, is perfectly mated with a rum-laced syrup and layers of rich mousse.

Chocolate Mousse Cake

GENOISE
4   eggs
½   cup sugar
½   cup all-purpose flour
2   ounces unsalted butter, melted

SYRUP
3½   ounces sugar
3½   ounces water
3½   ounces rum

MOUSSE
9   ounces baking milk chocolate
8   egg yolks
3   tablespoons unsweetened cocoa
1   pound 2 ounces unsalted butter, softened

FINISH
¼   cup grated chocolate

Heat oven to 400°. Combine eggs and ½ cup sugar; mix well. Heat in double boiler over hot water, beating vigorously until temperature reaches 113 to 122° or until mixture is smooth and foamy. Remove from heat; whip until completely cooled. Mixture should be quite thick and whitish. Gently fold in flour with a spatula. Stir in melted butter. Pour batter into 8-inch round cake pan (2 inches deep). Bake about 25 minutes. Combine 3½ ounces sugar and water; heat to hard boil. Cook 2 to 3 minutes; stir in rum. Melt chocolate over very low heat; set aside. Whisk egg yolks and cocoa in double boiler over hot water until mixture is smooth and foamy. Slowly stir in softened butter. Remove from heat; slowly stir in chocolate. If you desire a lighter mousse, fold in stiffly whipped cream for more fluffiness. Cut Genoise horizontally into 3 layers, spreading syrup over each. Put ¼ of the mousse on bottom layer, spread evenly. Repeat for next 2 layers. Spread remaining mousse mixture on top and sides; garnish with grated chocolate.

8 SERVINGS.

From the Spanish Village comes a cake very representative of the cuisine of the country where oranges and almonds are commonly used. A simple topping eliminates any need for frosting. This is a favorite at Village "restaurant" and "banquet" nights.

Orange-Almond Cake

CAKE

1¼	cups all-purpose flour
1	cup sugar
1½	teaspoons baking powder
½	teaspoon salt
¾	cup milk
⅓	cup shortening
1	egg
2	tablespoons grated orange peel

TOPPING

¼	cup sliced almonds
1	tablespoon sugar
2	tablespoons orange-flavored liqueur

Heat oven to 350°. Grease and flour 8-inch round cake pan. Combine all cake ingredients in large mixer bowl. Beat on low speed 30 seconds. Beat on high speed 3 minutes. Pour into prepared pan. Sprinkle with almonds. Bake about 40 minutes or until toothpick inserted in center comes out clean. Remove from oven; sprinkle with 1 tablespoon sugar and drizzle with liqueur.

8 TO 10 SERVINGS.

Testers found this fruit-sparked cake "very appealing and easy to prepare." Linda Johnson, Edina, MN., says it was a favorite of her mother-in-law who lived in the Finnish community of Menahga, MN.

Finnish Orange Cake

CAKE

½	cup granulated sugar
⅔	cup packed brown sugar
½	cup shortening
2	eggs
2½	cups all-purpose flour
2	teaspoons baking powder
1	teaspoon baking soda
½	teaspoon salt
1½	cups buttermilk
1	large orange
1	cup raisins
½	cup chopped nuts

FROSTING

1	cup reserved orange-raisin mixture
½	cup chopped nuts
1	cup powdered sugar
1	teaspoon butter

Heat oven to 350°. Grease and flour 13x9x2-inch pan. Cream sugars and shortening; add eggs and beat well. Combine dry ingredients; add with buttermilk to creamed mixture. Grind orange and raisins in food chopper or process in food processor, partially chopping orange before adding raisins. Reserve 1 cup of mixture for topping. Fold remaining ground fruit and nuts into batter. Pour into prepared pan. Bake about 40 minutes or until toothpick inserted in center comes out clean. Combine all frosting ingredients; blend well. Spread on cake while still warm. Serve with whipped cream, if desired.

12 TO 15 SERVINGS.

Tester Ann Hammer, Big Lake, MN., found this "moist and rich with a distinct orange flavor." Be sure to grease pan thoroughly so cake can be removed easily after cooling step.

Finnish Village Orange Cake

3	eggs
1¼	cups sugar
¾	cup butter, melted, cooled
1¾	cups all-purpose flour
2	teaspoons baking powder
½	cup hot water
1¼	cups orange marmalade
10	drops orange oil
1	teaspoon vanilla sugar or ½ teaspoon vanilla

Heat oven to 350°. Grease 12-cup bundt pan thoroughly; flour. Beat eggs well; gradually mix in sugar. Beat until light and fluffy; fold in butter. Combine flour and baking powder; stir into egg mixture. Combine water, orange marmalade, orange oil and vanilla sugar; fold into egg mixture. Pour into prepared pan. Bake about 60 minutes or until toothpick inserted near center comes out clean. Let stand 5 to 10 minutes; invert onto plate or wire rack to cool completely.

12 TO 16 SERVINGS.

Sofia Rizzo, Guatemala City, Guatemala, calls this "a very different fruit cake that can be thinly sliced to serve a crowd." Enthusiastic testers Jane and Stephen Chapco, Regina, Saskatchewan, called it "super fantastic" and said "the whole family loved it!"

Pastel de Navidad

½	cup butter
12	ounces cream cheese
2¼	cups sugar
6	eggs
2	teaspoons vanilla
3	cups all-purpose flour
2¼	teaspoons baking powder
½	cup raisins
1½	cups candied fruit
½	cup nuts, if desired

Heat oven to 350°. Grease 12-cup bundt pan. In mixer bowl, cream butter, cream cheese and sugar; beat in eggs and vanilla. Combine flour and baking powder; blend into creamed mixture. With mixer at low speed, add raisins, fruit and nuts. Turn batter into greased pan. Bake 60 to 70 minutes or until done. Cool; remove from pan. Cut into thin slices.

20 TO 30 SERVINGS.

This treasured holiday treat comes from Vicky Grablander, Baltic, SD., whose mother was an English war bride. "This is her favorite recipe and I always bake her one for Christmas. Add citron if you wish and be sure to make several weeks ahead of serving so flavors can blend." Tester Kathy Kinsey, Mason City, IA., describes it as "very pretty and quite tasty."

English Christmas Cake

1¾	cups chopped candied cherries
1¾	cups chopped candied pineapple
16	ounces raisins
3	cups broken pecans
¼	cup brandy
1	cup butter, softened
2¼	cups sugar
6	eggs
4	cups all-purpose flour
1½	teaspoons salt
½	teaspoon baking powder
1½	teaspoons cinnamon
1	teaspoon nutmeg
2	tablespoons brandy

Heat oven to 275°. Line 10-inch tube pan with foil. Combine fruit, pecans and ¼ cup brandy. Let stand, stirring occasionally. Cream butter; add sugar and beat well. Mix in eggs, one at a time, beating well after each addition. Combine dry ingredients; stir half into egg mixture with 2 tablespoons brandy. Stir remaining half of flour mixture into fruit and nuts. When coated, stir by hand into batter. Pour into prepared pan. Bake 3 hours, 45 minutes, with pan of water in oven. Cool 5 minutes; remove from pan. Cool completely. Wrap in brandy-soaked cheesecloth, then in foil. Store in refrigerator.

16 TO 20 SERVINGS.

For a fiesta finale, try this south-of-the-border sensation from Barbara Francis, Blytheville, AR. "Delicious and different with no shortening in the cake," says Barbara. Have icing ready so cake can be topped right from the oven.

Mexican Fruit Cake

2 cups granulated sugar
2 eggs
2 cups all-purpose flour
2 teaspoons baking soda
1 (16-ounce) can crushed pineapple in its own juice, undrained
1 cup pecans or walnuts, broken
1 (8-ounce) package cream cheese
2 cups powdered sugar
½ cup margarine, softened
1 teaspoon vanilla

Heat oven to 350°. Grease 13x9x2-inch baking pan. Combine sugar, eggs, flour, baking soda and pineapple; mix well. Fold in nuts; pour mixture into greased pan. Bake about 35 minutes or until cake springs back when lightly touched on top. Meanwhile, combine cream cheese, powdered sugar, margarine and vanilla. Remove cake from oven and ice while hot.

15 TO 18 SERVINGS.

For many, this stirs memories of holidays past. Contributor Beth Johnson Holod credits her mother, Mary Lu Johnson, Davenport, IA., for providing the recipe and the memories. Tester Beverly LeBeau, Fayetteville, NY., served it to company with enthusiastic results. She suggests adding a little Grand Marnier or Cointreau to the sauce for a sophisticated touch.

Cranberry Cake

CAKE
1 cup sugar
2 cups all-purpose flour
2 teaspoons baking powder
1 cup milk
1 tablespoon margarine, melted
2 cups fresh or frozen cranberries

SAUCE
1 cup sugar
¾ cup half & half
½ cup butter or margarine

Heat oven to 350°. Grease two 11x7-inch baking pans. Combine dry ingredients. Add milk to melted butter; stir into dry mixture. Stir in cranberries. Pour into greased pan. Bake 30 to 35 minutes or until toothpick inserted in center comes out clean. Combine sauce ingredients in heavy saucepan. Cook over medium heat until mixture comes to a boil, about 10 minutes, stirring frequently. (Watch carefully; it boils over very easily.) Serve warm cake with hot sauce.

10 TO 12 SERVINGS.

"Make this ahead and fill just before serving. Everyone likes it," says Liv Dahl, St. Paul, MN. She serves as Administrative Director of Heritage Programs for Sons of Norway International. Although frozen berries can be used, this dessert is particularly flavorful when fresh berries are at their peak.

Strawberry Torte

CAKE

3	eggs
1	cup sugar
1	cup all-purpose flour
7	tablespoons butter, melted, cooled

GLAZE

¼	cup butter
½	cup sliced almonds
1	tablespoon flour
1	tablespoon cream
⅓	cup sugar

FILLING

1	pint fresh or frozen, drained, strawberries
1	cup whipping cream, whipped

Heat oven to 350°. Grease and flour 10-inch round cake pan. Beat eggs and sugar together. Add flour and butter; mix well. Pour into prepared pan. Bake about 25 minutes. Meanwhile heat all glaze ingredients to a full boil; spoon glaze on top of cake and return it immediately to the oven for 10 minutes longer or until glaze is golden. When cake is cool, cut horizontally into 2 layers and fill with strawberries and whipped cream.

10 SERVINGS.

"This tastes sooo good!" says contributor Sarah Thompson, Fairfield, CT. Once the "log" is readied, she suggests writing or drawing pictures using colored tube frostings. Culinary grande dame, Julia Child, reminds creative cooks that this need not be just a holiday dessert —"decorate with flags and sparklers for July 4th, an ax for George Washington's birthday, etc."

Buche de Noel

CAKE

5	eggs, separated
¼	teaspoon cream of tartar
1	cup granulated sugar
1	tablespoon grated orange peel
2	tablespoons sherry
1	cup cake flour
¼	teaspoon salt
	Powdered sugar

FILLING

2	cups heavy cream
¼	cup powdered sugar

FROSTING*

3	ounces unsweetened chocolate
3	tablespoons butter
4	cups powdered sugar
⅛	teaspoon salt
7	tablespoons milk
1	teaspoon vanilla

LES CHAMPIGNONS

2	egg whites
¼	teaspoon cream of tartar
⅔	cup sugar
	Unsweetened cocoa

Heat oven to 375°. Line 15x10x1-inch jelly roll pan with foil. Beat 5 egg whites until foamy; add ¼ teaspoon cream of tartar and beat until stiff. Gradually beat in ½ cup sugar. In separate bowl, beat egg yolks until thick and lemon colored. Beat remaining ½ cup sugar, orange peel and sherry into egg yolks. Fold yolk mixture into whites. Combine flour and salt; fold gradually into egg mixture. Pour into prepared pan. Bake about 20 minutes. Turn out onto towel sprinkled with powdered sugar. Carefully remove foil. Roll up cake in towel so it looks like a log. Set aside to cool.

When the cake roll is cool, whip 2 cups cream and ¼ cup powdered sugar until thick enough to spread. Unroll cake and remove towel; spread with filling and reroll carefully. Refrigerate cake. For frosting, melt chocolate and butter together. Combine remaining frosting ingredients; stir in chocolate mixture and blend well. Let stand, stirring occasionally until of spreading consistency. Spread log with frosting. Run tines of a fork along the length of the log to suggest bark. Add a knot hole if you wish. Refrigerate until serving time. Just before serving, decorate with Les Champignons, if desired.

To make Les Champignons, line cookie sheets with foil or parchment paper. Heat oven to 250°. In small mixer bowl, beat 2 egg whites and ¼ teaspoon cream of tartar until foamy. Beat in ⅔ cup sugar, 1 tablespoon at a time, until meringue is stiff and glossy. Spoon meringue shapes on lined cookie sheets or pipe on with pastry bag and decorating tip. Lightly sprinkle mushroom caps with cocoa. Bake about 45 minutes or until firm and very delicately browned. Cool.

10 SERVINGS.

Tip: *Canned, ready to spread frosting can be substituted for frosting recipe.

Café Latté, St. Paul, MN., features this old world favorite along with a veritable smörgasbord of tantalizing sweets. The nutmeg-spiced cream frosting is attractively dotted with chopped pecans.

Swedish Apple Cake

CAKE

1	cup packed brown sugar
1	cup granulated sugar
¾	cup vegetable oil
3	eggs
1½	teaspoons vanilla
½	cup buttermilk
2½	cups all-purpose flour
¾	teaspoon salt
1	tablespoon baking soda
1½	teaspoons nutmeg
1	cup chopped pecans
3	cups finely-chopped apples

FROSTING

12	ounces cream cheese
1	cup powdered sugar
3	cups heavy cream
1½	teaspoons nutmeg
2	cups chopped pecans

Heat oven to 350°. Grease two 9-inch round cake pans. Combine brown and granulated sugars, oil, eggs, vanilla and buttermilk; mix well. In separate bowl, combine flour, salt, baking soda and 1½ teaspoons nutmeg; blend into wet ingredients. Stir in 1 cup chopped pecans and apples. Pour into prepared pans. Bake about 45 minutes or until knife inserted in center comes out clean. Blend cream cheese and powdered sugar; slowly stir in cream and nutmeg. Fill and frost cake, using 2 cups pecans to press on sides and sprinkle on top of cake.

12 SERVINGS.

This favorite from the German Village Cookbook is even tastier with "a scoop of ice cream or topped with whipped cream" says tester Carolyn Rice, Bloomington, MN. Dough chills for easy handling while apples are being prepared.

German Village Apple Cake

2   cups all-purpose flour

⅓   cup granulated sugar

½   cup plus 2 tablespoons cold butter

2   eggs

1   egg, separated

⅛   teaspoon salt

1½   tablespoons cold water

4   large baking apples

½   cup raisins

½   cup finely chopped walnuts

½   cup granulated sugar

2   teaspoons cinnamon

¼   cup butter, melted

    Powdered sugar

Combine flour and ⅓ cup sugar in bowl; cut in cold butter. Add whole eggs, 1 egg yolk and salt; continue folding ingredients and gradually add water. Work first with fingertips, then knead by hand into a medium-firm dough. Scrape side of bowl free of excess dough. Shape into a ball, adding a little more flour if necessary. Cover and refrigerate 30 minutes.

Heat oven to 350°. Peel and slice apples. Using a floured pastry cloth and covered rolling pin, roll dough into a 12x8-inch rectangle. Fold dough over back of hand and place it in 15x10x1-inch jelly roll pan. Cover sheet of dough with half of apple slices, leaving 1½ inch margin all around. Combine raisins, walnuts, ½ cup sugar and cinnamon; sprinkle half over apples. Repeat with remaining apples and raisin mixture. Fold margin of dough over filling, first the short sides, then the long sides. Spoon melted butter over filling; brush border of dough with lightly-beaten egg white. Bake 35 to 45 minutes or until golden. Cut into 1x5-inch slices; sprinkle with powdered sugar. **30 SERVINGS.**

The J. Edward Staab family, Indianapolis, IN., finds holiday gifts from their kitchen are much appreciated, particularly when this cinnamon-topped cake is presented. They love the versatility — "good for breakfast or dessert and wonderful to have on hand to serve unexpected guests."

German Apple Cake

1	cup packed brown sugar
1	egg
3	tablespoons margarine or butter, melted
1	cup all-purpose flour
1	teaspoon baking soda
1	teaspoon cinnamon
⅛	teaspoon salt
1	cup chopped apples
1	cup raisins
1	cup chopped nuts

Heat oven to 375°. Thoroughly grease 9x9x2-inch baking dish. Combine brown sugar, egg and margarine. Add dry ingredients and mix well by hand with a wooden spoon. (Batter will be very stiff.) Stir in apples, raisins and nuts. Pour into greased baking dish. Sprinkle top with cinnamon, if desired. Bake 35 to 40 minutes.

6 to 8 SERVINGS.

Karen Michael, Eden Prairie, MN., fondly recalls her grandmother making this sponge cake-like recipe. Tester Mary Brubacher, Hopkins, MN., loved the "very good flavor and old-fashioned appearance and texture." Potato starch is a flour made from potatoes.

Finnish Sugar Cake

	Dry bread crumbs
4 to	5 eggs (1 cup)
1	cup raw sugar
2	tablespoons cold water
¾	cup unbleached all-purpose flour
¼	cup potato starch

Heat oven to 350°. Thoroughly grease 9-inch round cake pan. Sprinkle heavily with bread crumbs. Beat eggs and sugar until thick, foamy and pale yellow. Add cold water to egg mixture; beat again until thick. Combine flour and potato starch; stir quickly by hand into egg mixture. Do not beat. Pour into prepared pan; put in oven immediately. Bake 30 to 40 minutes. Do not open oven for first 20 minutes. Serve plain or with fresh fruit.

12 SERVINGS.

"I hope you enjoy a little taste of Norge when you try this recipe," says Mary Zurcher, Glenburn, ND. "It was given to me by Kari Mahle, a Norwegian immigrant and special friend whose love for her homeland is very deep." Tester Amy Tervola, New York Mills, MN., prepared this for a family birthday party and said all tasters found it delicious!

Prinsesse Ragnhild Kake

CAKE

5	eggs
1½	cups powdered sugar
¾	cup all-purpose flour
¾	cup cake flour
2	teaspoons baking powder

SAUCE

1	cup warm water
2	tablespoons sugar
2½	teaspoons rum extract

SWEETENED WHIPPED CREAM FROSTING

2	teaspoons unflavored gelatin
6	tablespoons cold water
2	cups whipping cream
½	cup powdered sugar
2	cups preserves or jam
	Fresh fruit such as strawberries, blueberries, raspberries, peaches or kiwi fruit

Heat oven to 325°. Grease two 9-inch round or 9x9x2-inch baking pans. In large mixer bowl with electric mixer, whip eggs and 1½ cups powdered sugar until white in color. In small bowl, combine flours and baking powder.

Add to egg mixture; mix on low speed just until blended. Divide batter evenly between pans. Bake about 25 minutes or until toothpick inserted in center comes out clean. Cool cakes slightly. Combine sauce ingredients; pour over tops of both layers. Cool cakes completely; remove from pans.

Soften gelatin in cold water in glass measuring cup, about 5 minutes. Place measuring cup in hot water in saucepan; heat until gelatin is dissolved. Cool just to room temperature. Beat whipping cream slightly in a chilled medium bowl. Gradually add ½ cup powdered sugar, beating until stiff peaks form. Cover and refrigerate 10 minutes before frosting cake.

Place bottom layer on serving plate. Spread with preserves; place second layer over first. Frost sides and top of cake with Sweetened Whipped Cream Frosting. Place extra frosting in pastry bag fitted with decorating tip; decorate around edges of cake and/or make lattice strips across top of cake. Garnish with fresh fruit. Refrigerate until ready to serve.

12 TO 16 SERVINGS.

"During the five years my parents lived in Sweden, my grandmother would prepare this cake when we visited her," says Elinor Karlsson, Providence, RI. "This magnificent Swedish dessert goes back many years and it is unique for texture as well as taste." Be sure cake has thoroughly cooled before spreading with whipped cream.

Swedish Meringue Cake

5	tablespoons butter
1	cup powdered sugar
5	eggs, separated
⅔	cup all-purpose flour
1½	teaspoons baking powder
1	cup granulated sugar
1¼	ounces slivered almonds
1¼	cups whipping cream, whipped

Heat oven to 350 to 375°. Grease 12x16-inch baking pan. Mix butter and powdered sugar until creamy. Add egg yolks, one at a time, mixing well after each addition. Combine flour and baking powder; stir into butter mixture; spread in greased pan. Beat egg whites and granulated sugar until stiff peaks form. Spread unevenly over mixture in pan. Sprinkle with almonds. Bake about 20 minutes or until meringue has a little color and cake is dry. Let cake cool; remove from pan. Cut into layers as desired. Spread whipped cream on bottom half; add top, meringue side up.

12 SERVINGS.

"Easy, delicious and adaptable to many flavors of fillings and toppings" comments Mary Brubacher, Hopkins, MN., about this recipe for *"sockerkaka."* Testers Jon and Dagmar von Briesen, Forked River, NJ., pronounced it *"excellent and just plain easy!"* Mary's daughter, Sara, found that one reward of attending cooking school in Sweden was coming home with recipes like this to enjoy for years to come.

Swedish Sugar Cake

3   eggs
1   cup plus 2 tablespoons sugar
⅓   cup warm water
1   cup plus 2 tablespoons all-purpose flour
1½   teaspoons baking powder
     Sweetened whipped cream, custard or jam for filling
     Sweetened whipped cream and berries, sliced bananas*, grated chocolate, chopped nuts, etc. for topping

Heat oven to 350°. Butter and sugar one 9-inch round cake pan. Beat eggs and sugar together; stir in water. Blend flour and baking powder; stir into mixture. Pour into prepared pan. Bake about 25 minutes or until toothpick inserted in center comes out clean. Cool in pan 5 to 10 minutes; turn out. When cool, cut in half horizontally. Fill and top with your choice of filling and topping. Keep refrigerated; best eaten same day.

8 TO 10 SERVINGS.

Tip: *To keep bananas from browning, dip in 7-Up.

Ned Tervola, New York Mills, MN., says, "The real name for this is 'Suomen Tayte Kakku' and it makes a very special birthday cake." A wonderful show-off dessert particularly when fresh berries and peaches are available.

Finnish Fill Cake

4	eggs
1	cup granulated sugar
1	cup all-purpose flour
2	tablespoons cornstarch
2	teaspoons baking powder
½	teaspoon salt
2	cups whipping cream
¼	cup powdered sugar
1	cup each of 4 of the following fruits: sliced strawberries, sliced bananas, sliced peaches, blueberries, raspberries, well-drained mandarin orange segments, well-drained pineapple tidbits

Heat oven to 350°. Grease and line two 9-inch round cake pans with waxed paper. Beat eggs; add granulated sugar and mix well. Combine flour, cornstarch, baking powder and salt; stir into egg mixture; mix well. Divide batter evenly between prepared pans. Bake about 25 minutes or until toothpick inserted in center of cake comes out clean.

Cool cakes. Carefully remove from pans and remove waxed paper. Split cakes horizontally in half. Place one layer on serving plate, spread with whipped cream, add a layer of fruit and continue alternating to use all four cake layers, garnishing top with colorful fruit.

16 SERVINGS.

From the French Village and the province for which it is named, comes a simple, buttery cake. The first set of buildings at the permanent French site was modeled after those of Brittany.

Gâteau Breton

1	cup butter, softened
1¼	cups sugar
6	egg yolks
1¾	cups all-purpose flour

Heat oven to 375°. Grease 8-inch round cake pan. Cream butter and sugar; beat until fluffy. Beat in egg yolks until mixture is very pale and fluffy. Stir in flour. Pour into greased pan. Smooth top carefully; then run a large tined fork around the cake in a series of concentric circles. Bake about 40 minutes.

8 SERVINGS.

Known as "frystekaka" at the Norwegian Village where it is devoured with gusto, the batter is pastry-like. Staffer Linda Erceg suggests serving with a dollop of whipped cream and a good cup of coffee. Very popular at festive events, like weddings, in the "old country" and sometimes decorated with tiny flags.

Norwegian Almond Cake

CAKE

2   cups all-purpose flour

2   teaspoons baking powder

⅔   cup sugar

½   cup butter

1   egg, beaten

FILLING

½   cup finely-ground unblanched
    almonds

1   cup sugar

About ⅓ cup water

Heat oven to 375°. Combine cake dry ingredients in bowl. Cut in butter with pastry blender or fingertips. Add egg; mix well. Divide dough in half. Roll out one half large enough to cover bottom and side of 9-inch springform pan. Combine filling ingredients, using enough water to make a paste. Put filling on bottom crust in pan. Roll out remaining dough; cut into strips for lattice top and edging. Place over filling. Bake 25 to 30 minutes.

10 SERVINGS.

Ian Higgins, Spokane, WA., makes this a day ahead of serving for best flavor. "My mother ate this as a child — the German 'egg lady' sold it along her route each week. It keeps and freezes well." Tester Britta Ylikopsa, Hudson, WI., describes it as "very moist and delicious and wonderful with a glass of milk. This recipe could be renamed 'Vanishing Cake'," she adds.

German Crumb Cake

2   cups packed brown sugar

2   cups all-purpose flour

½   cup butter

¼   teaspoon salt

1   teaspoon cinnamon

1   egg

1   cup sour milk or buttermilk

1   teaspoon baking soda

Heat oven to 350°. Grease 13x9x2-inch pan (or two 9-inch round cake pans). Combine brown sugar, flour, butter and salt to make coarse crumbs. Reserve 1 cup of mixture; combine with cinnamon and set aside. Combine remaining crumbly mixture with remaining ingredients; mix well by hand. Pour into greased pan; sprinkle with reserved crumbly mixture. (Batter will be quite shallow in pan.) Bake 25 to 30 minutes or until toothpick inserted in center of cake comes out clean.

16 SERVINGS.

One of the many "Restaurant Night" favorites at the Spanish Village. Cake is intriguing because only one layer has cocoa added for very mild flavor. The rich, buttery frosting has wonderful mocha taste. Double frosting amounts if you wish to frost sides as well as middle and top of cake. Tester Marie Lacy, Edina, MN., served it at a party and said the frosting, especially, was an overwhelming success.

Pastel de Moca

CAKE

2	cups all-purpose flour
1	tablespoon baking powder
1	teaspoon salt
½	cup butter, softened
1	cup granulated sugar
1	teaspoon vanilla
2	eggs
¾	cup milk
1	tablespoon unsweetened cocoa

FROSTING

½	cup butter
1	cup packed brown sugar
2	teaspoons instant coffee granules
1	teaspoon unsweetened cocoa
¼	cup milk
½	teaspoon vanilla
2	cups powdered sugar

Heat oven to 350°. Grease and flour two 8-inch round cake pans. Combine flour, baking powder and salt; set aside. Cream ½ cup butter and sugar in large bowl until fluffy; add vanilla. Beat in eggs one at a time. Add flour mixture alternately with milk; begin and end with flour. Beat well. Spread half of batter in 1 prepared pan. Beat cocoa into remaining batter; spread in other pan. Bake 30 to 35 minutes or until toothpick inserted in center comes out clean. Cool; remove from pans. Melt ½ cup butter in large saucepan. Stir in brown sugar, instant coffee and cocoa. Heat to a vigorous boil; boil 2 minutes, stirring constantly. Remove from heat; add milk while stirring vigorously. Return to heat; heat to boiling. Remove from heat and let cool to lukewarm. Stir in vanilla and powdered sugar; beat until spreading consistency. Fill and frost cake.

8 SERVINGS.

"Olga, a French student spent a month with us and became our 'French daughter'," explains LaRon Croft, Chico, CA. "She brought this recipe to us and we made it many times together and since." The moist ingredients never completely "set" so cake cannot be tested for doneness with usual methods. Tester Nan Jakobson, Osage, IA., rated the flavor "excellent."

French Yogurt Cake

3 to 4 cups cut-up fresh fruit
1 cup plain or fruited yogurt
3 cups all-purpose flour
2 cups sugar
1 tablespoon baking powder
3 eggs
¾ cup vegetable oil

Heat oven to 350°. Grease 11x7x2-inch baking dish. Place fruit in dish to cover bottom. Combine remaining ingredients; mix well. Pour over fruit. Bake 40 to 50 minutes or until golden brown.

12 TO 16 SERVINGS.

Barbara Marick, Bloomington, MN., suggests this as a compatible base for a pudding mixture topped with fresh fruit or fruit covered with a clear glaze. Especially attractive with strawberries or blueberries.

Flan Cake

¾ cup sugar
¼ cup butter, softened
3 egg yolks
1¼ cups cake flour
2 teaspoons baking powder
½ teaspoon salt
½ cup milk
½ teaspoon lemon extract

Heat oven to 375°. Grease and flour flan or tiara pan. Combine sugar, butter and egg yolks; beat until fluffy. Combine flour, baking powder and salt; stir into fluffy mixture alternately with milk/lemon extract mixture. Pour batter into prepared pan. Bake about 20 minutes or until golden. Indentation on top can be filled with glazed strawberries, blueberries, raspberries, peaches, etc.

8 TO 10 SERVINGS.

A New Zealand dessert, honoring ballerina Anna Pavlova, which allows you to be creative in your patterning of colorful fresh fruits. Contributor Elinor Karlsson, Providence, RI., says this recipe has been handed down "by word of mouth" from grandmother to mother to Elinor. Include kiwi fruit if available since much of it is raised in New Zealand and it is named after their national bird.

Pavlova

6 egg whites
   Dash of salt
1 teaspoon vinegar
3 cups sugar
   Assorted fruits such as cherries, bananas, kiwi fruit etc.; as many colors as can be found
2 cups whipping cream, whipped

Heat oven to 350°. Line flat baking pan at least 16 inches on each side with parchment paper. In large mixer bowl, beat egg whites with salt until foamy; add vinegar. Beat in sugar, 1 tablespoon at a time; continue beating until stiff and glossy.

Spread meringue mixture on prepared pan in a circle about 15 inches in diameter and 1 to 1½ inches thick. Place pan in oven; reduce oven temperature to 300°. After 15 minutes, turn off oven; leave pavlova in oven with door closed 45 minutes to 1 hour longer. Cool completely; remove from pan.

Spread whipped cream over pavlova; arrange fruits in desired pattern. Cut into wedges.

20 SERVINGS.

"This is an elegant, tasty dessert that is easy to make," says Barbara Rottman, Dublin, OH. She suggests choosing your favorite variety of apple — sweet or tart — to suit your preference.

Bavarian Apple Torte

½   cup butter, softened
⅓   cup sugar
¼   teaspoon vanilla
1   cup all-purpose flour
8   ounces cream cheese, softened
⅓   cup sugar
1   egg
½   teaspoon vanilla
⅓   cup sugar
½   teaspoon cinnamon
4   cups diced peeled apples
¼   cup slivered almonds

Heat oven to 450°. Cream butter, ⅓ cup sugar and ¼ teaspoon vanilla; blend in flour. Spread on bottom and side of 9-inch springform pan. Combine cream cheese, ⅓ cup sugar, egg and ½ teaspoon vanilla; blend until smooth. Spread evenly over pastry lining. Combine ⅓ cup sugar and cinnamon; toss with apples to coat evenly. Arrange apples over cream cheese filling. Sprinkle almonds evenly over top. Bake 10 minutes. Reduce oven temperature to 400°; bake 25 minutes longer. Cool before removing springform pan rim. Refrigerate until chilled. Garnish with whipped cream, if desired.

6 TO 8 SERVINGS.

Tip: Because the butter in the pastry may "leak" during baking, place springform pan on a piece of aluminum foil.

This German specialty appeared in the Jordan, MN. Elementary School Cookbook. Tester, Linda Austin, Greensburg, PA., a professional cooking instructor, sent a mouth-watering color photograph of her results along with the critique. "This is best served warm," she advises. "It makes the kitchen smell wonderful."

Fresh Apple Kuchen

2	cups all-purpose flour
¾	cup sugar
½	teaspoon salt
¼	teaspoon baking powder
½	cup butter
1	pound apples
½	teaspoon cinnamon
¼	teaspoon nutmeg
2	egg yolks
1	cup heavy cream

Heat oven to 400°. Combine flour, 2 tablespoons of the sugar, salt and baking powder. Cut in butter until mixture resembles coarse crumbs. Pat firmly on bottom and sides of 9-inch round cake pan. Peel and core apples; cut into ½-inch wedges. Arrange in pastry-lined pan. Combine remaining sugar with cinnamon and nutmeg; sprinkle over apples. Bake 15 minutes. Beat egg yolks with cream; pour over apples. Bake 30 minutes or until golden brown. Place pan on wire rack; cool 10 minutes. Serve warm.

6 TO 8 SERVINGS.

This variation on the popular rice pudding theme comes from Britt Olson, Cavalier, ND. "My father really enjoys this old-fashioned recipe from the owners of a German restaurant. It is easy to prepare and everyone likes it." Tester Pam Fredericksen, Davenport IA., wholeheartedly agrees. "My husband and I pronounce this excellent!"

German Rice Pudding

1	cup uncooked long grain rice
3	cups water
¼	teaspoon salt
½	cup sugar
½	cup raisins
1	tablespoon butter
1	teaspoon vanilla
1	cup cream

In saucepan, heat rice, water and salt to boiling; reduce heat. Cover and simmer until all water is absorbed. Stir in sugar, raisins, butter, vanilla and cream. Cover and simmer over low heat 30 minutes. Serve warm or cold with cinnamon and cream, if desired.

8 SERVINGS.

"Guests love this," remarks contributor, Patricia Swanson Anderson, Montevideo, MN. "I usually mold it in a bowl, spoon it out into small dessert dishes and decorate it with the sauce and almonds." A wonderful make-ahead to enhance any menu.

Swedish Rice Mold with Raspberry Sauce

⅔	cup sugar
½	cup water
2	envelopes unflavored gelatin
½	teaspoon salt
2	cups milk
2	cups cooked rice
1	teaspoon vanilla
1	cup whipping cream
1	(10-ounce) package frozen raspberries, thawed
1	tablespoon cold water
2	teaspoons cornstarch
½	cup slivered blanched almonds

Heat sugar, ½ cup water, gelatin and salt in 2-quart saucepan over medium heat, until gelatin is dissolved. Stir in milk, rice and vanilla; cool. Whip cream until stiff; fold into rice mixture. Pour into ungreased 6-cup mold or serving bowl. Cover and refrigerate until firm, about 3 hours. Heat undrained raspberries to boiling. Combine 1 tablespoon water and cornstarch; stir into raspberries. Heat to boiling, stirring constantly. Boil and stir 1 minute. Purée in blender until smooth. Refrigerate to chill. Unmold rice pudding by dipping briefly in warm water and loosening edge with a spatula. Invert onto serving plate. Serve with small bowl of raspberry sauce or drizzle sauce over mold just before serving. Decorate with almonds.

8 SERVINGS.

"This is a favorite because it has been made and enjoyed by so many generations in our family," comments Lindsey Neva, Finley, ND. "My mother makes it on special occasions." Serve this famous Norwegian feast dish warm.

Rommegrøt

½	cup butter
¾	cup all-purpose flour
2	cups cream
2	cups milk
½	cup (scant) sugar
¼	teaspoon salt

Melt butter in saucepan; slowly stir in flour. Stir in cream, milk, sugar and salt. Cook and stir over medium heat until thickened. Pour into bowl and sprinkle with cinnamon and sugar, if desired. Serve warm.

8 SERVINGS.

Loretta Larson obtained this recipe from Amy Erickson, longtime Concordia College Food Service Manager. Loretta then adapted it for speedier microwave preparation and says, "It's quick and delicious and never scorches or is lumpy."

Micro Rommegrøt

1	cup butter
1	cup all-purpose flour
3	cups half & half
1	cup whole milk
¼	cup sugar
¾	teaspoon salt

Melt butter in large microwave-safe bowl. Stir in flour with wire whisk. Cook until mixture bubbles; cook 30 seconds longer. Heat half & half and milk together; slowly add to flour mixture. Stir with wire whisk while mixing. Return to microwave until mixture begins to boil, about 2 minutes. Remove from microwave; stir in sugar and salt. Microwave 30 seconds longer. Add more hot milk if necessary to reach desired consistency. Serve warm with melted butter, cinnamon and sugar, if desired.

16 SERVINGS.

"This recipe has been prepared by my family for four generations," says Charla Beukema, Marquette, MI. "A dearly-loved woman from Mexico shared it with us." Tester Gary Nichols, Edina, MN., describes it as "a total hit! It didn't last five minutes."

Spanish Cream

1	envelope unflavored gelatin
3	cups milk
½	cup sugar
3	eggs, separated
	Salt
1½	teaspoons vanilla

Soften gelatin in milk about 5 minutes. Place in double boiler over hot water. Stir in sugar until dissolved. Beat egg yolks; pour into mixture in double boiler, stirring constantly until mixture is well heated and coats spoon but is not thick. (Do not overcook or custard will curdle.) Stir in salt and vanilla. Remove from heat and cool slightly. Beat egg whites until stiff; fold cooked mixture into egg whites until thoroughly mixed. Pour into individual dessert dishes. Refrigerate until set.

6 SERVINGS.

A make-ahead from the Russian Village that can be crowned with fresh fruits or eaten as is. "I serve it with fresh raspberries and my guests love it," comments tester Gretchen Pracht, Edina, MN. "Light" sour cream works beautifully.

Russian Cream

1	envelope unflavored gelatin
1	cup cold water
2	cups whipping cream
1½	cups sugar
2	teaspoons vanilla
16	ounces dairy sour cream
1	cup raspberries, strawberries or other favorite fruit

Sprinkle gelatin evenly over water; do not stir. Combine whipping cream and sugar in heavy saucepan or double boiler over hot water. Heat over low heat to lukewarm. Stir in gelatin mixture. Heat gently until sugar and gelatin are thoroughly dissolved. Remove from heat; cool. When mixture begins to thicken, fold in vanilla and sour cream. Pour into pretty serving bowl or individual dessert dishes. Refrigerate until set, about 4 hours. Before serving, top with well-drained berries.

6 SERVINGS.

"When my students want to try an impressive French dessert, we use this recipe — a real pleaser without being difficult," says Kathy Uvaas, Fergus Falls, MN. Since hot topping melts ice cream rather quickly, you may want to freeze ice cream balls ahead, place them in dessert dishes and serve immediately with sauce.

Easy Cherries Jubilee

3	(16-ounce) cans dark, sweet, pitted cherries
¼	cup cornstarch
¾	cup sugar
	Dash of salt
	Several tablespoons brandy
	Vanilla ice cream

Drain cherries, reserving 1½ cups juice. Dissolve cornstarch in a little of the reserved juice. Combine cherries, juice, cornstarch mixture, sugar and salt in saucepan. Cook over medium heat, stirring constantly, until thickened. Pour brandy over top and light with a match. (Flame will extinguish itself when all brandy is burned up.) Serve immediately over scoops of vanilla ice cream.

8 TO 10 SERVINGS.

Janet Sadlack, Burnsville, MN., included this divine dessert in her newsletter,
The Microwave Times, *which has world-wide distribution.*

Micro Chocolate-Amaretto Mousse

4	ounces cream cheese
¼	cup semi-sweet chocolate pieces
1	tablespoon Amaretto liqueur
1	cup whipping cream
½	cup sugar

Combine cream cheese and chocolate pieces in 1-cup glass measure. Microwave (HIGH) uncovered, 40 to 50 seconds or until chocolate is softened. Stir to melt chocolate. Blend in liqueur; set aside. Beat cream and sugar until thickened. Fold in chocolate. Spoon into individual dessert dishes. Cover and refrigerate until set, about 2 hours.

4 SERVINGS.

"While living in Panama for ten years, we were introduced to many new foods. This particular recipe became a family favorite that we continue to prepare frequently," says Elisa Wright, Bloomington, MN. "It always brings back memories of good times," she adds. Pour caramelized sugar quickly into baking dish and tilt immediately so mixture doesn't harden before bottom is completely and evenly coated.

Panamanian Flan

⅓	cup sugar
1	(14-ounce) can sweetened condensed milk
5	egg yolks
1	(5-ounce) can evaporated milk
5	ounces water
½	cup regular milk
1	tablespoon vanilla
¼	teaspoon salt

Heat oven to 325 to 350°. Melt sugar in small skillet, stirring constantly until caramel colored. Pour into 1½-quart baking dish, tilting quickly to coat bottom and a little of the sides. In bowl, mix condensed milk and egg yolks. Stir in remaining ingredients; blend well. Pour into caramel-coated baking dish; place in pan of hot water. Bake 1 hour or cook in double boiler over medium heat 1 hour. Flan is done when knife inserted near edge comes out clean. Cool and refrigerate. Invert onto serving plate.

8 TO 10 SERVINGS.

"After our traditional Christmas meal, this dessert brings sweet memories of France to our table," comments Bonita English, Red Cloud, NE. Watch sugar and water closely during caramelizing step because once browning begins, it progresses quickly. Remove from heat before mixture is too dark.

Crème Caramel

¾ cup sugar
¼ cup water
¼ cup sugar
¼ teaspoon salt
5 eggs, slightly beaten
3 cups scalded whole milk

In heavy saucepan, heat ¾ cup sugar and water to boiling. Swirl contents of pan until sugar has dissolved and turned caramel color, about 5 minutes. Carefully pour caramel into 4-cup mold or 8 individual molds. Tip and swirl each mold to coat bottom and sides evenly with caramel; when caramel ceases to run, turn the mold upside down on waxed paper to cool.

Heat oven to 325°. Stir ¼ cup sugar and salt into eggs; stir mixture into scalded milk. Strain through a fine sieve into caramelized mold. Place mold in pan of boiling water placed in lower third of oven. Bake about 60 minutes or until knife inserted in center comes out clean. (If individual molds are used, baking time will be less.)

To serve custard warm, let it settle in a pan of cold water 10 minutes; unmold onto warm serving dishes. To serve cold, cool at room temperature; chill several hours and unmold. Pour any remaining caramel over unmolded custard and serve.

8 SERVINGS.

Tips: Because slow cooking is the secret of a desirable custard, take care that the water surrounding the mold does not even simmer during baking.
To unmold a chilled caramelized custard, it is sometimes helpful to place the bottom of the mold briefly in a pan of hot water.

"Scrumptious" is the word tester June Kohl, Cass Lake, MN., uses to describe this make-ahead and freeze dessert from Shirley Schmid, Hibbing, MN. An eye-catching refresher to serve following a holiday or other special occasion meal.

Cranberry Parfait

1½   cups fresh or frozen cranberries
4   egg yolks
1½   cups powdered sugar
3   cups whipping cream, whipped

Cook cranberries in water to cover until thick and juicy. Whip egg yolks, powdered sugar and cranberries; cook in top of double boiler over hot water until thick. Cool; fold in whipped cream. Pour mixture into 6-cup bundt pan or fancy mold. Freeze until firm. Serve garnished with cranberries dipped into powdered sugar, if desired.

8 TO 10 SERVINGS.

"I enjoyed this many times with my host family while in France," says Christine Lemley, Evanston, IL. Tester LaRae Ellingsen Hovland, Edina, MN., describes it as a "festive treat." In addition to firm, easily-managed fruits like strawberries and banana pieces, pieces of angel food or pound cake make tasty dippers.

Fondue au Chocolat

2   (8-ounce) bars semi-sweet cooking chocolate, cut up, or 1½ (12-ounce) packages milk chocolate chips
⅔   cup half & half
2   teaspoons whiskey and/or 2 tablespoons orange juice
      Fruit for dipping, such as grapes, apple slices*, pear slices*, banana pieces* or strawberries

Heat water to boiling in small skillet or saucepan. Combine chocolate and half & half in small ceramic or metal bowl; place in pan of boiling water, being careful not to get any water in chocolate mixture. Heat and stir until melted and smooth, about 10 minutes. Remove from heat and stir in whiskey or orange juice. Keep chocolate mixture warm and serve with fruit pieces. Use fondue forks or bamboo skewers for dipping.

4 SERVINGS.

*Tips: *Dip these fruits in lemon juice to prevent darkening.
Chocolate and half & half can also be heated over low heat in heavy saucepan.*

Dr. Roma Hoff, Eau Claire, WI., offers a new twist to an old-fashioned baked custard. "This is a unique and easy dessert," comments tester Kitty Winn, Edina, MN. A food processor makes short work of blending and coconut adds pleasant flavor and texture.

Apple Flan

4	eggs
1	(14-ounce) can sweetened condensed milk
14	ounces (1¾ cups) milk
1	teaspoon vanilla
1	cup sliced peeled apples
1	cup grated coconut

Heat oven to 350°. Combine all ingredients except coconut in food processor; process 30 seconds. Fold in coconut. Pour into 10x6-inch baking dish; place dish in 13x9-inch baking pan. Pour hot water into 13x9x2-inch pan to a depth of 2 inches. Bake 1 hour. Cool.

10 SERVINGS.

"This was given to me by our guest, Anne Garans, Marseille, France," explains Loretta Bebeau, Minnetonka, MN. "It is really delicious with a dollop of whipped cream or crème fraîche." Since the French prefer fresh ingredients, Loretta encourages use of fresh fruits. Make a day ahead of serving for ample setting time.

Couronne de Fruits Rouges

1	cup plus 2 tablespoons powdered sugar
2	tablespoons water
1¾	cups pitted sweet bing or black cherries
1	envelope unflavored gelatin
¼	cup water
1½	cups raspberries
1½	cups strawberries
1	cup fresh currants, if desired*
	Juice of 1 lemon
2	tablespoons Kirsch

*Tip: *If not using currants, amounts of other fruits can be increased by a total of 1 cup.*

Dissolve powdered sugar in 2 tablespoons water in 1-quart saucepan. Add cherries; simmer gently over medium to low heat about 10 minutes. Soften gelatin in ¼ cup water in 1-quart bowl. Remove cherries from heat, drain juice into softened gelatin. Add cherries to strawberries and raspberries in 3 to 4-quart bowl. Sprinkle lemon juice and Kirsch over fruit; gently toss. Pour cherry-gelatin mixture evenly over fruit; toss to coat all fruit. Pour fruit mixture into 6-cup ring mold. Cover and refrigerate overnight. To unmold, dip mold into warm water for a few seconds; loosen edges and invert onto dampened serving plate.

8 SERVINGS.

When Camille Assir, Sugar Land, TX., returned to the U.S. after living in Hamburg, Germany, she adapted this favorite from northern Germany to incorporate time-saving pudding mix. Amount of sugar added depends on tartness of fruits you choose to use.

Rote Grütze

2	pounds mixed fresh or frozen fruit such as cherries, currants, raspberries, strawberries, blackberries
	Powdered or granulated sugar
2	(3½-ounce) packages vanilla pudding and pie mix (not instant)

Place fruit in saucepan and cover with water. Heat to simmering; stir in sugar to taste. Remove from heat; stir in pudding mix. Pour into bowl, cover and refrigerate until firm. Serve with cream or vanilla sauce on the side, if desired. 6 TO 8 SERVINGS.

Nancy Thorson, Red Wing, MN., passes on a recipe given to her by friend Gisela Witgert who grew up in West Berlin. "This was a favorite dessert of her family," adds Nancy. Prepare the day before serving or at least three hours ahead of time. The six adults who taste-tested the creamy light torte agreed —"excellent flavor and texture."

Snowy Vanilla Torte

1½	cups fine vanilla wafer crumbs (about 33 wafers)
6	tablespoons butter, melted
¼	teaspoon nutmeg
¾	cup sugar
1	envelope unflavored gelatin
	Dash of salt
1¼	cups water
2	egg whites
¼	teaspoon grated lemon peel
1	tablespoon lemon juice
½	teaspoon vanilla
1	(1½-ounce) envelope dessert topping mix
1	cup dairy sour cream

Combine crumbs, butter and nutmeg; press firmly on bottom and up side of 9-inch springform pan. Refrigerate to chill. In saucepan, combine sugar, gelatin and salt; stir in water. Cook and stir over medium heat until gelatin is dissolved. Refrigerate until partially set. Add egg whites, lemon peel, lemon juice and vanilla; beat until very fluffy, 5 to 7 minutes. Refrigerate until partially set. Prepare dessert topping according to package directions. Fold into gelatin mixture with sour cream. Spoon mixture in prepared crust. Sprinkle lightly with nutmeg. Chill until firm, about 3 hours or overnight. 10 TO 12 SERVINGS.

"When I lived in Germany as an exchange student, this recipe was a favorite of my host family," recalls Nanette Rollene, Decorah, IA. *"My host mother went to great pains to make sure I could recreate the recipe at home for my American family to enjoy."*

Schwartzwalder Kirsch Torte

CAKE
¾   cup all-purpose flour
¼   cup unsweetened cocoa
¼   teaspoon salt
6   eggs, separated, room temperature
1¼ cups sugar
1   teaspoon vanilla

GLAZE
¼   cup sugar
1   tablespoon water
¼   cup brandy or similar extract

FROSTING
2 to 2½ cups whipping cream
¼   cup powdered sugar
2   tablespoons brandy or extract
     Shaved chocolate
     Maraschino cherries, well drained

Heat oven to 350°. Lightly grease and flour two 9-inch round cake pans. Combine flour, cocoa and salt in small bowl. In another small bowl, beat egg yolks until thick and creamy. Stir in ¾ cup of the sugar and continue beating until mixture is thick and light. Transfer to large bowl. In separate bowl, beat egg whites until frothy; gradually add remaining ½ cup sugar, beating until stiff peaks form. Fold egg yolk mixture into whites. Sprinkle flour mixture over egg mixture; add vanilla and blend. Divide mixture evenly between 2 prepared pans. Bake about 25 minutes. Cool 10 minutes.

Meanwhile, in small saucepan, combine sugar and water for glaze. Place over low heat and stir until sugar is dissolved. Remove from heat; stir in brandy. Remove cakes from pans; let cool on wire racks. Brush brandy glaze over top and allow to cool.

For frosting, chill whipping cream and powdered sugar together. Beat until thick and light; stir in flavoring. Place one cake layer on serving plate. Spread with whipped cream. Top with second layer. Use remaining whipped cream to frost sides and top. Sprinkle sides with shaved chocolate. Use pastry tube to decorate top of cake with whipped cream; garnish with cherries. Refrigerate.

8 TO 10 SERVINGS.

Danielle Mossner, Janesville, WI., received this culinary gift from her great grandmother who brought it from Germany. Baked-on almonds provide an attractive topping and complement the delicate vanilla flavoring of the cake and filling.

Blitzen Torte

TORTE

½	cup butter, softened
¾	cup sugar
4	egg yolks
1	egg white
1½	cups all-purpose flour
2	teaspoons baking powder
1	teaspoon vanilla
½	cup milk
⅛	teaspoon salt

MERINGUE

4	egg whites
⅛	teaspoon cream of tartar
1	cup sugar
1	cup sliced almonds

FILLING

1	egg yolk
1	cup milk
2	tablespoons butter
1	tablespoon flour
1	teaspoon vanilla

Heat oven to 350°. Grease two 8-inch round cake pans. Beat all torte ingredients together well. Pour into greased pans. Beat egg whites and cream of tartar until frothy; gradually beat in sugar by tablespoons, until smooth and glossy. Spoon mixture evenly onto layers in pans; sprinkle with almonds. Bake about 45 minutes or until toothpick inserted in center comes out clean.

In saucepan, combine all filling ingredients except vanilla; cook and stir until thick. Stir in vanilla. Let filling cool. Remove one meringue-topped layer from pan. Place on serving plate, meringue side down. Spread with filling. Place other layer on top, meringue side up.

12 SERVINGS.

From the Swedish Village, this is particularly appealing when served while still warm from the oven. Day-old bread is transformed into a taste treat!

Kajsa's Bread Pudding

4	slices day-old white bread
2	tablespoons butter or margarine
⅓	cup packed brown sugar
1	teaspoon cinnamon
⅓	cup raisins
3	eggs, slightly beaten
⅓	cup sugar
1	teaspoon vanilla
	Dash of salt
2½	cups milk, scalded

Heat oven to 350°. Butter 1½-quart casserole or 9x9x2-inch baking pan. Toast bread to a light, golden brown. Spread with butter; sprinkle with brown sugar and cinnamon. Put slices together, making 2 sandwiches. Trim away crusts and cut each sandwich into 3 or 4 rectangles. Arrange rectangles in casserole; sprinkle with raisins. Blend eggs, sugar, vanilla and salt; gradually stir in milk. Pour mixture over bread in casserole. Bake 60 to 75 minutes or until knife inserted in center comes out clean. Serve warm or cool, with or without cream.

4 TO 6 SERVINGS.

Keri Ricks, Appleton, WI., who "loves cooking ethnic foods" finds this an easy, delicious end to any meal, French or otherwise." The secret is sealing pastry edges thoroughly so none of the wonderful chocolate-almond filling escapes. Serve in wedges with a fork or in small squares as finger food.

French Pithiviers

1	(17¼-ounce) package frozen puff pastry, thawed
6	tablespoons butter, softened
½	cup sugar
¾	cup sliced almonds
2	tablespoons flour
1	teaspoon vanilla
2	eggs
2	ounces semi-sweet chocolate, cut into small pieces

Heat oven to 375°. Place 1 pastry sheet on ungreased cookie sheet. Cream butter and sugar; stir in almonds, flour, vanilla and 1 egg until well mixed. Spread filling over pastry, leaving ½ inch around edges. Sprinkle chocolate over filling. Beat remaining egg; brush around edge of pastry. Place second pastry sheet on top and press edges together, sealing well. Brush top with egg and pierce in a few places with a knife. Bake 10 to 15 minutes or until top puffs up and is golden brown. Let cool 10 minutes. Cut into wedges.

8 SERVINGS.

This recipe was printed on an oven mitt that Elizabeth Krysia of Appleton, WI., purchased in Austria. "I had tasted it in the courtyard restaurant of the Burg in Salzburg and loved it! It is simple to prepare and I make it when my middle school German students are studying native foods," she explains. Although the sweet soufflé-like texture makes an ideal dessert, it may also be served for brunch.

Salzburg Dessert Omelet

3   eggs, separated
1   teaspoon vanilla
½   teaspoon grated lemon peel
1   tablespoon flour
     Dash of salt
     Powdered sugar

Heat oven to 350°. Grease 9-inch round cast iron skillet, 8x8x2-inch or oval baking dish. Combine egg yolks, vanilla, lemon peel and flour in medium bowl. Mix with fork or rotary beater until no lumps remain. In another medium bowl, beat egg whites with salt until stiff. (Whites are beaten enough when they do not fall out of inverted bowl.) Fold egg yolks into whites, using long spatula (a slotted one works best). Fold just until well-blended; do not overfold. Pour into greased skillet, forming into mounds. Bake 10 to 12 minutes or until lightly brown on outside but soft on the inside. Sprinkle with powdered sugar. Serve at once.

6 TO 8 SERVINGS.

"Jam-filled pastries are popular in Russia and students in the Russian Club enjoy preparing this rich, easy-to-make pastry for 'Culture Day'," comments high school Russian instructor, *Sheryl Hall, Spirit Lake, IA. The Soviet people love sweets such as this to serve with popular black or green teas.*

Pirok

1	cup butter, softened
1	cup margarine, softened
1	cup granulated sugar
2	egg yolks
1	teaspoon vanilla
3	cups all-purpose flour
1	teaspoon baking powder
½	teaspoon salt
2	cups strawberry, raspberry or apricot preserves
	Powdered sugar

Heat oven to 375°. Cream butter, margarine and granulated sugar; blend in egg yolks and vanilla. In separate bowl, combine flour, baking powder and salt. Blend wet and dry ingredients together. Spread ¾ of dough evenly to 12x18-inch rectangle on ungreased cookie sheet; press down with fingers (dough will be sticky). Spread preserves evenly over dough to within ½ inch of edge. Dot preserves with remaining dough (dough can be dropped by teaspoonful over preserves). Bake about 30 minutes. Sprinkle with powdered sugar. Cool 30 minutes; cut into squares.

54 (2-INCH) SQUARES.

"My Aunty Marge (in her 90s) always provided this dessert at family festivities, by popular demand," says Barbara Rottman, Dublin, OH. Tester Christine Schulze, Moorhead, MN., calls it "a glorious ending for a gourmet meal." Christine advises that waxed paper must be cut to exact size of pans and adds, "Meringue mixture should be gently turned into pans so no air volume is lost."

Schaum Torte

1	cup egg whites (6 to 8)
½	teaspoon cream of tartar
2	teaspoons vanilla or 1½ teaspoons vanilla and ½ teaspoon almond extract
¼	teaspoon salt
2	cups granulated sugar
	Sweetened strawberries
2	cups whipping cream
¼	cup powdered sugar
1	teaspoon vanilla
	Whole strawberries

*Tip: *Nine-inch springform pan with bottom greased or lined with greased waxed paper can be used.*

Variations —

Butter Brickle: Substitute crushed butter brickle candy (Heath bars) for berries. Do not mix candy with whipped cream but sprinkle over layers of cream and on top of torte.

Mocha: Add 6 tablespoons unsweetened cocoa to whipped cream and increase powdered sugar to ⅔ cup. Add a few grains of instant coffee or substitute 1 teaspoon very strong brewed coffee for 1 teaspoon vanilla.

Rum: Substitute 1 to 1½ teaspoons rum flavoring for vanilla.

Heat oven to 300°. Grease two 9-inch round cake pans*; line with greased waxed paper. Beat egg whites, cream of tartar, 2 teaspoons vanilla and salt until stiff peaks form; gradually add granulated sugar, beating constantly. (Make sure all sugar is dissolved and beaten into egg whites; this may take up to 15 minutes.) Divide meringue evenly between prepared pans; spread evenly to edges. Bake about 40 minutes. Turn off oven and open door 1 to 2 inches. Allow torte to dry out in oven for 30 minutes longer with door partially open. Completely cool on cooling racks. Remove from pans, remove waxed paper. (Torte is very fragile and top may crack a bit during this process.)

Whip cream, powdered sugar and 1 teaspoon vanilla until stiff. Fold in sweetened berries, according to taste. (Or, keep separate and serve as layers of cream and berries.) Immediately before serving, place 1 meringue on serving plate. Spread with half of whipped cream and berries. Top with second meringue and add remaining cream and berries. Arrange whole strawberries on top and around sides.

10 TO 12 SERVINGS.

From the Language Villages German Cookbook comes this special flourless torte loaded with ground walnuts. "With a bit of whipped cream and a cherry, chocolate curl or walnut half, this dessert looks quite elegant," says Jan Traaseth, Moorhead, MN.

Walnut Torte

6   eggs, separated
½   cup granulated sugar
1   teaspoon grated lemon peel
     Juice of ½ lemon (1 to 1½ tablespoons)
¼   cup dry bread crumbs
2½   cups (about 12 ounces) finely ground walnuts
     Whipped cream or chocolate pudding
     Powdered sugar
     Walnut halves

Heat oven to 350°. Thoroughly grease 10x2½-inch springform pan. Beat egg whites until stiff; set aside. Beat egg yolks and granulated sugar until very light and foamy. Mix in lemon peel, lemon juice, bread crumbs and ground walnuts; blend mixture well. Fold into egg whites; blend until no white shows. Pour batter into greased pan. Bake 30 to 40 minutes or until springy to the touch. Remove outer ring from pan; let cool completely.

Slice torte horizontally into 2 layers. To slice with dental floss or string, slip floss around torte to desired height/thickness; cross the 2 ends of the floss over each other where they meet and pull gently. (This torte will be drier and more crumbly than are American cakes, so careful handling is required.)

Spread whipped cream or chocolate pudding between layers; sandwich them together. Allow torte to stand 1 to 2 days to blend flavors and allow filling to blend into torte. Before serving, sprinkle top with powdered sugar; decorate with walnut halves.

10 TO 12 SERVINGS.

When you spot those first tender rhubarb stalks, celebrate spring with this heritage recipe from German-born Ingrid Lenz Harrison, Wayzata, MN. Allow 30 minutes for dough-chilling step before continuing with preparation. Tester Carrie Rocke, Davis, CA., was very complimentary. "Delicious! Everyone wanted more."

Rhubarb Kuchen

1½	cups all-purpose flour
1	teaspoon baking powder
	Dash of salt
6	tablespoons butter or margarine
6	tablespoons sugar
1	egg
2	pounds rhubarb, cut into bite-sized pieces
¾	cup sugar
2	eggs
8	ounces dairy sour cream
2 to	3 tablespoons sugar

Combine flour, baking powder, salt, butter, 6 tablespoons sugar and 1 egg; mix together quickly and refrigerate 30 minutes. Grease 10-inch springform pan with butter or margarine. Heat oven to 400°. Roll out dough to fit bottom and side of pan. Bake crust 3 to 5 minutes. Add rhubarb and sprinkle with ¾ cup sugar; bake 30 minutes longer. Reduce oven temperature to 350°. Combine 2 eggs, sour cream and 2 to 3 tablespoons sugar; pour mixture over cake in oven; bake 30 minutes longer or until lightly browned and egg mixture is set. Turn off oven; let cake cool in oven.

12 SERVINGS.

Gary Tucker, Ogden, UT., adds this note with his recipe, "Kase Kuchen is an afternoon staple in Germany and is found in all the bakeries. It does need to stand 24 hours before serving." Tester Peggy Eichenberger, Marietta, GA., used a cheesecake pan and pronounced the results "beautiful and delicious."

German Cheesecake

DOUGH

1	cup all-purpose flour
¼	cup sugar
	Grated peel of 1 lemon (1½ to 3 teaspoons)
½	cup butter, softened
1	egg yolk

FILLING

3	ounces cream cheese, softened
3¾	cups sugar
3	eggs
8	ounces dairy sour cream
2	tablespoons lemon juice
¼	cup cornstarch

TOPPING

1	cup dairy sour cream
3	tablespoons sugar
	Dash of salt
1	teaspoon vanilla

Combine all dough ingredients; mix with hands until blended. Refrigerate 1 hour. Heat oven to 400°. Roll part of dough to ½-inch thickness; cut a circle to fit bottom of 12-inch springform pan. Bake 8 minutes or until golden brown. Remove pan from oven and cool. Reduce oven temperature to 325°. Butter side of pan; roll out remaining dough into a strip and press onto side of pan. Beat cream cheese until very smooth. Gradually beat in 3 to 3¾ cups sugar. Add one egg at a time, beating well after each addition. Stir in sour cream, lemon juice and cornstarch. Pour filling into dough-lined pan. Bake about 60 minutes. Cool cheesecake completely. While it is cooling, combine topping ingredients; pour over top of cheesecake. Refrigerate 24 hours.

12 SERVINGS.

Cindy Kryda's mother-in-law made this for Cindy and her husband when they were newlyweds and then shared the recipe since it was her son's favorite. Tester Helen Clark, Arden Hills, MN., comments, "My family enjoyed this dessert and what a surprise to cut into the cake portion and find pudding underneath!"

Mystery Mocha

CAKE

¾	cup granulated sugar
1	cup all-purpose flour
2	teaspoons baking powder
⅛	teaspoon salt
1	ounce unsweetened chocolate
2	tablespoons butter
½	cup milk
1	teaspoon vanilla

SAUCE

½	cup packed brown sugar
½	cup granulated sugar
¼	cup unsweetened cocoa
1	cup cold double-strength coffee

Heat oven to 350°. Grease 9-inch round or square pan. Combine ¾ cup sugar, flour, baking powder and salt. Melt chocolate and butter together; stir into flour mixture. Blend well. Combine milk and vanilla; add to chocolate mixture. Mix well; pour into greased pan. Combine sauce ingredients except coffee; sprinkle over batter. Pour coffee over top. Bake about 40 minutes or until top springs back when lightly touched. Serve warm or cold with whipped cream, if desired.

4 TO 6 SERVINGS.

"This is simple yet elegant and delicious," says Kathy Uvaas, Fergus Falls, MN. Tester Paula Anderson, West Fargo, ND., said "everyone in the family liked this" and she suggests using fresh peaches or blueberries for variety.

Salzburger Nockerln

1	pint strawberries
2	tablespoons granulated sugar
3	eggs, separated
⅛	teaspoon cream of tartar
¼	cup granulated sugar
1½	tablespoons flour
1	teaspoon grated lemon zest
1	teaspoon vanilla
	Powdered sugar

Butter 9-inch pie pan. Heat oven to 350°. Hull and slice strawberries; combine with 2 tablespoons sugar. Let stand while preparing dessert. In mixer bowl, beat egg whites until foamy. Add cream of tartar and beat until soft peaks form. Gradually add ¼ cup granulated sugar, 1 tablespoon at a time, beating until stiff but not dry peaks form.

In another mixer bowl, using same beaters or whisking by hand, beat egg yolks about 3 minutes until light in color and ribbons form when beater is lifted. Sprinkle on flour, lemon zest and vanilla; beat into yolks just until blended. Stir 1 heaping spoonful of beaten whites into yolks to lighten them; then fold yolk mixture quickly but gently into whites until no streaks of white remain. Using large spoon, make 4 distinct heaping mounds of soufflé mixture in prepared pan. (The mounds may touch each other.) Bake in lower center of oven 15 to 18 minutes or until golden brown. Remove from oven and sprinkle lightly with powdered sugar.

Serve immediately by separating mounds carefully with tines of fork and placing each soufflé on an individual dessert plate. Spoon strawberries and juice around soufflés.

4 SERVINGS.

From the Church family, Oxford, OH., comes a versatile showcase for fresh fruits. Made with sweet cherries, it is a specialty of the Limousin area of France. But, the Churches enjoyed it in other areas with prunes soaked in Armagnac and also with apricot halves. So, be creative and choose your personal favorites as they come into season. Vary sugar amount to correspond with tartness of fruit.

Limousin Fruit Flan

1	cup milk
3	tablespoons sugar
3	eggs
1	tablespoon brandy or vanilla
⅔	cup all-purpose flour
2	cups fruit such as sweet cherries; raspberries; blueberries; chopped rhubarb; halved, pitted apricots; sliced, peeled, cored apples
3	tablespoons sugar

Heat oven to 350°. In blender container, place milk, 3 tablespoons sugar, eggs, brandy and flour; blend 1 minute. Pour a thin layer into lightly buttered 10-inch ceramic flan dish. Bake about 30 minutes or until set. Remove from oven and distribute fruit evenly over baked layer. Sprinkle with 3 tablespoons sugar. Cover with remaining batter. Bake about 35 minutes or until top is brown. Serve at room temperature as is, or sprinkled with powdered sugar or topped with cream or ice cream, if desired.

4 TO 6 SERVINGS.

"As lovely in summer as it is festive during the holidays," remarks Nancy Bros, Edina, MN., about this rum-laced dessert. Ten tasters at a dinner party gave resounding approval and commented on attractive appearance as well as delicious flavor.

Olde English Trifle

1	family-size Sara Lee pound cake
½	(18-ounce) jar apricot preserves
¼	cup (2 ounces) rum
2	(3-ounce) packages vanilla pudding and pie filling mix (not instant)
2½	cups whole milk
1	tablespoon sherry
2	cups whipping cream
1	tablespoon sugar
1	teaspoon rum
1	pint strawberries, halved
4	macaroon cookies, crumbled
1	cup toasted slivered almonds
1	cup fresh or frozen blueberries

Cut pound cake horizontally into 3 equal slices; fit into ungreased 13x9x2-inch pan. Spread apricot preserves over cake; sprinkle with ¼ cup rum. Prepare pudding mix using 2½ cups milk; stir in sherry. Spread over apricot preserves. Whip cream with 1 tablespoon sugar and 1 teaspoon rum; spread over pudding. Layer with strawberries. Sprinkle with macaroon crumbs, then almonds. Add blueberries (at the last minute if using frozen).

12 SERVINGS.

Helen Clark, Arden Hills, MN., has adapted the traditional trifle to resemble one she enjoyed years ago at a New York City restaurant. They wouldn't reveal their recipe but Helen experimented in her home kitchen until she had perfected a scrumptious facsimile. Tester, Eileen Teska, Racine, WI., found it "very popular" with her family.

Trifle Chantilly

2   (3-ounce) packages vanilla pudding and pie filling mix (not instant)

1   sponge cake, cut or torn into bite-sized pieces

2   packages shortcake sponge cakes or lady fingers

1   (18-ounce) jar strawberry or raspberry preserves

1   cup heavy whipping cream
    Fresh strawberries or raspberries to taste
    Sliced or slivered almonds

Prepare vanilla pudding as directed on package; set aside to cool. Layer in trifle bowl or other glass serving dish, torn sponge cake, vanilla pudding, preserves and fruit. Repeat two or three times. Whip cream; spread over top of finished layers. Garnish with sliced almonds.

8 SERVINGS.

Tip: To make 12 servings, use 2 (4.6-ounce) packages pudding mix, 4 packages shortcake sponge cakes, more preserves and 2 cups whipping cream.

In this heritage recipe from Carol Frey, Chicago, IL., a golden brown, buttery pastry encases a rich almond filling. "Tasty and attractive," comments tester Loretta Larson, Fergus Falls, MN. She floured her hands for ease in shaping filling mixture for this "Dutch treat."

Dutch Banket

1	cup almond paste
1	cup sugar
1	egg
1	egg, separated
¼	cup cornstarch
2	cups all-purpose flour
1	cup butter
¼	cup water

Let almond paste, sugar, egg, egg yolk and cornstarch stand in a bowl at room temperature 30 minutes. Heat oven to 400°. Blend flour, butter and water in separate bowl; divide dough into 2 equal parts. Roll each part on floured surface into 13x8-inch rectangle. Cut lengthwise into 2 equal strips (four 13x4-inch strips). Combine almond paste with ingredients in bowl; shape into 4 rolls, each about 12 inches long. Place rolls on lengths of dough. Fold over ends, then long sides, moistening one side to seal before pressing. Place seam-side-down on ungreased cookie sheet. Prick holes on top. Beat egg white and brush tops of rolls. Bake 14 minutes; reduce oven temperature to 325° and bake about 20 minutes longer or until light brown. Cut into slices.

4 (13-INCH) ROLLS.

Tip: Can be prepared in advance and frozen until ready to bake.

When she was 18, Susan Barton, Janesville, WI., had the pleasure of traveling to France with her grandmother. Down a side street in a small town, they stopped at a patissiere and savored "the richest, most lemony tarts." After years of trying to duplicate the taste, Susan perfected this tempting facsimile. Tester Mary Hultgren, Arlington, MN, agrees they take time to prepare but comments, "The end product is well worth the work!"

Tartes au Citron

PASTRY

3	egg yolks
9	tablespoons frozen lemon juice, thawed
½	cup sugar
¼	teaspoon salt
1½	cups butter
4½	cups all-purpose flour

FILLING

6	egg yolks
1½	cups sugar
	Grated rind of 1 lemon (1½ to 3 teaspoons)
½	cup lemon juice
¼	cup cornstarch
¼	teaspoon salt
1½	cups boiling water
½	cup butter, cut up

In medium bowl, beat 3 egg yolks lightly; add 9 tablespoons lemon juice, ½ cup sugar and ¼ teaspoon salt. In large bowl, cut 1½ cups butter into flour with pastry blender. Stir egg mixture into flour mixture; mixing carefully with fork or hands. Divide dough into 3 or 4 parts. Wrap each in plastic wrap. Refrigerate 1 hour. Heat oven to 350°. Pinch off about 1 tablespoon of dough for each tart; press into miniature muffin pans. Bake 20 to 25 minutes. Remove from pans. Cool on paper towels.

Beat 6 egg yolks very well in mixer bowl. Add remaining filling ingredients except boiling water and butter; beat again thoroughly. Combine mixture with boiling water and butter in top of double boiler. Cook over hot water until mixture thickens, stirring often. Cook 5 to 10 minutes longer over simmering water, stirring occasionally. Cool 20 minutes before filling tart shells. May be served immediately or refrigerated, covered, overnight.

6 DOZEN (1½-INCH) TARTS.

Tips: Tart shells can be made ahead; store in airtight container. Tarts can also be made in larger muffin cups.

Soraya Cornick, Albert Lea, MN., received this recipe for "Donauwellen" from a German friend. "We sat at her kitchen table working together to convert measurements and other particulars — quite a task," recalls Soraya. "While fine-tuning the recipe I have tried to keep it as authentic as possible." Tester Kathy Cochran, Albertville, AL., comments "I can't wait to make this delightful dessert again. Unusual and not too sweet."

Danube Waves

1	pound (2 cups) unsalted butter, softened
1½	cups sugar
4	eggs
2½	cups all-purpose flour
1½	teaspoons baking powder
	Dash of salt
2	tablespoons unsweetened cocoa
2	(16-ounce) cans tart red cherries, drained
1	(3-ounce) package vanilla pudding and pie filling mix (not instant)
1¾	cups milk
	Flaked chocolate or chocolate curls

Grease 17x11x1-inch pan. Heat oven to 350°. Cream ½ pound of the butter and sugar; add eggs and mix well. Stir in flour, baking powder and salt. Spread half of batter in greased pan. Stir cocoa into remaining batter; mix until well blended. Spread chocolate batter over first layer. Spread cherries on top. Bake 20 to 25 minutes. Cool completely.

Prepare vanilla pudding according to package directions, using 1¾ cups milk instead of 2 cups. Let cool completely, stirring often to avoid skin forming on top. Add pudding, a large spoonful at a time to ½ pound butter, beating with electric mixer after each spoonful until well blended and smooth. Frost cooled cake. Sprinkle generously with flaked chocolate or chocolate curls.

24 SERVINGS.

Sem Sutter, Chicago, IL., revives "warm and happy memories of years as a student in Germany" by preparing this delectable dessert. Tester Rachel Thompson, Edina, MN., shared it with a French exchange student and they both enjoyed every fruit-filled bite.

German Plum Pastry

PASTRY
2   cups all-purpose flour
2   tablespoons sugar
1   teaspoon baking powder
    Dash of salt
¾   cup cold butter
1   medium egg, beaten
1   tablespoon rum
1   teaspoon grated lemon peel

FILLING
2   pounds fresh prune plums, halved, pitted
½   cup sugar
2   tablespoons sugar
1   teaspoon cinnamon
¼   teaspoon cardamom
2   tablespoons flour

Heat oven to 400°. Combine 2 cups flour, 2 tablespoons sugar, baking powder and salt. With pastry blender, cut in butter until mixture resembles fine crumbs. Add egg, rum and lemon peel; work with fingers until dough is smooth. Pat over bottom and up side of 9-inch round springform or cake pan. Place plum halves over bottom pastry, cut-side-down and sprinkle with ½ cup sugar. Combine remaining 2 tablespoons sugar with spices and flour; sprinkle over plums. Bake about 40 minutes or until pastry is golden brown and plums are bubbling. Serve warm or at room temperature.

6 TO 8 SERVINGS.

This creative venture evolved in the kitchen of Robert and Kay Kallos, Atlanta, GA. It began with a favorite dessert Kay enjoyed during her stay in Kassel, Germany. "As good as the Pflaumenkuchen of my memory was," says Kay, "my husband has made it even better by adding the delicious hazelnut cream filling." You will need a tart pan and ample time for the several preparation, chilling and baking steps.

Plum-Hazelnut Cream Torte

SWEET TART DOUGH
2	cups all-purpose flour
2	tablespoons sugar
¼	teaspoon salt
1½	teaspoons grated lemon peel
10	ounces (1¼ cups) unsalted butter
2	tablespoons water
1	teaspoon vanilla

FILLING
14 to 16 prune plums, halved, pitted
⅓	cup sugar
½	teaspoon cinnamon
½	teaspoon nutmeg
2½	tablespoons unsalted butter

HAZELNUT CREAM
1	egg
1	egg yolk
½	cup sugar
⅓	cup all-purpose flour
1	cup milk, scalded, cooled
3	tablespoons unsalted butter
½	teaspoon vanilla
1	teaspoon hazelnut liqueur
1	tablespoon rum
½	cup ground hazelnuts

Combine 2 cups flour, 2 tablespoons sugar, ¼ teaspoon salt and lemon peel. Cut butter into flour mixture until it is the consistency of coarse meal. Stir in water and vanilla. Put dough in a zip-lock plastic bag; let rest 30 minutes. (If room is warm, refrigerate dough.) Grease 10-inch tart pan with removable bottom. Press dough into greased pan. (Some dough may be left over.) Place pastry-lined pan in freezer 30 minutes. Heat oven to 400°. Bake tart shell 15 to 20 minutes or until well browned.

Arrange plums skin-side-down, in baking dish. Combine ⅓ cup sugar, cinnamon and nutmeg; sprinkle over plums. Dot with 2 tablespoons butter. Cover loosely with foil. Bake 20 to 30 minutes or until juices are released. Remove from oven; cool completely. Drain off juice and reserve in a small saucepan.

Beat egg and yolk; slowly add ½ cup sugar, beating until light in color. Stir in ⅓ cup flour; continue mixing until smooth. Add milk; mix well. Place in medium saucepan; heat to boiling, stirring constantly. Mixture will become thick and custard-like. Add 3 tablespoons butter, vanilla, hazelnut liqueur and rum. If lumpy; whip until smooth. Fold in hazelnuts. Pour mixture into bowl; place waxed paper directly on surface of filling to prevent a "skin" from forming. Refrigerate 60 minutes before serving.

Spoon cream mixture into shell. Top with plums skin-side-down. Cook reserved juice until thickened. Spoon over top of tart. Refrigerate 60 minutes before serving.

12 SERVINGS.

A "can't stop eating 'em" sweet snack that rates applause for flavor and versatility. Wonderful as part of a dessert buffet or tea table for that "something extra" and delightful as an ice cream topping or nibbler just about anytime.

Swedish Nuts

1½ cups blanched almonds
2 cups walnut halves
2 egg whites
1 cup sugar
Dash of salt
½ cup butter

Heat oven to 325°. Toast nuts 15 minutes or until light brown. Beat egg whites until frothy; gradually beat in sugar and salt until smooth and glossy. Fold nuts into egg whites. Melt butter in large baking pan. Spread nut mixture over butter. Bake about 30 minutes, stirring every 10 minutes, until no butter remains in the pan and the nuts are coated and evenly browned. Cool. Store in tightly covered container.

3½ CUPS.

Approximate
Metric Equivalents

¼ teaspoon	=	1.23 milliliters
½ teaspoon	=	2.46 milliliters
¾ teaspoon	=	3.7 milliliters
1 teaspoon	=	4.93 milliliters
1¼ teaspoons	=	6.16 milliliters
1½ teaspoons	=	7.39 milliliters
1¾ teaspoons	=	8.63 milliliters
2 teaspoons	=	9.86 milliliters
1 tablespoon	=	14.79 milliliters
2 tablespoons	=	29.57 milliliters
¼ cup	=	59.15 milliliters
½ cup	=	118.3 milliliters
1 cup	=	236.59 milliliters
2 cups/1 pint	=	473.18 milliliters
3 cups	=	709.77 milliliters
4 cups/1 quart	=	946.36 milliliters
4 quarts/1 gallon	=	3.785 liters

Converting to Metric

When converting to or from metric, be sure to convert *all* measurements. Otherwise, the proportions of the ingredients could be critically imbalanced.

When this is known...	Multiply it by...	To get
teaspoons	4.93	milliliters
tablespoons	14.79	milliliters
fluid ounces	29.57	milliliters
cups	236.59	milliliters
cups	.236	liters
pints	473.18	milliliters
pints	.473	liters
quarts	946.36	milliliters
quarts	.946	liters
gallons	3.785	liters
ounces	28.35	grams
pounds	.454	kilograms
inches	2.54	centimeters
Fahrenheit	subtract 32 multiply by 5 divide by 9	Celsius (Centigrade)

Converting from Metric

When this is known...	Divide it by...	To get
milliliters	4.93	teaspoons
milliliters	14.79	tablespoons
milliliters	29.57	fluid ounces
milliliters	236.59	cups
liters	.236	cups
milliliters	473.18	pints
liters	.473	pints
milliliters	946.36	quarts
liters	.946	quarts
liters	3.785	gallons
grams	28.35	ounces
kilograms	.454	pounds
centimeters	2.54	inches
Celsius (Centigrade)	Multiply by 9 divide by 5 add 32	Fahrenheit

Food Safety Reminder . . .

Several recipes call for raw eggs. For safety reasons, we suggest substituting commercially-prepared meringue powder for egg whites and pasteurized liquid eggs for whole eggs. Substitution equivalents are on product labels. Anytime raw eggs are used in any type of recipe preparation, they should be fresh with clean shells showing no cracks or other damage.

Temperature Equivalents
(Fahrenheit/Celsius Scale)

Fahrenheit	Celsius
32°F Water Freezes	0°C
40°	4.4°
50°	10°
60°	15.6°
70°	21.1°
80°	26.7°
90°	32.2°
100°	37.8°
110°	43.3°
120°	48.9°
130°	54.4°
140°	60°
150°	65.6°
160°	71.1°
170°	76.7°
180°	82.2°
190°	87.8°
200°	93.3°
212° Water Boils	100°
250°	121°
300°	149°
350°	177°
400°	205°
450°	233°
500°	260°

Contributors and Testers . . .

Concordia Language Villages is deeply grateful for the participation of the Villagers, parents, staff members, restaurateurs and other friends of the Program who made this unique collection possible. A very sincere thank you to recipe contributors and testers from across the country and abroad who shared special samplings of their heritage as well as time, culinary talents and best of all, enthusiasm.

We regret that due to similarities and spatial restrictions, we were unable to publish every recipe submitted. And we cannot claim that every selection is "original." However, we do attest that each is a cherished favorite of the contributor.

Jane F. Abel
Jane Ahlin
Aller Family
Lorraine Amundson
Cynthia Anderson and
    Family
Deborah Wangaard
    Anderson
Jane Anderson
Joseph Anderson
Mark Anderson
Patricia Anderson
Paula Anderson
Camille Assir
Delphine Aubourg
Linda G. Austin
Marianne Axboe
Judy Bahr
J.L. Baker
Marlene Banttari
Susan M. Barton
Ruby Bauer
Peggy Baumgaertner
Loretta Bebeau
Carey Benson
Karen Bergh
Julie Bernstein
Charla Beukema
Jennifer Dean Blair
John and Kathy Borge
Lynn and Ann Bose
Charlie Boone
Katherine Bradbury
Jenna Brooke Bratvold
Linda Bredeson
Evelyn Bress

Kathryn Brierley
Mary K. Broderius
Judy Broekemeier
Nancy Bros
Eric Brown
Joy Brown
Lois Brown
Lorraine Brown
Mary Brubacher
Jeanne Bruder
Mary Brumfiel
Philip Brunelle
Ann Burckhardt
Marsha Burt
Florence Bye
Christian and Marguerite
    Caille
Gretchen Calvit
David Caraway
Governor Arne and
    Susan Carlson
Elsa Carlson
Mary Carlson
Emily Carpenter
Jerry Cegla
Jane Alex Chapco
Tim Choy
E'Lise Christensen
Joanna Christensen
Linda Church
Ciatti's
Helen R. Clark
Judy Clifton
Hillary Rodham Clinton
Kathy Cochran
Julia Commons

Shareen Connors
Susan Conners
Sarah Coomber
Soraya Cornick
Helen Couper
LaRon Croft
Eileen Cumming
Monica Cummings
Diane Curtiss and Family
Marty Daggett
Liv Dahl
R. Naomi Dahl
Deb Dahlseng
Bonnie Damkroger
Carrie and Julian
    D'Andrea
Beverly Deeds
Noelle Deharpporte
Alison C. DeHart
John and Ginger Dell
Ann de Leon
Alyssa Derksen
Barbara Des Camps
Sharon Detert
The Dicksons
Janet Dillenburg
Orene Docken
Jason Dockter
Pamela S. Dorris
President Paul and
    Mardeth Dovre
Mary Theresa Downing
Eleanore M. Dryer
Mary Dunn
Virginia Dutcher
Joni Ebert

The Ediner
Maria Eggemeyer
Peggy Eichenberger
Barbara Eisinger
Amy Eld
Linnea Eliason
Bonnie Eng
Doris Engdahl
Stephen Engel
Bonita English
Lee English
Nancy English
Linda and David Erceg
Beth Anderson Erickson
Sharon Erickson
Shirley Erickson
Wiebke Erickson
Sue R. Essig
Everything Kitchen and
    Coffee
Kathie Fargione
Derrick John Ferguson
Anne Fischer
Jill E. Fischer
Willa Fisher
Mary Lee Fitzsimmons
Trudy Flage
The Fractions
Barbara Francis
Susan Francis
Pam Fredericksen
Carol Frey
Rita Frey
Gasthof zur
    Gemutlichkeit
Reidun Gauger

Jane Gillam
John Giordano
Doris Ann Girerd
Victoria Grablander
Alicia Granse
Helen Grant
Kristen Gray
Nancy Gray
Green Mill, Too
Suzanne Greenwood
Juneko Grilley
Diana Gulden
Carolyn Halbach
Sandra Hall
Sheryl Hall
Susan Hall
Ann Hammer
Annikiki Hammond
Sylvia Hansen
Ingrid Lenz Harrison
Sheri Hartjen
Dianne Haugen
LuAnn Haugen
Birgit Hemberg
Therese Hennemann
Krista Herman
Stewart Herman
Barbara Hernke
Hege Hertindahl
Ian D. Higgins
Helen Hill
Stephanie Hillman
Mary Hippe
Drs. Donald and Roma
  Hoff
Sarah and Jane
  Hollinshead
Heidi Hollonbeck
Ingrid Holm
Joanne Holm
Douglas and Beth
  Johnson Holod
Steve and Lynn Holter
  and Family
Hotel Sofitel
Rebecca Hotvedt
Elizabeth Hovland
LaRae Ellingsen Hovland
Jean Hughes
Anna Hultberg

Mary Hultgren
Shelly Jacobs
Nina Jahnke
Nan Jakobson
Ruth Jensen
Donna Jesperson
Annie Johnson
Dennis and Carole
  Johnson
Linda Johnson
Mary Lu Johnson
Vicki Jones
Jordan, MN. Elementary
  School
Paul and Janis Jordan
Nancy Jordet
Levi Kafka
Kafté
Patti Kahn
Robert and Kay Kallos
Elinor Karlsson
Donna Kastner
Scott Kee
Pamela and Margot
  Kelsey
Margaret and Ancel Keys
Heather Randall King
Kathy Kinsey
Ann and Larry Klueh
Angela Klus
June Kohl
Aino Koivastik
Marilyn Krasowski
Cindy Kryda
Betty W. Krysiak
Marjorie Kugler
Camille Kulka
Laura Kyllander
Marie Lacy
Judy Torvend Laing
Janelle Lamb
Laurene Lamping
Sue LaPean
Judith Larson
Loretta Larson
Beverly LeBeau
Amy Lecy
Christine Lemley
Greg LeMond
Ruthann Lewis

Kari Lie
Heni Lindberg
Kim Lobert
Arlene Lombard
Carol Lowell
Patricia Lund
Betsy Lykken
Michael Lykken
Ann Lynch
Kristin Lyons
Robert Male
Paulette Malecek
Ceil Manchester
Barbara Marick
Gary Mark
Ellen Markuson
Marsh Lake Preserve
Sadie Martin
Vivian Mason
Gail Mathisen
Corrine Matney
Alice Matsumoto
Claudia McGrath
James Mead
Mary Meuwissen
Mary Hockenberry
  Meyer
Patricia Meyers
Karen Michael
Kent Mitchell
Walter F. Mondale
Tracey Moorhead
Mia Morrill
Candace and Courtney
  Moser
Danielle Mossner
Chris and Alice Mounts
Carol Nasby
Lois Nehrus
Kathlyn Nelson
Lindsey Neva
Gary Nichols
Mary Nielsen
Maureen Nimis
Dr. Tim and April Nissen
Donna Nooleen
Patricia Nordahl
Linda Paulson
  Norderhaug
Esther Norha

Betsy Norum
Ellen Ochs
Daniel Ofstedal
Dorothea Ofstedal
Paul Ofstedal
Karen Ogdahl
Larry and Ilene Iverson
  Olson
Maren Olson
Mark, Jeri, Britt and
  Hans Olson
Maria Onheiber
Eleanor Ostman
David Palmer
Nicolle Pata
Noelle Paulson
Sonja Pavlik
Paige Pearson
Marsha Penti
Raynelle Perkins
Eric Peterson
Carolyn Petterson
Mary Ann and Errin
  Pfeifer
Susan Pfund
Maria Pino
Linda Poets
Dr. JoEllen Polzien
Gretchen Pracht
Karla Yukari Pratt
Becky Preston
Emily Pye
Quail on the Hill
Lois Rand
Peter Randall
Sue Reider
Jonathan Remund
Sandra Reuther
Pam Reynolds
Sharon Rhodes
Carolyn Rice
Mary Rice
Jay Richards
Mary Richards
Brent and Jackie Richens
Keri Ricks
Lisa Riddle
Verna Risko
Sofia Rizzo
Carrie Rocke

Miriam Rocke
Richard and Enid
　Roehrner
Elisa Rojas
Nanette Rollene
Susan Rollins
Jacquelyn Rosholt
Barbara Rottman
Carmen Rottman
Bryan Rubbelke
Carol Rueber
Marlis Runnberg
Janet Sadlack
Alma Jean Satran
Alice Sauer
Louise Saunders
Jenna Schieffer
Sue Schiess
Rachel Schlak
Mary Schlieckert
Robert and Shirley
　Schmid
Kara Schmitt
Andrea Schulze and Mike
　Seifert
Christine Schulze
James Schulze
Margaret Schulze
Cathy Schwinden

Matt Scott
Mildred Seidman
Shelly's Woodroast
Elizabeth Shoffner
Alma Shurb
Steven Sillers
Paul Simon
Peggy Singh
Brett Skaugstad
Marsha Skogheim
Conni Ellyn Sloth
Bill and Joelle Snyder
Carolyn Snyder
Susan Soenen
Barb Sommer
Rich Speers
Helen Spencer
Benjamin Squire
Harriet Squire
Mr. and Mrs. J. Edward
　Staab
Cora Stahn
Pam and Joe Stanoch
Audrey and Bill Stearns
Elie Steffensen
Daryl Stensgaard
Stacy Stromstad
Sturgis High School
Sem Sutter

Karen Swanson
Lois Swenson
Leah Switzer
Diane Syme
Dianne Taylor
Jennifer Teichmann
Pat Temple
Nancy Teply
Amy Tervola
Eileen Teska
Dana Thome
Susan Thompson
Rachel Thompson
Sarah Thompson
Maxine Thorkelson
Patty Thornton
Beverly Thorson
Nancy Thorson
Tour de France
Debbie Trowbridge
Gail Tsuboi
Gary Tucker
Tufte Family
Brad Turbes
Kathy Uvaas
Jean Donham Van
　Deusen
Bob and Laura Vogel
Ene Vogel

Dagmar von Briesen
Linda Wallenberg
Barbara Wang
Kathy Watts
Alan Wax
Ellen Weber
Gerda Weninger
Amy White
William Wiktor
Wild Rice Gifts Co.
Martha Willand
LaVonne Williams
Christie and Susie Wilson
L.C. Winn
Marilyn Wippl
Nancy Witt
Luann Woeltge
Kathy Wolf
Elisa Wright
Lai Ying
Ellen Ylikopsa
Kris and Britta Ylikopsa
Linda Young
Ann Zavoral
Michelle and Mary
　Zurcher

The title of this cookbook, *The Global Gourmet,* was submitted by Emily Virginia Christianson.

Index

361

The Global Gourmet
Concordia Language Villages
901 S. 8th Street
Moorhead, MN 56562

Please send _____copies of *The Global Gourmet* $22.95 each _____

Minneapolis residents add sales tax of 7% $1.61 each _____

Minnesota residents add sales tax of 6½% $1.49 each _____

Postage and handling ($3.50 for 1-3 books; $5.50 for 4-6 books) $ _____

TOTAL ENCLOSED $ _____

Name

Address

City   State   Zip Code

Make checks payable and mail to Concordia Language Villages.

If ordering in quantity, please contact Concordia Language Villages for cookbook and shipping costs.
Write or call 1 (800) 247-1044 in MN or 1 (800) 222-4750 outside MN.

— —

Concordia Language Villages
Chinese, Danish, Finnish, French, German, Japanese, Norwegian, Russian, Spanish and Swedish
One-, two- or four-week sessions for 7-18 year olds
Abroad trips for 15-18 year olds

Please send me more information about your summer programs.

Name

Address

City   State   Zip Code

Mail to: Concordia Language Villages, 901 S. Eighth Street, Moorhead, MN 56562 or call (800) 247-1044 in MN,
1 (800) 222-4750 outside MN.